VERDI

VERDI

JOSEPH WECHSBERG

G. P. PUTNAM'S SONS
NEW YORK

For My Giuseppinas

Designed by Humphrey Stone

SBN 399-11409-2
Library of Congress Catalog Card Number 74-81703

Printed in Great Britain

CONTENTS

1
AGONIES AND THE 'MIRACLE'

'Verdi is loved,' Carlo Gatti once told me. 'This, I believe, is the difference between him and other great composers. People are awed by Bach and Beethoven, they revere the divine Mozart, they often admire Wagner. But people love Verdi. He was one of us, simple, honest and human, a wonderful man and a wonderful musician, a rare combination.'

Gatti, one of Verdi's most important biographers – he died in 1965, at the age of eighty-nine – as a young man had known the composer and later knew more about him than anyone else. He loved Verdi and sometimes did not dwell on the problematic side of his complex character. But Verdi's complexity as a man does not diminish his genius as a musician, and makes him even more human. No man is perfect, and Verdi was no exception. After his death, the poet Gabriele d'Annunzio wrote an ode, ending: 'He loved and wept for all men.'

Verdi, the composer, expressed human emotions – love and hatred, sorrow and joy, jealousy and despair – in melodies that everybody understands instinctively, even people who do not know much about music. They hum 'La donna è mobile', they cry when Violetta dies, they are moved by Aïda and Radames, they hate Iago and suffer with Desdemona, and chuckle with Falstaff. The blessed music came out of Verdi as water pours from a mountain spring. His characters may wear strange costumes, acting out an implausible melodrama, but their emotions are timeless and true. People can identify with them. Verdi is still essentially a composer for our time.

Gatti first saw Verdi in 1892:

He was seventy-nine. I was sixteen, the leader of the boys' section of the chorus at the Milan Conservatory which had once rejected Verdi's application as a student. We were taking part in a performance of Rossini's oratorio, *Mosè in Egitto* – that year was the hundredth anniversary of Rossini's birth –

OPPOSITE Verdi conducting a performance of Aïda.

Verdi's birthroom at Le Roncole.

and Verdi conducted. In the first rehearsal something went wrong with our boys' section. Verdi became quite angry. And when Verdi was angry ...

Gatti puffed out his cheeks and spiralled his right hand upward:

He called me to the front and yelled at me. I was afraid he was going to throw his baton at me. Verdi was understanding when it came to the problems of an orchestra, but he was not very patient with singers. He used to say that singers, especially the famous ones, made rarely an effort to penetrate the spirit of his work.

I asked Gatti how Verdi had looked:

He was frail and elegant, with wonderful bearing. He had a fine head, with long white hair, and a proud nose, and there was fire in his eyes, though his face was serene. His manner was never intimate. Even his close friends would never think of putting an arm around his shoulder – and you know how informal we Italians usually are. Verdi just wasn't that kind of man. He had the pride of a peasant from Parma, and he wanted to be one of those peasants.

8

Giuseppe Fortunino Francesco Verdi was born at eight pm, on 10 October 1813, a Sunday, in Le Roncole, a tiny village in Parma. Verdi believed for a long time that he was born on 9 October 1814, as his mother had told him erroneously, until he found out the truth when he was sixty-three. To the end of his life he celebrated his birthday on the 9th. In 1813 the Duchy of Parma was part of Napoleon's Empire. Two days after Verdi's birth his father walked three miles to the nearby market town of Busseto, where the French authorities spelled his son's name 'Joseph Fortunin François Verdi'. At the parish register of Le Roncole his birth was recorded in Latin. Ironically, the name of the great Italian patriot was never registered in Italian.

The countryside between the cities of Parma, Cremona and Piacenza is flat and dull. In Cremona the Amatis, the Guarneris and Antonio Stradivari created the magnificent instruments which later sung the beautiful melodies of Verdi. 'Nature has bestowed no charm on this landscape,' wrote Antonio Ghislanzoni, the librettist of *Aïda*; 'The plain rolls monotonously on. Rich for the countryman, poor for the poet.' Summers are hot and winters often raw. But Verdi loved his region, his *paese*, with its dark, fertile soil. After he became famous and rich, he could have lived anywhere, but he spent much of his life on his farm in Sant' Agata, a short walk from Le Roncole and Busseto. Even when he was the most celebrated man in Italy, he proudly called himself 'a peasant from Parma'. His virtues – honesty, simplicity, common-sense – were those of a peasant. So were his weaknesses – a certain suspicion, the tendency to quarrel, often a lack of tolerance. Sometimes he could not forgive, and even after he forgave, he could not forget.

The house where he was born is still there and is maintained as a national monument by the Italian Government. The Verdis must have been very poor. The family had lived there for generations. Verdi's father, Carlo Giuseppe, kept the only store in Le Roncole, selling salt, wine, groceries, and ran a small *osteria* for the locals. After church on Sunday everybody would come into the tiny tavern for a glass of Lambrusco. Carlo and his wife, Luigia, never learnt to read or write. No one in the family was a musician; Verdi's genius was neither hereditary nor environmental. His only sister, Giuseppa, was mentally retarded after an attack of meningitis and died at the age of seventeen. Verdi seems to have inherited his dignity and integrity from his mother. He never got along with his father, who gave up the store and the tavern as soon as his son earned some money and afterwards lived for many years at Verdi's expense.

The boy learnt to read and write with the village priest, Pietro Baistrocchi, when he was seven. The next year his father bought him a spinet, now at the Scala Museum in Milan. By the time Verdi was ten

The spinet on which Verdi first learnt to play. It was repaired by a kindly neighbour, Stefano Cavaletti, who recorded that he had made the repairs 'gratuitously, seeing the good disposition the young Verdi has for learning to play this instrument, which is sufficient for my complete satisfaction'.

he was playing the three-manual organ at the village church. According to a local tradition, a group of Russian soldiers came through Le Roncole in 1814, looting and raping. Verdi's mother took her infant and hid at the top of the campanile where there is now a commemorative stone. But Verdi never mentioned the story and Gatti never believed it. Naturally enough Le Roncole now calls itself 'Roncole Verdi'. In 1872 the Marchese de Pallavicino, then the feudal lord of Busseto, had a commemorative stone put on Verdi's birthplace. Verdi was then living in nearby Sant' Agata, shortly after the world-wide success of *Aïda*. He was furious, but there was nothing he could do except ignore the whole thing. Later a statue of Verdi was placed in front of the cottage. Several plaques were added, with permission of the Department of Fine Arts; one in 1951 by the choral societies of Italy saying '*Pura espressione dell' anima popolare Italiana*' – 'the pure expression of the soul of the Italian people'.

As a small boy Verdi was called 'Beppino'. Later everybody called him 'Verdi', never 'Giuseppe'. His second wife Giuseppina sometimes called him 'Pasticcio', which means, literally, 'a baked dish topped by a crust'. Verdi could be quite crusty. She and some *very* close friends might also call him 'Mago', the sorcerer. In her letters she often simply calls him 'Dearest'. He always signed his name 'G. Verdi'. His signature has been much interpreted, by expert and amateur graphologists. He often wrote his name slightly upward, surrounding it with a sort of fence that became more enclosed as he got older and, in his final years, all but shielded his name from the outside world, protecting his privacy. About the slight upward tendency there can be no doubt: Verdi accepted his defeats as philosophically as his victories but there was never doubt about where he was going – up and up on the golden wings of his music.

His early musical talent was first noticed by the remarkable man whom Verdi all his life considered his real father. Antonio Barezzi, thirty-six when Verdi was ten, was the most prosperous merchant in Busseto. Verdi's father bought the groceries and the local Lambrusco wine from him. Barezzi was a music lover – people called him *maniacco dilettante* – and played the flute. He founded the small Philharmonic Society which rehearsed in his house (now called Palazzo Barezzi) in the main street.

Verdi never talked about his formative years although once he said to a friend, 'my youth was hard'. He was admitted, probably at the urging of Barezzi, to the *ginnasio* in Busseto. Though seemingly a sleepy town, Busseto had an interesting cultural life. The small cathedral kept a chorus and a string quartet, there was a music school, two 'academies' for Greek and Italian poetry, an old Jewish com-

The church at Le Roncole where Verdi played the organ.

Antonio Barezzi, a Busseto merchant, was the first to recognise Verdi's exceptional talent. He supported him financially throughout the struggle of his early years.

munity with its rabbinical school, and a few painters who had chosen to live there. For seven years Verdi had room and board in the modest house of the cobbler Pugnatta, paying thirty centesimi a day. His father paid half, and the boy earned the other half as organist in Le Roncole. Nothing at all is known about Pugnatta, whom Verdi saw every day; he never mentioned him later on. On Sundays and holidays the boy would walk the three miles to Le Roncole and back, sometimes barefoot, 'to preserve his shoes'. In Le Roncole they called him *maestrino*, little master.

The best musician in Busseto was Ferdinando Provesi, the cathedral's organist and director of the Philharmonic Society. He taught the boy to play the flute, the bass clarinet, the horn, the piano – Verdi was permitted to practise on a piano in Barezzi's house – and gave him some instruction in harmony and counterpoint. Provesi wanted Verdi to become a musician. But Don Pietro Seletti, a canon at the cathedral, and Verdi's schoolteacher, hoped Verdi would one day be a priest. Provesi, an Italian 'patriot', was known as a radical, while the priest was a reactionary, in favour of the Pope and Austria's domination over Parma, since the Congress of Vienna in 1815. Fortunately the organist at the cathedral failed to show up one day, the thirteen-year-old boy took over and did so well, improvising at the organ, that Seletti was impressed and agreed Verdi should study music. It was the first lucky accident in Verdi's life.

After finishing his *ginnasio* Verdi became Provesi's assistant, teaching Barezzi's children, composing, playing the organ and the piano. Later Verdi declared he had composed 'marches for brass band by the hundred, perhaps as many little sinfonie, serenades, cantatas, and various pieces of church music'. In 1828 (the year after the death of the revered Beethoven) Verdi wrote a 'new' overture for Rossini's *Il Barbiere di Siviglia*, for a performance by the members of the Philharmonic Society. This was not unusual; perhaps the original overture was too difficult to perform for the local amateurs. Verdi never permitted his early compositions to be published and he had most of them burnt.

At seventeen he was teaching, composing, copying scores, conducting and also helping Barezzi with the ledgers and accounts in the store. The following year he moved into Barezzi's house and fell in love with Margherita, the eldest daughter, whom he had known since childhood. She was a few months younger than Verdi, gentle and pretty. The prosperous bourgeois Barezzi made no objections to his daughter's marrying the once-barefoot peasant boy from Le Roncole. Barezzi soon realized that Busseto had become too small for Verdi's talent; Milan's celebrated Conservatory would be the place to study. Barezzi discussed it with Provesi and Verdi's father. Carlo Verdi would apply for a monthly stipend to the Monte di Pietà e d'Abbondanza, a seventeenth-century charity in Busseto, supported by most of the well-to-do citizens, and Barezzi himself would lend Verdi money if more was needed.

The scholarship was granted but was to begin months later, in the autumn of 1833, at twenty-five francs a month. For decades thereafter, the people of Busseto said that Verdi had not been 'grateful' enough – which enraged him and created exasperating problems. Until the stipend came through, Barezzi alone supported Verdi; he also financed Verdi's first trip to Milan, then in a foreign state. (The Habsburg Emperor Franz I was King of Lombardy-Venetia, of which Milan was the capital. The Austrians also 'advised' the former Empress Marie-Louise, then Duchess of Parma.) Verdi got a passport issued by

Ferdinando Provesi, the cathedral organist at Busseto and Verdi's music teacher.

Parma's Ministry of the Interior, describing the colour of his hair ('chestnut-brown') and eyes ('grey'), his forehead ('high'), nose ('aquiline'), complexion ('pale'), and special peculiarities ('pock marks').

The Milan Conservatory turned down Verdi's application 'without explanations'. For almost a century the rejection was considered a typical example of a young talent turned down by the conservative Establishment until in 1931 Carlo Gatti published the truth in his biography, after much study in the old Conservatory files. The Conservatory had been overcrowded, Verdi was a 'foreigner' and 'too old', and he had held his hands 'incorrectly' while playing the piano. Verdi never discovered the reasons in his lifetime and remained bitter about the refusal. Many years later, when the Conservatory asked Verdi for permission to be named after him, he said: 'They wouldn't have me young. They cannot have me old.'

Once again Verdi's musical career was saved by Barezzi, who said that Verdi could stay in Milan, at his expense, and study privately with the best teacher, Professor Vincenzo Lavigna, a good musician, mediocre composer, and very strict. Lavigna's favourite composer was Giovanni Paisiello, whose masterpiece, *Il Barbiere di Siviglia* (1782), preceded Rossini's by thirty-four years. Lavigna worked with Verdi on Palestrina (whom Verdi later called '*in primis et ante omnia*'), Corelli, Haydn, Mozart, and Beethoven. Verdi remembered that Lavigna had been 'very strong on counterpoint. . . . I did nothing but canons and fugues, fugues and canons of every sort.' He learnt his lessons well and proved it in his great ensembles and the magnificent fugue, the finale of *Falstaff*. At Lavigna's advice Barezzi bought Verdi a season-ticket for La Scala and got him a pianoforte. Verdi worked hard in Milan, up to fourteen hours a day. Eventually he paid back every lira to Barezzi, but he never ceased feeling deeply grateful.

When his old music teacher, Provesi, died in Busseto in July 1833, Verdi was sad but could not afford to attend the funeral. A month later his sister Giuseppa died, and again Verdi had no money. He did not realize that Provesi's death would create many problems. Barezzi and Verdi's friends at the Philharmonic Society wanted the young man to become Provesi's successor as organist, choirmaster and director of the Philharmonic. Lavigna said, no; Verdi needed 'at least another year of study'. Meanwhile a second group in Busseto, led by the Provost of the cathedral, imported their own candidate, Giovanni Ferrari, choirmaster from nearby Guastalla.

The small-town feud became bitter and political, the (liberal) 'Verdians' against the (clerical) 'Ferrarians'. At one point the Verdians of the Philharmonic Society invaded the cathedral and removed their music. The situation became so critical in June 1834 that Barezzi asked

The young Verdi teaches a piano pupil, who may be Margherita Barezzi, daughter of his patron.

Verdi to come back to Busseto, to prove to his enemies how good he really was. On the day Verdi arrived the Provost appointed Ferrari as organist and choirmaster. This *fait accompli* created terrific excitement in town. While Ferrari performed at the cathedral, Verdi conducted outdoor concerts, always for larger audiences. Six months later the ducal Governor decreed that the position would be filled 'by competition', and Verdi returned to Milan and his studies. The competition was postponed, however, and the situation in Busseto became so difficult that Barezzi asked Verdi to return for good. Lavigna gave Verdi a final certificate: 'Signor Verdi ... pursued his studies in a praiseworthy fashion, of fugues with two, three, and four voices. ... While with me, he has always been most quiet and respectful and moderate in his dress. This is the pure truth.' In Italy in the 1830s a good musician was not expected to be a wild bohemian but a young man with good manners – at least in Lavigna's honest opinion.

In Busseto, Verdi told Barezzi he needed a job. He wanted to marry Margherita and pay back his debts. He began working on an opera; the libretto had been written by a friend in Milan, Antonio Piazza. A letter from Lavigna informed Verdi that a good job was available as organist at the Monza cathedral. But Barezzi asked him to stay, there was Margherita – and by December Verdi was still in Busseto. He wrote of his plight to Lavigna:

The Philharmonic Society reminded me of the pledges made, the insults they had been subjected to, the benefits I had received from the home town. ... They even threatened to hold me in Busseto by force if I made any move to leave. Except for the fact that the people here would turn against my benefactor Barezzi I would have left at once and neither their reproaches nor their threats could have held me. ...

The situation in Busseto slipped from bad to worse. For a while the government forbade the playing of music in the local churches. Later, music was permitted again but the Provost would not let Verdi play the organ in the cathedral, whereupon the Franciscan Friars outside the town invited him to play in their church. Thereafter, the Franciscan church was crowded on Sundays while the cathedral was nearly empty. There were enough intrigues, threats and curses for an early Verdi opera. Eventually the competition took place in Parma before Maestro Giuseppe Alinovi, the respected court organist. Ferrari had bowed out, discouraged, but a certain Rossi from Guastalla entered the lists against Verdi. After the competition – playing the piano and writing a fugue on a theme by Alinovi – the old man told Verdi: 'You should be Maestro in Paris or London, not in Busseto. I could not have done in a whole day what you did in a few hours.'

In April 1836 Verdi received his contract as Busseto's *Maestro di Musica*. On 4 May he married Margherita. They were not yet twenty-

OPPOSITE Verdi's birthplace at Le Roncole.

three, and much in love. Barezzi had 'arranged' for an apartment in a nice house, the Palazzo Tedaldi, and Verdi began teaching, composing, conducting. He had finished his first opera, *Rocester*. Some biographers, among them Gatti, claim that *Rocester* later became *Oberto*, Verdi's first produced opera. Others believe they are different works and that *Rocester* is lost, together with most other early Verdi compositions. Verdi talked many years later to Giulio Ricordi about *Oberto*, but his recollections are contradicted by early letters mentioning *Rocester*, which remains a minor Verdi mystery that may never be solved.

Verdi hoped to have *Oberto, Conte di Bonifacio* produced at La Scala, with the help of Lavigna, but his old teacher died suddenly in September. Verdi was very sorry; he had been fond of Lavigna. Professionally it was a frustrating time, though he and Margherita were happy with their baby, Virginia Maria Luigia. Verdi wrote a few songs. On 11 July 1838 their second child was born, a boy named Icilio Romano, and there was much happiness. It did not last: four weeks later the little girl, Virginia, seventeen months old, died of an unknown childhood disease. Verdi wanted to get away for he began to feel that Busseto had brought him nothing but bad luck. They would go to Milan. Margherita agreed, but what about the money? Verdi sat down and wrote to Barezzi (who lived five minutes away) asking for 'an additional 120 to 130 francs. This will be a straight loan and short-term. If you think favourably of this, tear up this note, keeping the loan a secret between us. . . . I am most eager to repay you quickly, and so is your daughter. I salute you from the heart. Yours most affec. G. Verdi.' Barezzi lent them the money and they went to Milan.

Merelli, the impresario, accepted *Oberto* for La Scala's spring season of 1839, but the production had to be postponed and in September Verdi had to ask Barezzi for another loan, 350 lire, as down payment on a small house in the Via San Simone: 'While I am working on my opera, I cannot raise the money by taking another job.' Then came another tragedy. On 22 October little Icilio died, sixteen months old. Again the cause of death was undetermined. The young parents were heartbroken but Verdi had to go on with the rehearsals.

Oberto was only a minor success and disappeared after fourteen performances – it was later produced in Turin, Genoa and Naples – but Merelli had faith in Verdi and gave him a contract for three more operas to be produced at La Scala and at the Kärntnertor-Theater in Vienna. The fee was four thousand lire and a share of the profits: a fortune for the young composer. He and Margherita hoped the bad days were over. They were still young, they could have children again, and he would write better operas.

Verdi began working on *Un Giorno di Regno* ('King for a Day') but

OPPOSITE Magherita Barezzi, Verdi's first wife.

19

went down with a bad attack of angina and had to stay in bed several weeks. Late in May, when he was better, Margherita became very ill. Verdi grew desperate and asked Barezzi to come to Milan. Barezzi arrived on 18 June — one hour before Margherita died. They buried her at San Giovannino Cemetery in Milan. The house in the Via San Simone was locked up, and Barezzi took Verdi to Busseto. A friend there later said that Verdi was 'on the point of mental aberration'. Verdi kept the wedding-rings he and Margherita had exchanged in a small copper box, with a lock of Barezzi's hair, and wrote on the box 'Mementoes of my poor family'. He never quite recovered from the shock, and he never talked about his loss.

Verdi's severe depression after his wife's death was not the last in his life, as it turned out: the genius who gave so much melodious beauty to mankind suffered all his life from spells of melancholy. For a while he lived in Busseto, miserable and lonely, in his brother-in-law's house but he had signed the contract with Merelli and had started on his second opera before his wife died. He had to finish it: he always kept his word.

The bill for the funeral of Margherita.

Unfortunately it was an *opera buffa*, though there is little comedy in the libretto, a sort of operetta about mistaken identity with a silly happy ending. *Un Giorno di Regno* was his worst failure. According to custom, the composer had to be in the orchestra pit during the premiere, sitting between the cellos ready to 'help out' during an emergency. Verdi never forgot the humiliation – the shouts, the laughter, the catcalls. After the premiere the opera was withdrawn. In a biographical sketch which his friend and publisher Giulio Ricordi wrote thirty-nine years later, probably after Verdi had talked to him, the composer is quoted:

Un Giorno di Regno did not please. Certainly some of the fault was in the music; part, too, in its execution. With a mind tortured by my domestic disaster, embittered by the failure of my work, I persuaded myself that I had nothing more to find in music and I decided never to compose again.

Verdi gave up the house in Milan – he had already sent the furniture back to Busseto – and lived in a furnished room in the Piazzeta San Romano. He had become apathetic, saw no one, occasionally ate something at a small trattoria nearby. He was in bleak despair; it was the worst time in his life.

'I was discouraged and gave no thought to music', Verdi much later dictated to Giulio Ricordi in his autobiographical reminiscences. 'Then, one winter evening, as I was leaving the Galleria De Cristoforis, I met Merelli on his way to the theatre. The snow was falling in large flakes. He took me by the arm and asked me to accompany him to La Scala. . . .' That was the beginning of *Nabucco*, the turning-point.

Bartolomeo Merelli, the powerful impresario who managed Milan's La Scala and the Kärntnertor-Theater in Vienna, showed him a libretto asking him to read it. According to Ricordi, Verdi remembers:

It was a thick bundle written in a large hand, as was the style then. I made it into a roll, took leave of Merelli, and started for home. On the way I felt a sort of uneasiness, a great sadness, an anguish that swelled up my heart. . . . At home I threw the manuscript with a violent gesture on the table and stood rigid before it. The libretto, falling on the table, opened itself, and without quite realizing it, my eyes fixed on the page before me at one particular line, 'Va, pensiero, sull'ali dorate'.

'Fly, thought, on golden wings', the magnificent chorus in *Nabucco*, became the (unofficial) anthem of the Risorgimento, the Italians' revolt against foreign oppression. On the stage of La Scala it was sung by the Israelites, captive in Babylon under Nebuchadnezzar ('Nabucco'), as they dream of their lost homeland, of freedom. But La Scala's first-night audience, and later, Italians everywhere, understood the deeper meaning and immediately identified themselves with the Hebrews in Babylon. Since then Verdi's chorus remains an almost supra-national hymn, like Beethoven's *Ode to Joy*, or perhaps *La Marseillaise*, that may be sung by people anytime, anywhere.

Verdi then describes with touching simplicity how he read the magic words and was deeply moved, 'particularly since they almost paraphrased the Bible, which I have always loved to read'. He went on reading the whole libretto, still resolved never to compose again, but ... 'sleep would not come, I got up, I read the libretto, not once, but twice, three times, and in the morning, it's fair to say, I knew it by heart. Even so, I decided not to change my mind. The next day I returned to La Scala and handed the manuscript to Merelli.'

One sees Verdi, seventy, nodding, musing, remembering, as he talks to Ricordi:

'Beautiful, eh?', he said.
'Very beautiful.'
'Well, then, put it to music!'
'No, never. I want no part of it.'
'Put it to music, put it to music!'
And Merelli stuffed the libretto into my overcoat pocket, seized me by the shoulders, and not only shoved me out of his office but closed the door, and locked it in my face. Now what? I went home with *Nabucco* in my pocket. Today, a verse; tomorrow another; one time a note, another a phrase ... little by little, the opera was done.

On the morning after the *Nabucco* premiere on 9 March 1842, Verdi literally woke up and found himself famous. His father called it a miracle. Barezzi said it was no miracle, it was exactly what he had hoped for during the years of Verdi's struggles. Verdi was glad to be able to pay off his debts and to have some financial security. The sudden fame meant little to him though. He was still too deeply wounded by the death of Margherita and the children and by his failures. Gradually he began meeting people again. The men of Milan loved to spend hours sitting in the cafés talking, mostly politics. Many admired the shy young man from Busseto who had written that wonderful hymn. Many had never heard *Nabucco* but everybody could sing 'Va, pensiero'; and many did, especially when some of the hated Austrian officers walked by. When Verdi was inspired to write the music of 'Va, pensiero', he was not consciously trying to write a patriotic song. He *was* an Italian patriot, a liberal republican. After the coronation of the Austrian Emperor, Ferdinand I, at the Duomo in Milan as King of Lombardy and Venetia, Verdi wrote to Busseto, 'The Emperor is gone and the brothel is over'. Doubtless, he thought of his own people when he wrote about the oppressed Hebrews in

The opening of the chorus 'Va, Pensiero' from *Nabucco*, arranged for piano and voice.

Nabucco; he was young, full of ideals, and his great chorus had fire and passion. It was written, as Beethoven might have said, from the heart to the heart, and the people felt it right away. But Verdi could not have anticipated that his hymn would arouse the soul of his nation during the years of the Risorgimento.

It was inevitable that Verdi found himself invited into the literary and social salons of the beautiful, fascinating women of Milan. Among his early friends were Andrea and Clara ('Clarina') Maffei. He was from Trento, had been educated in Munich, a knight of the Austrian Monarchy, and a Habsburg loyalist. The Contessa, charming and beautiful, came from an ancient, noble family in Bergamo, and dreamt of an independent, united Italy. Their political disagreements and Andrea's way of life – he was a gambler, spent his wife's money, and was always involved with other women – eventually broke up their marriage. The Contessa later lived with Carlo Tenca, the editor of the distinguished literary magazine *Rivista Europea*. Maffei, an

Countess Clarina Maffei, in whose salon Verdi first mingled with the intelligentsia of Milan. Clarina and her husband Andrea were to become his life-long friends.

amateur poet, translated Shakespeare, Schiller and Milton. Verdi remained a lifelong friend of both. He was never 'involved' with Clarina, as the gossip-columns reported, and when the Maffeis decided to separate in 1846 Verdi witnessed the separation agreement.

Clarina Maffei had the leading intellectual salon in Milan. The young peasant from Le Roncole was soon accepted by the sophisticated circle of poets and politicians. He was not only respected as the composer of *Nabucco*: that would not have lasted. But Verdi was well informed about politics, literature and, above all, he seemed to have a mature attitude toward life. This was surprising since he had never been outside of his native *paese* and Milan, while most of the others had been to Paris, London, Vienna. And he was only twenty-nine. People felt that he was intellectually honest; there was no pretence about him, nothing phoney.

Between 1842, when Verdi began to be seen in the salons of Milan, and 1849, when he was living with Giuseppina Strepponi in Paris, his name was often mentioned in connexion with interesting women. A whole literature exists about his assumed or alleged love-affairs, mostly written by Italians who obviously feel compelled to sustain the popular notion that Italians are great lovers and that Verdi, a national hero, must have been a very great lover indeed. How could Verdi (the argument goes) have expressed passions so truthfully on the stage if he had not lived through such passions himself? This argument completely misunderstands the nature of artistic creation, which remains inexplicable and mysterious. A somewhat more prosaic argument was based on Verdi the man – good-looking, healthy, young, famous, and fascinating to many women: of course (they say) he must have had affairs, preferably with married women who know so much, or with women of the theatre. It was almost his duty. Clarina Maffei was often mentioned, and so was Giuseppina Appiani.

Unfortunately for the chroniclers Verdi believed that his private life, and particularly his love life, was his and nobody else's business. Of course he liked attractive women and looked at them, even when he was happy with the woman who became his mistress and then his wife, Giuseppina Strepponi, but he never talked about the women he knew. He has left many letters but not a single love note and was strict about protecting his private life. However, Milan in the 1840s was not a big city, about 150,000 inhabitants, and the circle of artists, poets, musicians, and theatrical people was limited; gossip and speculation were unceasing.

Even the local biographers have never been able to agree on Verdi's relationship with Giuseppina Appiani. She was the daughter of Conte Antonio Strighelli, sixteen years older than Verdi, a widow with children, probably six. She was socially ambitious. Her salon was as famous in Milan – though somewhat different – as Clarina Maffei's. Madame Appiani collected musical celebrities, including Bellini and Donizetti who lived for some time in her house. There were rumours linking her romantically with her guests, and with Verdi but there is no evidence that she was more than 'a music-loving lady of society, kindhearted, hospitable and generous' as Frank Walker writes in *The Man Verdi*.

Much nonsense was written about the artistic 'rivalry' between Donizetti and Verdi, sixteen years younger. Proof now exists that Donizetti had heard *Nabucco*, liked it and praised it. Later he was quite pleased with the success of Verdi's *Ernani* in Venice. On 18 May 1844 Verdi wrote to Donizetti:

Honoured Maestro,
It was a pleasant surprise for me to read your letter to Pedroni [Giacomo Pedroni was a mutual friend] in which you so kindly offer to help at the rehearsals of my *Ernani*. I have no hesitation at all in accepting, with the deepest gratitude, your courteous offer, convinced that my music can gain a lot if *Donizetti* deigns to give it his attention. Thus I can hope that the spirit of the work will be fully appreciated. I beg you to occupy yourself both with the general direction and with such minor adjustments as may be necessary, especially in Ferretti's part. ... To you, Sig Cavaliere, I pay my compliments. You are one of those few men who have sovereign gifts and no need of individual praise. The favour you bestow on me is too great for you to doubt my gratitude. ... With profoundest esteem,
Your humble servant,
G. Verdi

It is clear that there was mutual admiration between the two composers. When Donizetti became very ill in 1845, Verdi wrote to Madame Appiani: 'If you can give me news of the sick man you will be giving me the best of presents. Others will not believe me sincere, but you will. If I don't love Art for myself I am interested in it for his sake, and for the sake of the prestige it brings to our country.'

Verdi's next opera was based on a libretto by Temistocle Solera who had written *Nabucco* and has acquired a measure of immortality as the poet of 'Va, pensiero'. *I Lombardi alla Prima Crociata* was after a poem by the Milanese poet Tomasso Grossi, about the Lombards trying to liberate Jerusalem from the Saracens. It was Verdi's first conscious effort to write a 'patriotic' opera to express the feelings of his compatriots under Austrian occupation. His new opera also involved him, for the first time, with censorship problems. In one scene a Saracen is converted and baptized by the Christian Maid, and the Archbishop of Milan called it a sacrilege to show baptism (a sacrament) on the opera stage.

Milan's clerical groups were against Verdi and the anti-clerical claque for him; it was Busseto all over again, only worse. The premiere on 11 February 1843 was a popular success though the work has since been forgotten. The listeners immediately identified themselves with the Lombards; the Saracens were, naturally, the hated Austrians. When the tenor sang '*La Santa Terra oggi nostra sara*' ('The Holy Land today will be ours'), the people shouted '*Si! Si! Guerra! Guerra!*'

I Lombardi pleased the audience better than the critics, who wrote that Verdi had created theatrical effect rather than true drama. There was a beautiful violin solo, almost a short concerto, as prelude to the third act, and there was already a typical Verdi trio, later repeated in *La Traviata* and other works – one lover who dies, one who survives heartbroken, and a father-figure exuding noble resignation. Verdi dedicated the score to 'Her Majesty, the Imperial Princess Maria Luigia of Parma, Austrian Archduchess'. It was an act of gratitude as Marie-Louise had done much for the arts in Parma. (Verdi had dedicated *Nabucco* to Archduchess Adelaide of Austria, but even his patriotic friends did not mind for Adelaide lived in Milan, and later married Vittorio Emanuele, Duke of Savoy, who in 1860 became the first King of united Italy.) Marie-Louise was pleased and received Verdi in audience. He was given a gold pin with his monogram set in diamonds.

At the Teatro Regio in Parma Verdi supervised a new production of *Nabucco*. Giuseppina Strepponi, who had taken the part of Abigaille at the premiere in Milan, sang again. Ever since there has been a tradition among the Parmigiani that the great love-affair began, naturally, in Parma.

2
GIUSEPPINA

'Not everyboby can write *Aïda*,' Giuseppina once said, 'but some-body has to pack and unpack the trunks.' Giuseppina understated her lifelong role as the woman behind Verdi. She did much more. She encouraged him after he played her the score of his first opera, *Oberto*. She helped him during his depressions, often just by being there. She had her faults but she was often wise and patient, and always loved and admired him. She never interfered with his work – she had too much respect for his creative genius – but she was often the first who heard his new melodies, and she was his most influential critic. Her letters tell us much about Verdi. She signed them 'Peppina', sometimes 'Your poor nuisance'. He might have created less if she had not been always around. Yet she managed to keep a certain, admirable independence; she paid for her clothes out of her own money. They often agreed to disagree. She even understood that he could be an agnostic yet deeply religious in his soul. It was a mature, civilized relationship.

Giuseppina Strepponi was born in Lodi in 1815, two years after Verdi. Her father, Feliciano Strepponi, *maestro di cappella* at the Monza cathedral (the job was later offered to young Verdi) and a minor composer, died early, and there were four children and no money. Giuseppina, the oldest, then studied singing at the Milan Conservatory (where they had rejected Verdi), was granted a scholarship, made her debut in Adria and Trieste in 1834, two years after her father's death, and at once began supporting her family. She was nineteen, managed by Alessandro Lanari, a noted Florentine impresario.

Lanari and his competitor, Bartolomeo Merelli, were powerful figures in the nineteenth-century operatic world. They virtually owned their clients, leased them to opera houses, were consulted about parts and productions. 'There is no better support for a singer,' writes Gatti, 'than the protection of the powerful impresario who dispenses fame and money, and creates the glory and wealth of his dependents.' Not much has really changed since then, though the powerful figures are no longer called impresarios.

Giuseppina Strepponi as she appeared for a benefit performance in Venice.

In the five years following her debut Strepponi appeared in more than twenty opera houses in Italy. She sang too much and ruined her voice early. Gatti reports that Lanari 'ceded' her to Merelli, who took her to Vienna in 1835. Her biographer, Mercede Mundula, writes: 'The prima donna becomes the mistress of the conquering impresario. ... A child is born of that union that Merelli, legally married, cannot legitimize: Giuseppina's existence will be bound to that child of sin, as to a cross, for many years. ...' This is the style of the Sunday-supplement, and the content of truth is nil. Actually Giuseppina had a second child, after a miscarriage. She certainly was no 'innocent victim of circumstances', as described by her adoring biographer, but neither was she an adventuress, and certainly not 'a theatrical whore', as another biographer calls her.

Modern research confirms that Strepponi met Napoleone Moriani,

Bartolomeo Merelli, the
impresario of La Scala.

then a famous tenor, in Bologna in April 1837, when she was twenty-
two. They fell in love. Their son, Camillino, was born in April 1838.
They appeared together in many opera houses, carrying on a hectic
love-affair. Strepponi soon tried to break away from Moriani, hoping
to marry a certain 'M. of Verona' (as she calls him in some letters)
whose identity remains unknown. She was always discreet; even at
that early age she wanted, above all, peace and security which the stage
could never give her. For a year or so she had no contact with Moriani
but in March 1841 Lanari brought them together again for appearances
which were good box office. Late that year her second child was born.
Apparently Moriani would not marry her. Strepponi wrote in despair,
'I would shut myself up among the nuns, guarded from sight, so as not
to give him the satisfaction even of a glance.'

Early in 1842 she had a nervous breakdown. She had sung too much, perhaps the wrong parts. Her great successes were *La Somnambula*, *I Puritani*, *Cenerentola*, *Norma*, *Lucia di Lammermoor*; in Venice, Bologna, Rome, Florence and at La Scala. She must have been very good to be able to sing such extremely difficult parts, but the excitement with Moriani and the pregnancies were just too much. A medical report of 3 March 1842, signed by three well-known doctors, says: '... Signora Strepponi has a delicate constitution. Her loss of weight has become very considerable. She is tormented by frequent coughing, with an unpleasant feeling of irritation all along the trachea and larynx, especially after the effort of singing. Her pulse is weak and rapid . . . .' The doctors declared that this might lead to consumption 'unless Signora Strepponi ceases to exercise her profession . . .'.

Five days later Strepponi sang the part of Abigaille in the premiere of *Nabucco* which brought Verdi his first triumph. According to G. Romani in *Il Figaro* she was the only member of the cast who had no success. But she sang in the eight scheduled performances of the season: she needed the money. After the triumphal premiere Merelli offered Verdi a new contract, leaving it to the young composer to state how much money he wanted. During the second performance Verdi went to see Strepponi in her dressing-room, asking for her advice. She told him he should not ask more than Bellini had been paid for *Norma*. Later, she often remembered their meeting. Verdi was shy and awkward then.

A few days after the *Nabucco* premiere Donizetti informed an impresario in Rome that 'Strepponi was the only one who never got any applause, that her Verdi did not want her in his own opera, but the management imposed her on him'. There has been speculation about Donizetti's reference to 'her' Verdi. He knew that Strepponi was interested in the young composer, but he also knew there was no love-affair between them at that time. But there was always gossip in the small, excitable world around La Scala.

For a year after La Scala's *Nabucco*, Giuseppina did not sing. She was trying to nurse herself back to health, and she was very unhappy. She told Lanari that 'the distant prospect of matrimony with someone not very rich' had not come off, and she had to support her small children and the rest of her family. She was twenty-seven, felt spent and finished. She remains out of sight until her appearance, again as Abigaille, at the Teatro Regio in Parma where Verdi supervised the production. Despite exaggerated local claims, nothing indicates that she and Verdi liked and respected each other more than as artists.

During the following years Strepponi appeared in some smaller houses. Milan, Venice and Rome would no longer engage her. She sang in *Nabucco* and later in *Ernani*, in Bergamo and Palermo. The reviews were discouraging. Strepponi's final performance was on

11 January 1846, in *Nabucco*, singing 'her' Verdi for the last time. At thirty-one she was finished as a singer, though this was long before our own hectic jet age which has ruined many artists prematurely.

But she had courage and determination, and made a bold decision. She would go to Paris, where she was completely unknown, and try to build a new career as a teacher. Paris was then Europe's musical centre, more so than even Vienna. *La France musicale* on 15 November printed an announcement, 'Singing Lessons by Madame G. Strepponi', which ended:

... Mme Strepponi comes to propagate in Paris, in the world and by tuition, a style, a method, which are in harmony with our tastes and constitution. We are convinced that this winter this eminent artist will enjoy a vogue in the fashionable world of Paris. Her lessons will take place at her house, twice a week, on Tuesdays and Fridays, from three to five o'clock. There will be eight lessons a month, at the price of forty francs. For three months, a hundred francs.

Exactly *when* the friendship with Giuseppina Strepponi became a real love-affair remains another unsolved mystery in Verdi's life. Neither he nor Giuseppina ever gave any hint. Verdi might have said it was nobody's damned business but their own. The biographers are reduced to guesswork. Some venture the opinion that the affair started at the time of *Nabucco*, in Milan, in 1842, but this does not explain why Verdi never spent much time with Giuseppina in the years that followed. The conclusion today is that they became lovers in Paris, late in 1847.

Verdi had not gone there for the express purpose of visiting Strepponi. He had produced his new opera *I Masnadieri* (after Schiller's *Die Räuber*) for the British impresario, Benjamin Lumley, at Her Majesty's Theatre in London. It was Verdi's first opera written for a non-Italian production, an exciting event for him and for London, where no important Italian composer had ever had a premiere – neither Rossini, Bellini nor Donizetti. *I Masnadieri* had been a success, and on his way back to Italy Verdi decided to stop over in Paris and take it easy for a while. He had enough money and he was tired. These were the 'years in the galley'. He had written too many operas since *Nabucco* and some, he knew, were rather bad.

He knew, of course, that Giuseppina Strepponi was in Paris and he went to see her. She had a nice house, enough pupils, even a few acquaintances – though perhaps not exactly friends. Within less than a year she had made the difficult comeback from a famous ex-prima donna to a successful teacher. She was able to support herself, her family, and her children, whom she had left in Italy.

Autumn, not spring, is the loveliest season in Paris, and the autumn

A street scene in Paris in 1852 painted by Gucard.

of 1847 must have been very special for Verdi and Giuseppina. What happened no one knows, but by the end of the year they were openly living together. They had not rushed into this like a couple of adolescents with romantic notions. They had known each other for eight years, since the spring of 1839, when Verdi, carrying the score of *Oberto*, had called on the prima donna in Milan. Since then, both had gone through their private agonies. It was perhaps suffering and compassion, as much as love and passion, that brought them together. Each had learnt about life, painfully. Now, together at last, they were mature beyond their years. Verdi was only thirty-four, and she was two years younger.

Still, some mysteries remain. Strepponi's younger child, born late in 1841, seems to have died in infancy, because she never mentions the baby. We do not know its name; we do not even know whether it was a boy or a girl. But she often mentions Camillino in her letters. When she began living with Verdi in Paris, Camillino was nine years old, probably living in Florence. Strepponi's friend, Giovannina Lucca, the wife of the music publisher, later the competitor of Ricordi, occasionally looked after the boy, and there is no doubt that she told Verdi about him. But why did Giuseppina not have Camillino with her, at least for some time? Why did Verdi never want to see the boy? Again, these are questions that no research has been able to answer.

Nor do we know what Giuseppina told Verdi about the father of her boy. She is extremely cautious in her correspondence, referring to a mystery man she calls 'M'. Gatti accepted the version told him by members of the Barezzi family who had known Verdi – that Merelli was the boy's father: 'Verdi himself, pointing her out one evening in the theatre [La Scala] to his sister-in-law Marianna, Margherita's younger sister, speaks about it, mentioning the son she is said to have had by him.' Perhaps Giuseppina thought that it would be easier to accept Merelli, then a powerful impresario, as the father of her child than a colleague, a tenor. After 1850 Giuseppina never mentions Camillino in her letters. Moriani, who had retired two years after Strepponi, was then living in Florence. Did he take care of Camillino? We do not know. 'A vague tradition at Sant' Agata holds that Camillino died in an institution in Florence at about fourteen or fifteen years of age,' concludes Frank Walker, the most thorough biographer of all.

A portrait of Verdi by an unknown artist.

3
THE GALLEY SLAVE

Later in his life Verdi called the years between March 1842 (*Nabucco*) and March 1851 (*Rigoletto*) 'the years of the galley slave'. He wrote fourteen operas in nine years, among them two half-baked masterpieces, *Macbeth* and *Luisa Miller*. Nearly five hundred new operas were written in Italy in those years. The insatiable Italian public, who had been brought up on opera, were forever demanding new works from its popular composers. The operas were supposed to be routine stuff, more or less alike, written according to certain conventions. Some fine, sensitive composers could not stand the murderous pace and cracked up. Bellini died, aged thirty-four, of dysentery, weakened, a victim of overwork. Donizetti died in a lunatic asylum. Rossini, immensely gifted, stopped writing operas when he was thirty-seven though he lived another thirty-nine years. Only Verdi was sufficiently hard and flexible to stand the atrocious demands. For years he gave the public what it wanted, often writing mediocre music, although almost all his early operas have moments of genius. Some are occasionally revived, but only briefly.

Verdi wrote fast and furiously in his 'galley years'. He was for a long time still suffering under the shock of having lost Margherita and their children. Work was the best antidote to his prolonged moods of depression. The impresarios were beginning to compete for his operas, and the money was tempting. 'Who knows whether I shall not wake up one morning a millionaire!,' he once wrote to Emilia Morosini, a friend in Milan; 'What a lovely word, with a full, lovely meaning! And how empty, in comparison, are words like "fame", "glory", "talent", etc.' Verdi knew that money was not everything but it would buy a lot. He was no exception. Great artists, from Shakespeare and Michelangelo to Mozart and Beethoven, were often preoccupied with the sordid subject of money. Characteristically, Verdi used his first earnings, after paying off his debts, to buy some farmland in his native village, Le Roncole.

OPPOSITE The first performance of Victor Hugo's *Hernani* at the Comédie Française in 1830, painted by Besnaud. This provocative play was the basis of Verdi's *Ernani*.

In his later years Verdi paid for the sins of writing too fast and too much. He could not bear to hear some of his early, popular music. In Montecatini, that haven for spa doctors and organ-grinders, he once paid money to all local organ-grinders asking them not to come near his hotel when they were playing 'La donna è mobile' or Father Germont's aria from *La Traviata*. But one day in Rome he heard an orchestra playing the beautiful prelude to the fourth act of *La Traviata* and started to cry. He also wept when, toward the end of his life, he heard the magnificent vocal quartet from the last act of *Rigoletto*, 'Bella figlia dell' amore', one of the greatest ensembles on the opera stage, on a par with the sextet from *Lucia*, the quintet from *Die Meistersinger*, the trio from *Der Rosenkavalier*. Verdi created a miracle of emotional counterpoint in his quartet: each voice has its own melodic line yet the four voices are perfectly blended. When the quartet is beautifully sung (which does not happen often because it demands four equally excellent voices), the chamber texture of the quartet becomes quite transparent and its emotional impact as a blend is enormous. This was probably what Verdi had vaguely in mind when he spoke of an 'Italian vocal quartet' contrasted to the Viennese string quartet.

After *I Lombardi* at La Scala Verdi signed a contract with the Teatro La Fenice in Venice, then and now one of Italy's leading opera houses. He told his friends in Milan that after four operas in four years 'La Scala needed a rest from Verdi'. It was no secret though that he was getting angry about Merelli's sloppy productions at La Scala. All great opera houses have their ups and downs, and La Scala was no exception. The orchestral playing was bad, the sets were often ridiculous, there was no co-ordination between stage and orchestra pit. Verdi was also dissatisfied with Merelli's production of *Nabucco* at Vienna's Kärntnertor-Theater. He had gone there with the impresario, his first trip outside Italy. Donizetti later told everybody at Madame Appiani's salon that the Italians had been received in Vienna 'almost with scorn'. It has been suggested that Verdi's resentment against Merelli may have had something to do with Giuseppina Strepponi, but this has never been proved.

Having signed the contract with Conte Carlo Mocenigo, the director of the Fenice, Verdi faced the problem of the libretto. Instinctively, Verdi sensed the deep affinity between Italian patriotism and French Romanticism. He became fascinated by Victor Hugo's drama *Hernani*. Hugo was a revolutionary Romanticist who dared challenge the Establishment followers of the Classicists, Corneille and Racine. *Hernani* was provocatively anti-Classical, full of passion and violence, with several suicides onstage. For the premiere at the Comédie

Française in 1830, Hugo had organized his claque of revolutionary long-haired poets, led by Théophile Gautier in green trousers and a dress coat with velvet lapels. Verdi loved it. He had only three months to deliver the score of his opera; not one line of the text was written. Verdi did an outline and the house poet at the Fenice, Francesco Maria Piave, would do the verses. No problem. How wonderful to be gifted and twenty-nine! It did not bother Verdi that earlier the great Bellini had started work on his own *Ernani* but had given up under pressure from the Austrian censors and simply used much of the *Ernani* music for *La Somnambula*.

The less said about the story of Verdi's *Ernani* the better. Bernard Shaw liked much of the music but parodied a scene from the opera in *Arms and the Man*. (A Swiss soldier runs away from a battle and gets into a lady's bedroom while munching some chocolate.) Yet the melodic genius of young Verdi turned this contrived nonsense into an exciting opera. The seductiveness of the music was irresistible; a critic wrote that people leaving the opera house were humming some of the melodies, exactly as seven years later, when they heard 'La donna è mobile' at the Fenice. Verdi had some fights with Sophia Loewe, the difficult prima donna and after the third performance he left, having personally thanked everybody in the cast except Madame Loewe, who received a cool, polite note. The former peasant boy from Le Roncole was learning fast the subtleties of operatic diplomacy.

Ernani (9 March 1844) was followed by *I Due Foscari* (3 November 1844) at Rome's Teatro Argentina and, only three months later, came *Giovanna d'Arco* (15 February 1845) at La Scala. Everything went wrong. During the rehearsals 'Verdi shouted like a madman and stamped his feet so much he looked as though he were playing the organ', his pupil Muzio wrote to Barezzi. Verdi had rows with everybody. Erminia Frezzolini, the prima donna – who was rumoured to be having an affair with Verdi – spent most of her time crying instead of singing. But Verdi's fury was directed mostly against Merelli. A few weeks after the premiere of *Giovanna d'Arco*, Merelli produced *I Due Foscari*, putting the opera's third act *before* the second. Verdi said he was finished with La Scala – and he did not come back until 1869, twenty-four years later.

Only six months after *Giovanna d'Arco*, Verdi produced the premiere of *Alzira* (12 August 1845) at the Teatro San Carlo in Naples, and then came *Attila* (17 March 1846) again at the Fenice in Venice. The mere physical effort of writing so many scores in so short a time seems miraculous unless one remembers what Mozart could do in an incredibly short time, or that Donizetti composed the last act of *La Favorite* in five hours. Somehow, most of Verdi's operas were well

Sophia Loewe, the temperamental German soprano who quarrelled with Verdi over the production of *Ernani*.

received by the public (though not by the critics). People liked the exciting melodies, the marches and choruses, his ability to convey a patriotic meaning to his operatic characters in the years before 1848. (He was certainly 'with it', and the people loved his 'message'.)

Take *Attila* for instance, based on a play by Zacharias Werner about the invasion of Italy by the Huns. In a great scene between Attila and Pope Leo 1 (based on historical fact) the Pope persuades Attila not to invade Rome. Piave, a hard-working hack, wrote the libretto but Verdi found it lacking in excitement and gave the book to Solera, who had written *Nabucco* and could be relied on to create some stirring verses such as 'Va, pensiero'. Unfortunately Solera was having one of his lazy spells. The faithful Muzio reported indignantly to Barezzi in Busseto that 'the poet was still in bed at eleven o'clock in the morning'. Solera delivered his version and promptly went off to Spain where he was said to have had an affair with Her Majesty the Queen, which delighted Solera's many friends in Milan. Verdi had to ask Piave to

Temistocle Solera, the librettist of *Nabucco, Il Lombardi, Giovanna d'Arco* and *Attila*.

help out once more while he did the music. He was suffering from rheumatism, and Muzio wrote: 'We rub him [Verdi] continually.'

The premiere of *Attila* at the Fenice was a great patriotic event, though less of an artistic one. When the Huns arrived at the Adriatic, people began shouting *'Italia! Italia!'* Solera had written an exciting line for a Roman saying to Attila, *'Avrai tu l'universo, resti Italia a me'* ('You take the universe, leave Italy to me'), and Verdi had a fine melodic idea. People in the audience jumped up, shouting *'L'Italia a noi!'* ('Italy for us!'). It must have been a great evening. The censors were so stunned they did not even object. But Verdi was no fool where his music was concerned, and after *Attila* he wrote to Contessa Maffei, 'It is not inferior to the others'. The good Muzio wrote to

Benefactor Barezzi: 'Verdi does nothing in the way of writing but amuses himself [in Milan] with walks or drives in one of the five or six carriages at his disposal. All the lords and ladies who pay court to him compete among themselves to amuse him. . . . He goes to bed early and sleeps well. He will soon be completely restored again.'

Verdi had been lucky to find Emanuele Muzio, who became his pupil, then his secretary, and finally his trusted friend for life. Muzio's early history resembles Verdi's, but he lacked Verdi's genius. Eight years younger, the son of a poor cobbler, he came from Zibello, a small village near Busseto. He studied music there and became the local organist. Then Verdi's benefactor, Barezzi, supported Muzio (who, as Verdi before him, got a small pension from the local charity, Monte di Pietà). Eventually Muzio came to Milan, trying to get admission to the Conservatory, and was rejected, as Verdi had been. It was Barezzi who got them together. Barezzi noted in his cash book on 10 April 1844 that he gave Muzio a loan of 180 lire and 80 centesimi and that 'Verdi and Muzio left together for Milan'.

Afterwards Muzio kept Barezzi constantly informed on what they were doing and his letters, often naive and with excessive detail, give an intimate picture of the composer. Muzio remained forever loyal to 'Mio Signor Maestro Verdi'. Once he wrote to Barezzi, 'My Signor Maestro has a grandeur of mind, a generosity, a knowledge, a heart, such as that to find a good parallel one would have to set beside it your own and say that you and he are the most generous hearts in all the world'. Muzio's devotion is often touching and his information always accurate. He worshipped Verdi, who treated him like the son he never had: 'This morning [Verdi] asked me, "How do you think you are getting on since you've been studying with me?" I told him, "I have been born again".' Besides studying music with Verdi he took care of the household and business details, talked to people Verdi did not want to see, kept many bores away. Later Muzio composed four operas and was for several years director of the Théâtre Italien in Brussels. But he devoted much of his life to protecting Verdi. He is among the most genuine, and endearing of the people associated with Verdi.

Verdi needed Muzio; he was often sick in these years while he was, according to his enemies, 'composing as fast as his pen could write'. He was not happy, and some of his illnesses were probably psychosomatic. (He was heard to remark while composing *Attila* that he was 'almost dying'.) While he was working on an opera he often complained of a chronic sore throat. Verdi always wrote mainly for the voice, treating even the orchestra as a blend of human voices. While developing his melodies he may have subconsciously strained his vocal chords, without even singing. Only in his later years, when he wrote *Otello* and *Falstaff*, did he no longer strain his inner voice. He was then thinking of words, sounds and music as a whole; he was no longer writing melodies. But while he suffered a lot during the 'years in the galley', he was learning a lot, preparing himself for his master-pieces. He learnt to develop character and action through vocal lines. Very few composers were capable of it: Monteverdi, Gluck, and above all Mozart, whose melodic lines (as Richard Strauss once remarked wistfully) go on and on and on. Verdi could do it, surpassing the melodic but somewhat static lines of Bellini. He had the true Italian gift of expressing a dramatic situation, a lyrical moment, a passionate climax through melody. As he later said, he had learnt 'to bend the notes'. It took time though, and Verdi knew it. Of *Alzira*, one of his galley-years operas, he later said, *'Quella è proprio brutto'* ('That one is really terrible').

Verdi had a contract with the publisher Francesco Lucca to deliver an opera 'for the Carnival of 1848', but he refused Lucca's advance and sent him a doctor's certificate stating that 'Verdi could not write music without grave risk to his health and perhaps even to his life', which sounds like a line written by one of his early librettists. He was also terrified of Lucca's wife, Giovannina, a somewhat melo-dramatic lady who once made a terrible scene in Verdi's apartment, telling him that he was wonderful while her husband did 'nothing but sigh in bed', and, incidentally, what about the promised new opera? Verdi sent another certificate to the impresario Benjamin Lumley in London who wanted another Verdi opera, having successfully staged *Ernani* at Her Majesty's Theatre in 1845. Lumley, familiar with the Italian propensity for drama and death, wrote back that 'Royal applause would cure any ill'.

In July 1848 Verdi and his friend Andrea Maffei went to the spa of Recoaro in the Venetian Alps. The Maffeis had just agreed to separate and Andrea was deeply depressed. So was Verdi, who did not feel well. The two poor men were congenial company. Fortunately Verdi soon got bored with the spa, a sure sign that he was not dying, though some newspapers reported that he was 'close to death'. He was thinking of his next opera, with three ideas in mind: an opera based on Schiller's *Die Räuber*, translated by Maffei, which later became *I Masnadieri*; another based on Grillparzer's *Die Ahnfrau* which he never composed; and a third project, based on *Macbeth*, by his favourite playwright.

As always, Verdi's first thought was who would pay for the operas. Lucca would have to get one, Lumley in London the other, and Alessandro Lanari, the brilliant impresario of the Teatro della Pergola in Florence, the third. Lanari was a shrewd businessman. He had

OPPOSITE Giuseppina Strepponi with the music of *Nabucco*.
OVERLEAF Costume designs for Rigoletto at La Scala.

44

successfully produced *Attila*, sending long reports to the 'dying' Verdi that contributed to his miraculous recovery, and later he visited the composer in Milan, presenting him with an album about Florence, dedicated by the city's leading families 'with respectful admiration'. Incidentally, the leading families had already subscribed to the premiere of the new (as yet unwritten) opera. Verdi might have smiled ironically, but he could not help being impressed. Florence was synonymous with two of his gods, Dante and Michelangelo, and Florence meant much to his idol, Alessandro Manzoni. Lanari mentioned a brilliant young conductor, Angelo Mariani, just twenty-five, whom he might be able to get. (He did not get him: Mariani was offered more money in Copenhagen.)

Verdi began working on the music for *I Masnadieri* and at the same time wrote a long scenario for *Macbeth*. Eventually, he decided to do *Macbeth* first because he heard the part of Macbeth as a baritone, and there were a few good ones around. He heard Karl Moor in *I Masnadieri* as a tenor, and his favourite tenor, Gaetano Fraschini, would not be available. These are the prosaic facts that influence the great compositions: thanks to the unavailability of a great tenor, Verdi wrote *Macbeth*, his earliest masterpiece, though an imperfect one. And when Lumley got nervous and came to Milan, Verdi promised him *I Masnadieri*, to be premiered three or four months after the first performance of *Macbeth* in Florence. Verdi, having been 'close to death' a while ago, signed the contracts, confident he would write two operas in ten months. Lucky Italians – Rossini, Donizetti, Verdi, who dashed off wonderful operas in no time at all, unlike poor Beethoven who tortured himself ten years with *Fidelio*, still a somewhat imperfect work.

Verdi began working on *Macbeth* in October 1846, and thanks to the faithful Muzio we know all about his daily routine. There was three hours' work in the morning, Verdi sitting at one end of a long table, Muzio at the other. Once in a while Verdi would walk over to the piano, and play and sing a melody. He had lunch with Muzio, at home or elsewhere and in the early afternoon played billiards with him. In the evening, Verdi might call on Clarina Maffei or Madame Appiani, often with Muzio. When Barezzi wrote to Muzio that a good post near Busseto was open, Muzio declined regretfully though he knew his family would need the money. His first loyalty was to Verdi. 'Please explain this to my mother,' he wrote to Barezzi; 'I haven't the heart to write to her.'

In *Macbeth* Verdi changed his style of composing. Before, he often wrote the melodies and arias first, and later put them into the score, while rehearsing the singers at the theatre. This time he thought of scenes, the beginning and the end, leaving in between space for the

OPPOSITE La Rocca di Busseto in 1857.

49

arias that he already sensed or perhaps heard in his mind, which made for continuity. This was the beginning of his own kind of music drama, which had no relation to the *Musikdrama* that Wagner had not as yet evolved, though *Der fliegende Holländer* had been produced three years earlier. Verdi felt that the attempted continuity was essential to translate the spirit of Shakespeare into music. He was still a long way from succeeding: the path led by way of *Don Carlos* to *Otello*; but he was at the beginning.

As Verdi became involved in his first Shakespeare opera, he got passionately attached to it. *Macbeth* caused him much heartache – more than any other opera. The problem began with Piave's poor libretto which Verdi was unable to improve. And there were casting problems. Sophia Loewe, the prima donna Verdi respected although she had been very difficult, had lost her voice and acquired a husband, Prince Liechtenstein. Marianna Barbieri-Nini, who sang Lady Macbeth, later wrote in her memoirs about the thirty-three-year-old composer:

More than a hundred piano and orchestra rehearsals of *Macbeth* were held. Verdi was never satisfied and demanded that the singers give a more and more concentrated rendering of their parts. In the morning and evening when the Maestro came to rehearse, all eyes would search his face to see whether he had some new torture for us. . . . Incredible though it sounds, the duet with the baritone, 'Fatal mia donna,' was rehearsed a hundred and fifty times. There was no such thing as defying Verdi's will. He was a tyrant to be implicitly obeyed.

After Lady Macbeth's sleepwalking scene during the premiere, the *diva* was in her dressing-room, exhausted but exhilarated. Suddenly Verdi came in: 'He gesticulated and his lips moved as if he were trying to make a speech but not a word came out. I could not speak either, only laugh and cry. I saw that Verdi's eyes were red too. He squeezed my hand hard and rushed out. That moment was a magnificent reward for those months of hard work and continuous strain. . . .'

For a few days after the premiere Verdi was euphoric, but gradually his analytical mind told him that something was very wrong with *Macbeth*, probably with the libretto. Andrea Maffei tried to improve Piave's text and made it even worse, but Verdi sent him a gold watch and thanked him for rewriting the sleepwalking scene. Some biographers mention Maffei among the people whom Verdi treated badly. Maffei's letter contradicts this theory. He writes that he needs Verdi's 'kindness and affection', admitting that 'the loneliness in which I find myself would be sweet to an egotist but I need friendship, and yours in particular. You could not take it from me without breaking my heart. . . . My pen and poor talent are for all time your servants. *Addio*.' This is not the language of a bitterly disappointed friend.

Eighteen years later Verdi revised *Macbeth* again for a production at the Théâtre-Lyrique in Paris, changing the orchestration, adding some numbers and a ballet; but the new version was not successful either. People were not yet ready for a psychological music drama. They expected melodies and arias from Verdi. He admitted that '*Macbeth* was a fiasco. Amen. I must say though that I did not expect it.' Could it be, he asked himself, that he did not understand Shakespeare, his favourite poet whom he had read and re-read since childhood? Saint-Saëns, who had planned his own version of *Macbeth*, wrote, 'It was an utter failure and cost Carvalho thirty thousand francs.'

Even in his younger years Verdi realized his inability to make a compromise. He wrote to the impresario Vincenzo Flauto, who had suggested that the composer's presence in Naples might help with the production of *Macbeth*:

Do not believe it! I am a sort of savage, and if the Neapolitans noticed so many defects in me the first time, it would be no different the second. I have been in Paris now for a year and a half, in the city where one is supposed to acquire good manners, but I must confess I am more of a bear than before. I have been wandering from country to country, and I have never said a word to a journalist, never begged a friend, never courted rich people to achieve success. Never, absolutely never! I shall always despise such methods. I do my operas, as well as I can. For the rest, I let things take their course without ever influencing public opinion to the slightest degree. . . .

In *Macbeth* Verdi was trying something new, but he did not dare go all the way towards music drama. As a concession to popular taste he added some traditional arias. However, in the sleepwalking scene he used no effects of vocal virtuosity – as Donizetti had done in *Lucia* – but wanted the aria to be sung almost in an anti-vocal style. He wrote about a production of *Macbeth* in Naples:

. . . Mme Tadolini has a wonderful voice, clear, liquid, and powerful, and Lady Macbeth's voice should be hard, stifled, and dark. Mme Tadolini's voice is the voice of an angel, and Lady Macbeth's should be the voice of a devil. Please bring these remarks to the notice of the directors of Maestro Mercadante, who will understand my ideas better than anyone, and of Mme Tadolini herself. . . .

Verdi was experimenting with something that (he sensed) was essential for Shakespeare, but he was not secure yet, making things difficult for his audiences and for himself. Only in his final master-pieces, *Otello* and *Falstaff*, had he learnt to turn Shakespeare into music, Italian music. *Macbeth* audiences missed a love story and a great tenor part. Macbeth is a baritone, perhaps the first true baritone part in the style of Verdi. His baritones are lyrical and often reach the lower

Emanuele Muzio, Verdi's devoted pupil and assistant, painted by Boldini.

range of the tenor voice. Don Giovanni and Figaro and Almaviva are bass baritones. Macbeth, Rigoletto and Luna (in *Il Trovatore*) are Verdi baritones. Verdi knew the importance of tenors, who often seem to radiate an audible sexual attraction, but Macbeth was the voice of his hometown people in Parma, who were natural baritones, not tenors.

Ten days after the premiere in 1847 Verdi wrote to Barezzi:

Dear Father-in-Law,
    For a long time I have wished to dedicate an opera to you who has been for me a father, benefactor and friend. ... Now here is *Macbeth* which I love more than all my other operas and which I think the most worthy to present to you. It comes from my heart: let yours receive it, and let it be always a witness of the gratitude and affection borne for you by
                                        Your most affectionate G. Verdi

In the past twenty years *Macbeth* has been recognized by many people as a masterpiece, though it will never become a popular success.

Between *Macbeth* (1847) and *Rigoletto* (1851), his first worldwide success, Verdi wrote five new operas. Two of them are still remembered, both after plays by Schiller whom Verdi admired most after Shakespeare. He had signed a contract with Lumley for *I Masnadieri* ('The Robbers') in London, and late in May he went there with Muzio. It was a long trip and he was worried; he spoke neither German nor English. Muzio wrote to Barezzi that Verdi and he were shocked 'to travel throughout all these provinces and kingdoms without being asked for our passports'. Their trunks were examined only once, in Belgium. On the short trip from Busseto to Milan 'you always have your trunks open to show what's inside' and passports were examined repeatedly. In Strasbourg Verdi 'got the whim' to go down the Rhine to Cologne, and there they took the train to Brussels, 'We passed through twenty-four tunnels, some five miles long.' Always meticulous, Muzio estimated that the trip from Milan to Paris had lasted $91\frac{3}{4}$ hours.

Verdi stayed two days in Paris while Muzio went to London to settle the details. Verdi, already a star composer, did not want to get involved in minor matters, and he was getting tough with his impresarios, 'If [Lumley] says a single word that doesn't suit me, I shall give him back ten for an answer and leave immediately, whatever happens.' The proud language that a Parmigiano of a later generation, Arturo Toscanini, might have used. Verdi had no reason to be displeased with Lumley. Jenny Lind and Luigi Lablache, the great basso, were to sing, and Verdi also liked the tenor, Italo Gardoni, another Parmigiano. In Paris he went to the Opéra and wrote to

Clarina Maffei that he thought it 'mediocre'. It is not known whether he visited Giuseppina Strepponi in Paris.

Verdi arrived in London, which he and Muzio found 'a chaos'. Muzio wrote to Barezzi: 'What a confusion! People shouting, the poor weeping, steam engines, steamboats flying along, men on horseback, in carriages, on foot, and everybody howling like the damned. My dear Signor Antonio [Barezzi], you cannot imagine.' Verdi wrote that the climate was 'horrible' and proved to be a shrewd and accurate observer:

I took an extraordinary liking to the city. It isn't a city, it is a world. Its size, the richness and beauty of the streets, the cleanliness of the houses, all this is incomparable. You stand amazed, feeling very small, when in the midst of all this splendour you look over the Bank of England and the docks. Who can resist these people? The surroundings and the countryside are marvellous. I do not like many of the English customs, or rather, they do not suit us Italians. How ridiculous it looks when people imitate the English in Italy!

The premiere of *I Masnadieri*, on 22 July 1847, was certainly a social event, attended by Queen Victoria and Prince Albert, the Duke of Wellington and all the *hoi polloi*. Most critics liked the opera, except Henry Fothergill Chorley who felt about Verdi as Hanslick felt about Wagner. Chorley called *I Masnadieri* 'the worst opera which was given in our time at Her Majesty's Theatre', and flatly stated that 'Verdi is finally rejected'. Even Jenny Lind was no help, 'so utterly worthless was the music'. Maffei's pedestrian libretto was no help either, but there is a great 'Verdi trio', father and son and soprano, and some fine arias and rousing choruses.

Verdi left London after the second performance, having turned down Lumley's offer to become musical director of Her Majesty's Theatre. Verdi was to direct the productions, conduct some of them, and compose one opera a year. He would receive the (enormous) salary of sixty thousand lire, an apartment, a carriage, and he would have four months every year to himself. Lumley was prepared to sign this fabulous contract for ten years. Verdi wisely said no. He would have had to rebuild the orchestra, he was still under contract to Lucca and, above all, he wanted to remain an independent composer. Instead he went to Paris, 'to be quiet, free, away from all annoyances, seeing neither managers nor publishers'. He was thirty-four, he had money, he liked Paris. And there, as we have seen, he fell in love with Giuseppina Strepponi.

4
GETTING NOWHERE FAST

Late in 1847 Verdi was getting increasingly concerned about the political future of his homeland. He and Giuseppina were ardent Italian patriots. In his letters Verdi shows more concern about politics than about his work. Though he had come to Paris to be free, 'seeing neither managers nor publishers', he agreed to accept the offer of the directors of the Opéra, submitted through his agent Escudier. Verdi was to do a revised version of *I Lombardi*, adding a few new numbers and a ballet. The Lombards became Frenchmen, the action was shifted from Milan to Toulouse, and the new package would be called *Jérusalem*. Verdi wrote to Clarina Maffei that the production, scenery and costumes were 'absolutely magnificent, for here they spare no expense'. He said little about the artistic side of the project but he did not have to; Clarina had learnt to read between his lines. It was strictly a commercial matter and Verdi liked the money. Later Ricordi had an Italian translation made and published a vocal score with Verdi's dedication 'to the distinguished singer, Signora Giuseppina Strepponi'. She deserved a better opera.

Verdi had invited Antonio Barezzi to Paris for a visit. After several weeks Barezzi returned to Busseto, telling everybody what a fine time he had with Verdi and Signora Strepponi, which is interesting when one considers what happened a little later in Busseto.

Verdi also worked on another 'commercial' project, his opera for the publisher Lucca, *Il Corsaro*. Piave's libretto was based on Byron's poem *The Corsair*. Verdi showed an appalling lack of interest. He sent the score to Lucca and forgot about it. He neither prepared the production, nor conducted the premiere at the Grande Teatro in Trieste; he did not even go there. *Il Corsaro* remains best forgotten. The only man praised by the critics was the man who had painted the scenery.

Verdi had reached a trough in his artistic creation. There was Giuseppina, much more important than any new opera. And there were the political events in Italy. On 13 March 1848 the revolt began

The scene in Milan near Santa Maria delle Grazie during the insurrection in April 1848.

in Vienna and soon turned into revolution. Metternich left Vienna the next evening; the most powerful man of the past decades (and the most hated by the Italians) was finished. Communications were slow and the news reached Milan only five days later. (Local revolts flared up in Budapest, Berlin and elsewhere.) There were fifteen thousand Austrian soldiers in Milan. Many of them were Hungarians and Croats who spoke no Italian, had not been infected by the Italian patriots, and remained loyal to the Austrian military commander, General (later Field-Marshal) Joseph Wenzel von Radetzky.

The revolt in Milan began on 18 March when a crowd collected in front of the Governor's palace. The soldiers fired at the demonstrators but the Milanese were not frightened off: on the contrary. They set up barricades. Housewives poured boiling water from the windows on to the Austrian soldiers in the streets. This was the beginning of *Cinque Giornate* ('The Five Days'), Milan's – and, as it turned out, Italy's – finest hour. Hundreds of barricades were set up in the streets

56

(which were much narrower than today). During the first three days people were exhilarated, almost drunk with the sweet scent of freedom. Manzoni, always afraid of crowds, had to be persuaded to appear on the balcony of his house in Via Morone, while people shouted 'Viva l'Italia! Viva Manzoni!' His sons were fighting in the streets and one was later captured by the Austrians and held hostage. It was a glorious time. The revolutionaries captured several city gates. Supplies were brought in and volunteers came from everywhere. Radetzky wanted to shell Milan but the foreign consuls protested vehemently and he hesitated, which encouraged the revolutionaries. On the fifth day the Austrian troops began to retreat toward the north. The next day the Austrians were gone. Milan was free for the first time since 1815.

News of the *Cinque Giornate* reached Paris late in March. Verdi immediately left and arrived in Milan in early April. It was all over, but the barricades were still up in the streets. Happy and elated, Verdi wrote to 'Citizen Francesco Maria Piave', then a soldier of the revolution in Venice:

Dear Friend, ask yourself whether I wished to remain in Paris, when I heard of the revolution in Milan! I left immediately but was only able to see these stupendous barricades. Honour to these brave men! Honour to all Italy which at this moment is truly great! Be assured, the hour of liberation has struck. ...

You talk of music to me! What are you thinking of? Do you imagine I want to occupy myself now with notes, with sounds? There is and should be only one kind of music to please the ears of the Italians of 1848 – the music of the guns! I would not write a note for all the gold in the world: I should feel immense remorse for using up music paper which is so good for making cartridges. My brave Piave, and all you brave Venetians, banish every petty municipal idea! Let all we Italians reach out a fraternal hand, and Italy will yet become the first nation of the world. ... I am drunk with joy. Just think, there are no more Germans [sic!] here. ... Farewell, my friend.

It is a fine, exciting letter, signed 'Giuseppe', not 'G. Verdi'. He was drunk with joy, but his joy was premature though all seemed well for a while. Manzoni and other leaders in Milan appealed to Carlo Alberto, King of Piedmont (the only independent part of Italy), and the Piedmontese troops marched into Lombardy. In Venice the 'brave Venetians' ousted the Austrians and proclaimed the Republic under Daniele Manin as President. But it soon became apparent that unification of Italy was a long way off. Carlo Alberto was having some second thoughts. Suppose he helped Lombardy to become a republic, how would this affect his own monarchy? Worse, the Milanese, who had all been united during the glorious Five Days, could not agree on

proclaiming their republic. The republicans among the patriots –
including Mazzini and Verdi – became infuriated and disenchanted.
Some people were in favour of a monarchy, under Carlo Alberto.
Others listened to Vincenzo Gioberti, a charismatic Roman Catholic
priest, who urged a federation of the Italian states under the Pope as
'President'. Once again, the revolution was devouring its own
children.

The news from Vienna was encouraging for the patriots. Emperor
Ferdinand and his court had fled, and a second wave of revolt swept
Vienna in May 1848. A Viennese newspaper published a poorly
written but exciting poem, *Greeting from Saxony*, by Richard Wagner,
Kapellmeister, in which he exhorted his fellow Saxonians to follow the
example of the Vienna revolutionaries. The revolution of 1848 remains
the only major issue on which Verdi and Wagner agreed. By 1871,
when Germany defeated France, Wagner was jubilant, an ardent
monarchist; while Verdi, deeply unhappy, was in his heart still a
republican, though he supported the King of Italy for the sake of his
beloved homeland.

Verdi went from Milan to Busseto to see Barezzi and his parents.
Piacenza had already joined Piedmont; Parma followed in May, by
plebiscite. Life went on much as usual in sleepy Busseto. Verdi sold
his farm in Le Roncole and bought a much larger estate near Busseto,
in the small village of Sant' Agata, and began talking to builders. It
was a good time to buy land since prices were depressed, owing to the
political complications.

The situation in Milan was moving from bad to worse. The various
factions could not settle their differences, and there were endless
squabbles. Mazzini wrote to George Sand in Paris: 'Reaction prevails
here. They threaten us. ... They send me anonymous letters telling
me to prepare for death by the dagger.' Everybody agreed that the
Austrians must be driven out of Italy but that was the only aim agreed
upon; what kind of Italy would they have when they were free? And
meanwhile Radetzky was rebuilding his army not far from Milan,
between Verona and Mantua.

Mazzini, Verdi, and their friends who pleaded for a republic were a
minority. Pope Pius IX – who had been hailed as a liberal, even a
progressive Pope after his election in 1846, when he had granted an
amnesty to more than a thousand people in Rome who had been
involved in the revolt of 1831 and 1832, shocking the conservative
powers all over Europe – now spoke out in an Allocution against an
Italian republic under his 'presidency', and even against a war of
independence. At the same time, the Pope secretly appealed to
Emperor Ferdinand for peace. The Pope suggested that Austria and

Italy observe their natural boundaries, which caused some cynical comment at Vienna's Ballhausplatz. 'Austria possesses her Italian provinces by the same treaties that have reconstituted the Temporal Powers of the Pope,' the Emperor was quoted as saying, which would indicate that he was not as 'feeble-minded' or 'mentally backward' as some historians have described him. The Austrians had no intention of giving up Lombardy-Venetia, one of their richest provinces. And the Pope would not even think of relinquishing *his* richest province, the area between Pesaro and Bologna. So much for the natural boundaries.

Late in May Verdi returned to Paris, bitterly disappointed. He knew that for the time being the fight was lost. He wrote to Salvatore Cammarano in Naples, asking him to start work on the libretto for the patriotic opera that the poet had earlier suggested. They had met three years before in Naples, where Cammarano was much loved by his friends for his bizarre ideas and eccentric behaviour. He was older than Verdi, tall and quiet and, as he said, 'often tired'. When he was tired he went to sleep no matter where he was. He was famous for the libretto of Donizetti's *Lucia di Lammermoor*; Verdi respected him, and

Barricades in the streets of Naples, May 1848.

had liked working with the poet on his *Alzira*. Now he wanted a 'patriotic' libretto from Cammarano. Verdi realized that manuscript paper was no good 'for making cartridges' after all. He now knew that he could not help Italy as a politician or a soldier; but maybe he could rouse the spirit of his countrymen by writing music. He had done it once, more or less unintentionally, with *Nabucco* and 'Va, pensiero'. Perhaps he could do it again, this time with all intention.

In Paris he and Giuseppina rented a house with a garden in Passy, which was then a quiet suburb, and later they lived in the Rue de la Victoire. The news from Italy was bad. Late in July Radetzky defeated the Piedmontese at Custozza. King Carlo Alberto signed an armistice, was called a Judas by the patriots, and had to escape from his headquarters where some patriots wanted to hold him prisoner. The glory of the Five Days was followed by shame and contempt. Early in August Milan and Parma were again occupied by Austrian troops. Many Milanese, afraid of reprisals, had already left town. Manzoni went to his wife's villa at Lago Maggiore, in Piedmont. Mazzini went to Lugano.

Verdi was deeply depressed. He wrote to Clarina Maffei: 'If we know how to seize the right moment and wâge the war that must be fought, the war of insurrection, Italy can yet be free. But God save us from putting our trust in our kings and foreign nations!' Clarina Maffei also went to Switzerland; so did Muzio, and Verdi sent him some money from Paris. To the revered Mazzini he sent his music for a patriotic poem, *Suona la Tromba* ('Sound the Trumpet'), written by Goffredo Mameli, a young poet from Genoa. Verdi wrote to Mazzini that he had tried to be 'more popular and easy than may have been possible for me', and he asked him to do with it what he wished: 'Burn it if it doesn't seem good enough.' Obviously, Verdi did not think that the music was very good; he never fooled himself about his own work. But as a wistful afterthought he wrote, 'May this hymn soon be sung among the music of the cannon on the plains of Lombardy.' His musical instinct had been right. Verdi's hymn did not become a sort of Italian *Marseillaise*. Another Mameli poem, *Fratelli d'Italia* ('Brothers of Italy') had earlier been set to music by Michele Novaro, now otherwise forgotten. *Fratelli d'Italia* became a popular song of the Risorgimento and, after 1946, the national anthem of the Italian Republic. It was one of Verdi's great regrets that he failed to give his country its national hymn.

Cammarano's patriotic opera, *La Battaglia di Legnano*, was based on a historical event, the battle of Legnano in 1176, when Frederick Barbarossa, the German King and Holy Roman Emperor, was defeated by the cities of the Lombard League. Verdi hoped the deeper meaning would be understood by Italian audiences, and it was. The premiere, at the Teatro Argentina in Rome, on 27 January 1849, was a great patriotic event. Verdi conducted and had to repeat the fourth act, which has a prayer, choruses, the death of the hero, and a final chorus. There was much chorus singing of *la patria*, and the audience went wild. In the end they shouted '*Viva Verdi!*' But patriotism does not seem to breed good music, and there is no reason to revive *La Battaglia* today. Many composers, from Beethoven to Shostakovitch, have failed when they tried to write patriotic music.

By July 1849 Rome was occupied by foreign troops, after a short, glorious interlude during which Garibaldi's four thousand volunteers were putting up a brave and hopeless fight against seventy thousand foreign troops. Garibaldi, the great guerrilla leader of the Risorgimento, retreated to San Marino, and eventually managed to escape from Italy. He went to New York and stayed away for ten years. In August 1849 it was all over bar the reprisals. Field-Marshal Radetzky wrote to his daughter: 'These Italians have never loved the Germans. Persuaded that they cannot liberate themselves by force, they have surrendered. We are avenged.'

Verdi and Giuseppina left Paris in the middle of August. There was another outbreak of cholera. But they left largely because Verdi did not want to live among Frenchmen at that time; he was thinking of the French troops that had occupied Rome, after the short and wonderful interlude of the Roman Republic. They went back to Busseto.

The Duchy of Parma had been relatively quiet for the past two years and was still almost an island of peace. There were no Austrian troops in the streets of Busseto – a sight that would have been too much for Verdi. The Parmigiani knew they were not as well off as the people in independent Piedmont, but they were certainly better off than those in occupied Milan, Venice or Rome. Thus Verdi's decision to live there for a while makes sense; but he was not alone, he was with Giuseppina and they were not married. Although Verdi knew the small-town atmosphere and had suffered much from it during the political fights before his appointment as *maestro di musica*, he does not seem to have worried about Busseto's reaction to his mistress. Giuseppina was more realistic. She had gone for a few days to Florence to look after her son, Camillino. From there she wrote to Verdi: 'Do not send any-one but come yourself to pick me up in Parma. I would be most embarrassed to be introduced into your house by someone other than yourself.'

The 'house' was the Palazzo Cavalli (now the Palazzo Orlandi), the finest in town. Verdi was Busseto's most famous citizen, and possibly its richest. The town's attitude became obvious the moment he helped Giuseppina to get out of the carriage. A few people happened to be standing around. A few minutes later the news was all over Busseto: Verdi and *that woman* from Paris had arrived. Oh, well, a woman of the theatre. What can you expect from such a person? A scandal, here in our nice, clean, peaceful Busseto.

Afterwards the scandal never stopped. The town revelled in its gossip. People ignored and humiliated Strepponi. When she went shopping they turned their backs to her. When she went to church they moved away from her. They all felt virtuous and above blame, and they let her know it. Why had Verdi decided to bring her to Busseto, of all places? He must have known that it would be different to Paris, where no one had really cared about them. Perhaps he wanted to be there to supervise the building of the new house on his Sant' Agata estate. But that could have been done by Muzio or someone else. It is more probable that Verdi became furious with the Bussetani and decided not to back out; he was going to show them. He still had old enemies in town who told each other how ungrateful he was 'after all we have done for him'. They talked as though they had done everything for him; as though he owed them his education, his talent, even his genius. Perhaps some political feelings were involved. There were many conservatives among his enemies, and Verdi, the republican revolutionary, wanted to rebel against convention and the Establishment. He disliked the philistine attitude of the petty-bourgeois in the town. He talked to no one, living with Giuseppina in splendid isolation, with half a dozen servants. For some time he even broke off relations with the much-loved Antonio Barezzi after he was told that Barezzi's wife had said that a visit to the Palazzo Cavalli was out of the question while Verdi lived there with 'that kept woman'. Barezzi told his wife how much he had liked Strepponi in Paris and his wife said, 'Why didn't you stay there with them?' It nearly broke Barezzi's heart. Fortunately, he got together again with Verdi and Giuseppina. Verdi's parents had also made some remarks about Giuseppina and Verdi never forgave them.

Before leaving Paris he had started work on another opera with Cammarano. After the fall of Rome, Verdi knew that this was not the moment for musical patriotism. The national movement had been suppressed all over the peninsula; the occupation troops were back. Verdi had long been attracted by Schiller's drama *Kabale und Liebe*. A titled father refuses to allow his son to marry a commoner. The two lovers commit suicide. Verdi liked the social significance and the anti-Establishment spirit of the play; he felt a great affinity for Schiller, the lifelong revolutionary. There would be no trouble from the censor, he hoped; and he was right.

The premiere of *Luisa Miller* (named after the heroine) in Naples, on 8 December 1849, was a success. The opera is still being performed

OPPOSITE An engraving of Busseto and Sant' Agata.

everywhere; many people feel, perhaps arbitrarily, that it is the beginning of Verdi's middle period, which gave us *Rigoletto* and other great successes. The critics sensed that Verdi had tried something new, an intimate, tender musical language which he later perfected so beautifully in *La Traviata*. Such divisions are meaningless for an artist's development is continuous, his style does not change from one day to the next. Verdi had written intimate love music before, even in some of his patriotic operas. But though the three acts of *Luisa Miller* were called 'Love', 'Intrigue', and 'Poison' – which is the outline of the plot – Verdi pursued his evolution with melodious recitatives, fewer breaks and longer melodic phrases, using melody more skilfully than before to develop character, plot, situation. He was, in short, rapidly learning how to write music drama. He composed a fine overture which has dramatic unity instead of being simply a medley of arias. *Luisa Miller* is perhaps the most interesting opera of his younger years. Nine years after the premiere it was produced in London and Chorley wrote, 'There are staccato screams in it enough to content any lover of shocking excitement.' Unwittingly, Chorley had praised Verdi's development. Verdi sensed that the days of *bel canto*, in the sense of Cherubini and Bellini, were over. The singer's voice was no longer a vehicle for vocal trills but had become an instrument of the music, the drama. Chorley died in 1872. Had he been around to hear *Otello* and *Falstaff* he might have agreed.

Verdi had signed a new contract with the House of Ricordi, which had published most of his operas, 'to produce a new opera in November 1850, in one of the leading opera houses of Italy, except La Scala of Milan'. Three years earlier, when negotiating the *Macbeth* contract with Giovanni Ricordi, Verdi had written: 'I cannot and must not allow a performance of *Macbeth* at La Scala, at least not until there has been a change for the better. . . . This stipulation which I now make for *Macbeth* goes for all my operas from now on.' Now, in February, he had not even decided on a libretto, and Ricordi was already talking to the directors of the Teatro Grande in Trieste where Verdi's *Il Corsaro* had failed completely two years before. His new opera, *Stiffelio*, was also a disaster. Thereafter Verdi avoided Trieste, but the elegant Triestini remained proud of him and in 1936 renamed their opera house Teatro Communale Giuseppe Verdi.

Verdi had done much reading in the past months. He was attracted by another drama of his favourite French playwright, Victor Hugo, who expressed in beautiful verse many things Verdi could not express in words (though certainly could in music). The play was *Le Roi s'amuse* and later became *Rigoletto*. Verdi was also interested in a bizarre drama by the Spanish playwright Antonio Garcia Gutiérrez,

and wrote to Cammarano about it, 'It seems to me very fine, rich in ideas and strong in situation.' The play was *El Trovador*, and Verdi's *Il Trovatore* has remained one of his enduring successes. And, not for the first or last time, he was thinking of *King Lear*; in February he sent a complete outline to Cammarano in Naples. But it was hard to keep in touch with Cammarano, who was often off on some eccentric pursuit; it was easier to work with Piave in nearby Venice. Piave was less gifted than Cammarano but more reliable; he wrote the libretto of *Stiffelio* based on an obscure French play.

They worked in a great hurry but that does not excuse Verdi for using such a silly story. An evangelical minister somewhere in Germany forgives his wife her adultery and, after noble soul-searching, suggests a divorce so she can marry her lover. But the lady still loves her husband and would rather die than divorce him. During the final scene the minister addresses his congregation. Suddenly he sees the Bible, open (by accident, no doubt) on the page where Christ forgives the adulteress. *Voilà!* The minister forgives his wife. Curtain. Let us hope they lived happily ever after. Perhaps the dramatic impact of the final scene fascinated Verdi. But he never really became interested in the characters, and if he tried to make adultery appear almost a virtue – a possible anti-Establishment thought – he failed.

Giovanni Ricordi (left) and his son Tito who succeeded him as head of the Ricordi publishing house in 1853. Despite frequent disagreements the House of Ricordi published nearly all Verdi's operas. Tito's son Giulio succeeded him in 1888.

The best that can be said of the music is that it was not too bad. The wonder is not that Verdi bothered with such nonsense but that only four months after the premiere of *Stiffelio* in Trieste he conducted his new opera *Rigoletto*, also written by Piave, in Venice. *Rigoletto* was his first worldwide success and remains one of the most frequently performed operas among the forty-two thousand that have been written since this strange and wonderful art-form was created in Florence around 1600. Genius, fortunately, remains unfathomable and unpredictable.

Until Verdi – then seventy years old – began working with Arrigo Boito on *Otello*, he was often unlucky with his librettists. He created some of the greatest successes – *Rigoletto*, *Il Trovatore* – not with the help of his 'poets' but despite them. Verdi's melodic power saved operas with miserable libretti. In 1781, seventy years before Verdi wrote the music of *Il Trovatore*, the twenty-six-year-old Mozart wrote to his father: 'Why do Italian operas please everywhere, in spite of their terrible libretti, even in Paris where I myself witnessed their success? Because the music reigns supreme and when one listens to it, all else is forgotten. :..' Mozart knew the truth early and remains the greatest genius of the lyrical theatre. Verdi learnt the truth relatively late, but when he did he gloriously carried Italian opera to a climax that has never been reached since his death.

Verdi understood the laws of the stage but not as completely as Mozart, whose letters to his father and Lorenzo da Ponte prove his enormous feeling for drama. Verdi usually sensed when something was wrong with a libretto but was not always able to suggest how to put it right. He was way ahead, though, of Rossini and Donizetti who often paid no attention at all to the libretti, using left-overs of music from earlier works.

In his early operas Verdi followed the operatic pattern of his age. The singers would perform almost as in a concert although they wore costumes and made certain 'dramatic' gestures, indicating some sort of libretto. The sloppy orchestral playing in Italy (which changed only when Wagner's operas became known there) was accompanied by sloppy staging and acting. Convention decreed that there must be a chorus scene at the beginning of the first act. (Even Bizet, who wrote an almost perfect opera, stuck to the convention at the beginning of *Carmen*.) After the chorus scene, a singer would perform a slow, melodious aria that had a final, fast part, called the *cabaletta*. In Italian *cavallo* means 'horse', and a *cabaletta* sometimes makes you think of a galloping horse. The *cabaletta* was technically difficult, demanded considerable vocal virtuosity, and created a furore if it was brilliantly sung. Everybody was happy, and the new opera was already virtually

The playbill announcing the first performance of *Stiffelio* in Trieste, 1850.

regarded a success. Later there would be another chorus scene, more arias, and duets between the protagonists. The drama, whatever there was of it, was developed in recitatives which usually bored the audience. People in Italy came to hear beautiful voices singing great arias. Convention also decreed that the *grande finale* brought together the stars, and if possible the chorus, in a rousing ensemble. Curtain, cheers, encores, applause.

In his earliest operas Verdi had not yet attained great skill in characterization through melody and had to use recitatives to express the action. His orchestra often accompanied in brass-band style, hm-tata, hm-tata; he had conducted such bands as a young man in Busseto. The critics were often right when they talked of 'hurdy-gurdy' music. The audiences did not mind so long as there were fine melodies, ideally with a high C at the end.

During his short political career, as Deputy in the first Chamber of a reunited Italy, Verdi was once asked by Quintino Sella, a fellow-deputy sitting next to him, how he worked when he was composing. Verdi disliked questions concerning the intimate sphere of artistic creation but he respected Sella, a noted geologist and economist. 'When you are composing,' Sella asked, 'how does the idea present itself to your mind? Do you work out the main theme first and later add the accompaniment, deciding only then how the accompaniment should be played, by flutes or violins and so on?'

'No,' Verdi said; 'The idea comes complete. I feel the colour [of the accompaniment], whether it should be for flutes or violins and so forth, as you say. My difficulty is to write down the musical thought quickly enough to capture it in its totality just as it comes into my mind.'

Creation is almost always painful and Verdi's case was no exception, as we know from Giuseppina's letters. When he was alone with himself, trying to get it off his chest, or heart, or mind, she would keep everything away from him that might interfere, and would take care of his needs. While he was working on *La Forza del Destino*, Giuseppina made detailed arrangements for the trip to St Petersburg where the new opera was to be performed. They would take two servants along, and she ordered large shipments of rice, noodles, macaroni, cheese and salami for four persons, even the wines – a hundred bottles of ordinary Bordeaux, twenty bottles of vintage Bordeaux, twenty bottles of champagne, possibly for celebrations. To a friend she said:

The noodles and macaroni will have to be well cooked to keep him in a good humour in the midst of all that ice! ... And I plan to let him be right in everything from the middle of October to January. I know that while he is composing and rehearsing the opera, it isn't the moment to persuade him that he might be wrong even once.

The problem of the libretto was often complicated by the problems of censorship. One could never foresee what might happen. The censors in various states, regions and duchies of Italy might object to different things in the libretto. Paradoxically, Verdi had less trouble with the Austrian censors in Milan and Venice than with the Italian censors in Rome and Naples. The Italians were afraid of being fired if they were too lenient. The Austrians cared little about losing their jobs because they would be sent home. The Austrian censors were, naturally, looking out for anything that might incite patriotic feelings among the Italian audiences and, God forbid, make them erupt into anti-Habsburg demonstrations. It took great skill to fool them, by making the chorus of the Israelites sing the stirring 'Va, pensiero' melody in *Nabucco*, or talk of 'invaders' in *Attila* when everybody in the audience knew that the Austrian or French occupying troops were meant. In Naples, under Bourbon rule, the censors would permit no reference that might be interpreted as undermining the principles of the Holy Alliance, such as the God-given rights of the ruler. The censors in Rome would watch out for anything that might offend religious beliefs (such as the baptism shown on stage in *I Lombardi*). Often the censors demanded a different title. *Ernani* had to be renamed *Elvira d'Aragona*, *Il Proscritto*, and *Il Corsaro di Venezia* in various states, but these changes fooled no one in the audience. Verdi understood that the human story was what really mattered, not the costumes and the historical background. People did not come to the opera house to see sets and costumes but to hear beautiful melodies sung by great voices, and perhaps to identify with the characters. Verdi's outline based on Victor Hugo's *Hernani* reads like a parody. But Hugo sensed that the composer managed to express the poet's words in music. Verdi did not hesitate to change the name of the heroine from Doña Sol to Elvira, which is easier to sing.

Then there were the many business details. Verdi was up against some shrewd impresarios and cold-blooded managers and publishers, but he was no unworldly artist. He had learnt something about figures and money while keeping the account-books and ledgers in Barezzi's store. When he received contracts to do his first opera for the Teatro La Fenice in Venice, he wrote to Conte Carlo Mocenigo, the director, on 25 May 1843:

... since neither you nor I would like to get ourselves into litigation, I have made some modifications which of course you can accept or refuse. I cannot bind myself to Article 2 of the contract, because the Director might refuse both the first and second libretto, and we might never see the end of it. ... I cannot bind myself to Article 3 because I always do the instrumentation during the piano rehearsals, and the score is never completely finished before the rehearsal preceding the dress rehearsal.

A tenth article must be added [stating that] Maestro Verdi is to be paid twelve thousand Austrian lire, in three instalments, the first on arrival in the city, the second at the first orchestra rehearsal, the third after the dress rehearsal is held. The artists who are to take part in the new opera of Maestro Verdi shall be chosen by the Maestro himself from the roster of the company.

I am not sending back the contract because it would be too voluminous. But I shall return or destroy it, as you direct. ...

Not bad for a thirty-year-old composer, well known in Italy but not yet world-famous. Everything is exact and quite explicit. And Verdi shrewdly did not return the contract with his letter because Conte

Mocenigo might tear it up in a rage. But this would not have worried Verdi too much as he could always find another opera house. Writing an opera was a pretty commercial business in those days. Composers were switching impresarios and theatres as authors are now switching publishers. After his very first opera, *Oberto*, written 'on speculation', Verdi never wrote another one without a contract, drawn up to his specifications. Conte Mocenigo and all other managers always agreed to Verdi's demands, which were mostly reasonable. But even the best contract could not protect him against a bad libretto and censorship problems.

5
THREE MASTERPIECES

After the disastrous failure of *Stiffelio* in Trieste, Verdi realized that he was getting nowhere fast. He had written sixteen operas in eleven years, some better than the others, always in a hurry, always under pressure from managers, impresarios, publishers. He was now thirty-seven; he was living with Giuseppina; he had large expenses and was aware of his responsibilities.

Early in 1850 Verdi had signed a contract with the Teatro La Fenice for delivery of an *opera seria* (a conventional opera based on arias, duets, choruses) to be staged during the Carnival in February 1851. He did not start writing until after the premiere of *Stiffelio* in November 1850, but he had been thinking of a subject for many months. He suggested the Spanish play *El Trovador* and *Kean*, by Alexandre Dumas *père*, but later he decided he was going to do Victor Hugo's *Le Roi s'amuse*. He greatly admired the Romantic dramatist because (he later explained) 'the great characters produce the great situations, and the dramatic effects follow naturally' – a brilliant analysis. Verdi also instinctively sensed the musical flow in Hugo's poetic language.

The directors of the Fenice and Piave, the librettist, had grave objections. They admitted that Hugo's play was dramatically sound. Everything planned, planted, and executed. Nothing had to be explained that had happened either before the curtain went up or during the interval. Nothing had to be assumed. The hunchback court-jester Triboulet, at the court of François I, discovers that the courtiers (who hate him) have kidnapped his daughters. He turns on them, calls out the names of some great old families of France, and says, 'Your mothers slept with their lackeys, you bastards!' This line brought the Paris premiere to a sudden halt as the audience jumped up protesting. There was a first-rate scandal and the play was banned.

Verdi must have known that the Austrian censors in Venice would never permit a play about a king who was a lecher and libertine. He was not surprised when the director of the Fenice informed him: 'The

Austrian Military Governor has rejected the libretto. He directs me to communicate his profound regret that the poet Piave and the celebrated Maestro Verdi have not chosen some other field to display their talents than the revolting immorality and obscene triviality of the libretto. ... His Excellency has decided that the performance must be absolutely forbidden.'

The censors also objected to Verdi's title *La Maledizione* ('The Curse'). Verdi remained in Busseto, wisely keeping away from the censors while the poor Fenice directors and Piave tried to straighten things out with them. Gradually, the French King was made the Duke of Mantua, and the hunchback Triboulet (Triboletto) became Rigoletto, and provided the title for the opera. All this took time and it was late in January, only four weeks before the scheduled premiere, that the censors released the new version. Hugo was so furious that his noble, poetic drama had been demoted to a mere libretto that he tried to prevent a Paris production for six years. But at last he realized that Verdi once again had expressed the very atmosphere of his play and grew to admire the opera. At least he never challenged Verdi to a duel, as Maurice Maeterlinck later challenged Claude Debussy after *Pelléas et Mélisande*. (Maeterlinck heard Debussy's masterpiece only two years after the death of the composer and said, 'I was completely wrong and he was a thousand times right.')

Rigoletto is unabashed melodrama but also Piave's best job for Verdi. Piave, a great womaniser, may have identified himself with the lecherous ('La donna è mobile') Duke of Mantua. Giuseppina Strepponi called Piave *Gran Diavolo* ('Big Devil') and worried about his 'bad influence' on Verdi. He was a charmer; once she thanked him for the 'delightful purse sent me through the Big Bear', who was Verdi. And why, she wondered, did Piave carry new ladies' stockings in his suitcase? Why indeed? Once she wrote to her Verdi who was then in Venice: 'Thank "Big Devil" for the lines he wrote to me and tell him not to show his friendship by leading you astray. I know he has great talent for that occupation. Please exhort him to show his erotic zeal with friends who resemble himself.'

It seems that during the rehearsals for *Rigoletto* Verdi had been flirting with a Venetian lady who later wrote to him *poste restante* in Cremona; but somehow Giuseppina found out about it, and that was the end. She also knew that Piave once approached a woman friend he had known, and sang to her 'La donna è mobile', in St Mark's Square. The lady was not amused and dismissed him. Back in Busseto, Giuseppina must have had some anxious moments while she knew Verdi was in Venice with Piave.

According to a myth that never dies, Verdi wrote the score of *Rigoletto* in forty days. The actual writing did not take much longer

OPPOSITE Designs by Giuseppe Bertoya for the second act of *Rigoletto* at the Teatro La Fenice, Venice.

73

OPPOSITE Francesco Piave whose libretto of *Rigoletto* was the best of the many libretti he wrote for Verdi.

LEFT Verdi's handwritten score for the quartet in the last act of *Rigoletto*.

BELOW The announcement of the opera's first performance.

but he had been thinking about the opera for a long time. (He never made sketches of ideas and melodies but kept them in his head.) Verdi fulfilled the terms of his contract with the Fenice: *Rigoletto* is certainly an *opera seria* with fine arias and exciting ensembles. He did much more though. *Rigoletto* is a long step forward on the way that began with *Macbeth* and *Luisa Miller*. The conversation between Rigoletto and Sparafucile is not just a duet but a dramatic conspiracy. The melody is played in the orchestra, and the two men discuss the terms of the murder in a sort of *parlando*. 'La donna è mobile' may be an old-fashioned aria (and remains one of Verdi's most popular melodies) but it is also a perfect character-sketch of the cynical seducer, the Duke. Of the magnificent quartet in the last act, 'Bella figlia dell' amore', Verdi said to Felice Varesi, the baritone who sang the part of Rigoletto, that he would probably never write a better ensemble. As always in musical matters, he was right. The quartet has been called 'a triumph of emotional counterpoint', by W. Brockway and H. Weinstock. None of the arias, duets, ensembles interrupts the action: on the contrary, they further the drama.

Rigoletto is a masterpiece, and the audience at the Fenice, on the evening of 11 March 1851, recognised it. Within four years the opera was performed all over Europe and in America. Routine performances do not always convey its greatness. The accompaniment must not be played in hurdy-gurdy style, and the tenor should be intelligent and vocally excellent to convey the idea of 'the frivolous, licentious character of the Duke', as Verdi said, performing with elegance and a sense of irony. *Rigoletto* belongs to the gold reserves of the repertoire and remains the darling of box-office managers. If Verdi had written nothing else, he would have been rich, and still famous today.

After the triumph of *Rigoletto*, Verdi and Strepponi moved out of the Palazzo Cavalli in Busseto to their new home in Sant' Agata. There they lived together, mostly (though not always) happy, for almost fifty years. For decades Verdi kept adding, rebuilding, altering; he loved the sound of hammering in his house. Strepponi explained her feelings once in a letter to Clarina Maffei, 'Except for the kitchen, the cellar and the stables, we have slept and eaten our meals in every nook of the house.'

Busseto, just a short walk away, remained enemy territory even after they became married. Sometimes Verdi might have been willing to forgive, but not Giuseppina. She had suffered too much there; as time went on, her bitterness if anything increased. She would have nothing to do with Busseto; she avoided the town like the plague. When she and Verdi arrived later on, from Genoa or Paris, they would get off the train at Borgo San Donnino (now called Fidenza) in order to avoid going through Busseto. The carriage would be waiting

OPPOSITE Giuseppina Strepponi.

77

and took them straight to Sant' Agata. Verdi would not permit a bridge to be built across the small Ongina river, which ran in front of his house. Sant' Agata became his fortress. With few exceptions – Barezzi and Angelo Carrara, his lawyer friend – no one from Busseto was admitted to Sant' Agata. Muzio, of course, was always welcome, as was Ricordi from Milan. In May 1851 Strepponi went to Florence again to look after her son Camillino and wrote to Verdi, 'I beg you with clasped hands not to connect yourself too intimately with your parents.'

Giuseppina's feelings were not a secret in Busseto and people said 'she stood between Verdi and his parents'. It is also hard to understand why she never brought Camillino home with her to Sant' Agata. Perhaps under her influence, Verdi had arranged for his parents to live in Vidalenzo, 'for his own peace of mind,' not far from Sant' Agata but not too close nearby either. His mother died that year on 28 June, and Verdi was deeply shocked. Should he have done more for her?

While Verdi and Giuseppina were alive, it was never explained why they did not marry until 1859, when they had known each other for more than seventeen years. The only one who had asked that question was Barezzi. Verdi wrote to him, early in 1852:

Dearest Father-in-Law. . . . After all these years I did not expect to receive such a cold letter from you. . . . If it were not signed Antonio Barezzi, that is, my benefactor, I would have replied curtly or not at all. I'll try as best I can to persuade you that I do not deserve such a reproof. . . .

You live in a town that has the bad habit of meddling in the affairs of others, of disapproving of everything that does not conform to its ideas. From this comes the gossip, the whispers, the disapproval. . . . I have no hesitation in raising the curtain that hides the mysteries closed within our four walls, and to tell you about my life at home. I have nothing to hide. In my house there lives a lady, free and independent, who like me prefers a solitary life. . . . What rights do I have over her, and she over me? Who knows whether or not she is my wife? And if she is, who knows what reasons or ideas there may be for not announcing it publicly? Who knows if it is good or bad? Could it not be a good thing? And, even if it were a bad thing, who has the right to damn us? I will say this, however: in my house she is entitled to equal or greater respect than I, and no one is allowed to fail in it for whatever reason. And finally she has every right to it by her conduct, her mind, and the special courtesy she always shows to others. . . .

This cannot continue. But if it must, then I am the man to defend myself. The world is large, and the loss of twenty or thirty thousand francs will not stop me from finding another country. In this letter nothing should offend you, but if anything does, consider it not written. I have always and do now consider you my benefactor. And I make it my honour and my boast. *Addio*, *addio*, with all my usual friendship.

G. Verdi

The letter did not answer Barezzi's question. Nor does any other letter.

Barezzi, a kind-hearted man, did not get angry but accepted Verdi and Giuseppina as they were. Various explanations were later given for Verdi's behaviour, none convincing. It was suggested that he was afraid to marry Strepponi because his first wife had died and a curse, as in *Rigoletto*, might threaten her – hardly plausible because Verdi, with his healthy common sense, would not worry about such things. Or it was said that Verdi had made a secret vow to the dying Margherita that he would never remarry – likewise implausible because Verdi did not behave like a character from one of his early operas. Was it that Strepponi refused to marry him because 'she did not feel worthy of Verdi'? But this too is unconvincing; we know from her letters that she understood well what she meant to him. Curiously, some English or American biographers who have known Verdi very well cannot hide their sense of shock because he lived for years with his 'mistress', and cannot see Verdi's point that sometimes a mistress deserves 'equal or greater respect' than quite a few married women. The fact is that within two years after the *Rigoletto* premiere he wrote two other immortal operas, *Il Trovatore* and *La Traviata*. Obviously his problems with Busseto, or with Giuseppina, did not interfere with his genius. And that is all that matters to us.

1852 was a blessed year in Verdi's creative life. He wrote, almost simultaneously, two completely different operas, *Il Trovatore* and *La Traviata*, that have remained among his most popular successes. In Rome, Verdi rehearsed with the orchestra and cast his new *Trovatore*, finishing the score at the opera house, as was his custom. At night he worked in his hotel suite on *La Traviata*. In the same year Wagner began writing the libretto of the *Ring*. Wagner, too, would work on two different levels when he wrote the music of *Tristan* and at the same time devised the libretto of *Die Meistersinger*.

The libretto of *Il Trovatore* is probably the most bizarre in the current operatic repertory. Non-Italian audiences consider it quite ludicrous. No one really tries to understand what goes on. Yet Verdi was right when he had become excited by Gutiérrez's Spanish melodrama, *El Trovador*. He sensed the dramatic possibilities in the sinister cast of characters and their burning passions. He returned Cammarano's first outline and wrote one himself which he enclosed, 'As a man of talent and exceptional character you won't mind if I, a very low man, take the liberty of saying that if we cannot do our opera with all the bizarre quality of the play, we'd better give up.' But 'the bizarre quality of the play' makes *Il Trovatore* the parody of a melodrama. Much of the story takes place twenty years before the opera begins. The early happenings in fifteenth-century Spain are told during the prologue by an old basso retainer of Count di Luna. How could Verdi and Cammarano make such a mistake? Surely they knew the cardinal rule that the stage shows action and must not provide explanation. Perhaps everything might have turned out differently if Cammarano had not died suddenly in July. He left the complete outline but no verses for part of the third and all of the last act. Verdi was deeply shocked. 'I cannot describe the depth of my sorrow,' he wrote to a mutual friend, Cesare de Sanctis; 'You loved him as much as I did and will understand the feelings I cannot express in words. . . .' He paid the widow more money than he had owed the poet, and asked a young poet from Naples, Leone Emanuele Bardare, to complete the libretto.

The story defies analysis. The central character is Azucena, the gypsy woman whose mother was long ago burnt at the stake by the local lord. She takes revenge by stealing one of the Count's two babies, a boy, and burns the child at the same stake. At this point the audience is asked to believe that during the confusion Azucena 'made a mistake' and instead burnt her own baby! She raises the other baby, Manrico, who grows up believing Azucena to be his dear mother. Manrico falls in love with Leonora. The young Conte di Luna (the other son of the lord who started all the trouble) is also in love with Leonora. No one but Azucena knows that Manrico and Luna are brothers. The audience may know it, provided it has read the libretto carefully. In the end, after two wonderful hours of drama and excitement Manrico is captured by Luna's men; Leonora takes poison and dies in Manrico's arms; Luna has Manrico executed and is told, *only then*, by Azucena that he has just killed his own brother. 'Mother, you are avenged!' the gypsy woman shouts. Curtain.

The genius of Verdi makes this improbable nonsense one of the most successful operas ever written. *Il Trovatore* is exciting from beginning to end. Most people love it even though they have no idea what is going on. It is heroic, and beautiful, and the melodies are magnificent. The vocal parts are very demanding. Azucena, a mezzo-soprano, has to sing a high C. Luna, a baritone, has to hold a high G. Manrico's *stretta* is a tough test of a tenor's power and vocal technique. Leonora's 'D'amor sull'ali rosee' is a *bel canto* masterpiece: a seventeen-note run, from the high C to low A, always following the orchestra's speed. Yet many critics deplored *Il Trovatore* as the end of the *bel canto* tradition, and others were shocked by what they called 'the vulgarity' of the music.

But once again the audience was ahead of the critics. People sensed the integrity of Verdi's melodic passion. Nothing is contrived in his music, everything is genuine, and people immerse themselves in love and hatred, jealousy and vengeance. The audience made the premiere

OPPOSITE The frontispiece to the score of *Il Trovatore*.

80

Al suo venerato ed ottimo amico, l'egregio Avvocato

ANTONIO VASSELLI

L'EDITORE

TITO DI GIO. RICORDI

IL TROVATORE

Dramma in quattro parti di Salvadore Cammarano

POSTO IN MUSICA DAL MAESTRO

GIUSEPPE VERDI

Cavaliere della Legion d'Onore

REGIO STABILIMENTO ✠ TITO DI GIO. RICORDI

MILANO-NAPOLI

FIRENZE, Ricordi e Jouhaud. — TORINO, Giudici e Strada. — MENDRISIO, Bustelli-Rossi.

at Rome's Apollo Theatre, on 19 January 1853, a fantastic success. During the 'Miserere' several women fainted. Other people were so overcome with emotion they had to leave. It is a wonderful scene. Manrico, not seen in the high prison tower, sings his farewell to Leonora. Leonora, alone in front of the stage, vows that she will never forget him. Offstage, on a third level, the monks chant the 'Miserere' chorus for Manrico who is soon to be executed. Verdi creates drama and contrast on three levels and fuses the scene by the power of his beautiful music. If the scene is well done the effect is simply colossal. But many people were shocked by the brutality. Solera, the librettist of *Nabucco*, said that 'Verdi is a great composer but weak as a woman to accept librettos from that ass of a Piave, or from that muddler Cammarano who for having written *Il Trovatore* deserves a life-sentence to the galleys . . . .'

Verdi accepted all criticism and all praise with equal detachment. To Clarina Maffei he wrote: 'People say the opera is too sad and there are too many deaths in it. But after all, death is all there is in life. What else is there?' He had reached that final conclusion at the age of thirty-nine.

Il Trovatore has been performed in many countries, continents, and languages – including Croatian, Slovenian, Lettish, Bulgarian, Serbian, Hebrew, Estonian, Lithuanian and others. Tamberlik, Caruso, Slezak, Martinelli, Lauri-Volpi, Jussi Björling, Bergonzi, Corelli and Domingo are among the stars who have sung the title role. After more than a hundred and twenty years *Il Trovatore* shows no signs of ailing or ageing.

Verdi, returning home from Rome, was met by Giuseppina in Leghorn. In these years he never took her with him, being afraid to expose her to the hectic excitement of the final rehearsals, and possibly to a failure. Perhaps the catcalls after the Scala premiere of *Un Giorno di Regno*, thirteen years ago, were still in his ears. He worked very hard that winter. The premiere of *La Traviata* at the Fenice in Venice was scheduled for 6 March 1853 – only forty-six days after the premiere of *Il Trovatore*.

Verdi had read Dumas *fils*'s novel *La Dame aux camélias* in Paris, during his 'honeymoon' with Giuseppina. Later he had seen Dumas's play, based on the novel. He knew that the story was partly auto-biographical. Everybody in Paris knew that Alphonsine Plessis had been Dumas's *dame aux camélias*; she is now buried near Dumas at the Cimetière de Montmartre. Some Verdi biographers have wondered whether the heroine of his opera, Violetta, 'the kept woman', might have been Giuseppina, and some even called *La Traviata* 'Verdi's autobiographical opera'. But Verdi was an Italian realist, a great craftsman who would not have let his innermost private life interfere with his music. Wagner worked that way, but not Verdi. He had been moved by the story of Violetta, he sensed that Dumas's play offered possibilities for beautiful music, he had heard the sadness and the beauty in his inner ear for a long time. Only thus can it be explained that he wrote the great music within a few weeks.

He conceived some of the most beautiful melodies at a time when he was terribly depressed about the recent events in Milan. On 6 February a disastrous revolt had broken out. Mazzini and some five hundred revolutionary members of his secret societies attempted to capture the fortress held by twelve thousand Austrian soldiers. It seemed an improbable task, even if each of Mazzini's men had been a hero carrying out several suicidal missions. The attempt failed badly; most people in Milan considered it a senseless quixotic adventure. Within a few hours it was all over, but several Austrian soldiers were killed. Field-Marshal Radetzky ordered the hanging of eighteen revolutionaries and many were sent to prison. He declared a state of siege, expelled all suspicious strangers, and had the assets confiscated of all who had been involved in the foolish conspiracy.

Though Mazzini became discredited in Italy for his failure, he had unwittingly convinced many Italian patriots that isolated revolts would not liberate and unite the peninsula. The foreign troops would have to be defeated in battle. Only the Piedmontese army could do that. The action would have to start in Piedmont, the only independent state in Italy, with its own army and foreign policy. Many Italian patriots were convinced republicans and had no use for the King of Piedmont; Verdi was one of them. But they had to admit, reluctantly, that the fight would have to begin there, first by diplomatic and possibly by military methods. The stage was set for Count Camillo Cavour, the Piedmontese nobleman, who owned a large estate and published a newspaper. He was also a patriot with ideas.

Piave had been asked to come to Sant' Agata to work on the libretto of *La Traviata*. Time was getting short. Poor Piave, who liked to stroll around St Mark's Square in Venice, looking at beautiful women, was totally lost in Sant' Agata. 'When it's raining,' he wrote to his friend Guglielmo Brenna, 'it's a case of looking at oneself in the mirror to see if one is still in human form or whether one has been changed into a toad or a frog.' But he left a workable libretto, skilfully condensing Dumas's play to create time for the important arias and ensembles. Everything considered, it was a good libretto. Later, Verdi would spend long hours in his study. Then, toward the evening, he might ask Giuseppina to come in and play her one of the new melodies. Sometimes he handed her a few pages. She was the first person who sang 'Sempre libera' from *La Traviata*. She was a severe critic. She was also a woman, in love with him, and she often wished he would spend less time in his study and more with her. She once wrote to him:

Like me, you can say that you long for your little room in Sant' Agata! If it were not for the opera contract we could enjoy, in Sant' Agata or some other quiet place, our tranquil existence, and the pleasures that are so simple and for us so delightful. Sometimes I fear that the love of money will re-awaken in you and condemn you to many more years of drudgery. My dear Mago, you would be very wrong. Don't you see? A great part of our lives has gone by and you would be quite mad if, instead of enjoying the rewards of your glorious and honoured labours in peace, you were to sweat to accumulate money. ... We shall have no children (since God, perhaps, wishes to punish me for my sins, in depriving me of any legitimate joy before I die). Well then, not having children by me, I hope you won't cause me sorrow by having any by another woman. Without children you have a fortune more than sufficient to provide for your needs, and a bit of luxury besides. ...

Don't you agree. If only you knew what a sad life I lead these days! ... You haven't got your poor Nuisance in a corner of the room, curled up in an armchair, to say, 'That's beautiful ...', 'That's *not!*' ... 'Stop!' ... 'Repeat that, that's really original ...'.

This beautiful letter is one of the few truly intimate exchanges between the creative genius of Verdi and Giuseppina, who heard many of the immortal melodies first and always told him what she felt about them. She asked him to take her to Venice for *La Traviata*, but he would not hear of it. This time he was really worried. He arrived in Venice on 21 February, with no score at all; he is said to have orchestrated the opera in thirteen days, during the rehearsals.

The score shows signs of feverish haste. Verdi's biographer, Carlo Gatti, kept a photostat copy of *La Traviata* in his study because, he said, it showed so much of the man's genius. After jotting down the first bars of the allegro brilliante, the melody of 'Sempre libera degg'io folleggiare di gioja in gioja', Verdi had not even bothered to write the rest of the melody. He had merely noted, in his fine, precise hand, '*Alle fine et cetera*'.

Gatti had said the page never failed to amuse him: 'One of the greatest melodies ever composed and Verdi just writes, "To the end, et cetera," as though everyone knew it already. Et cetera for whom, I ask you? Not for you and not for me and not for anyone except a genius like Verdi. Fortunately, in a later draft, he took time to write out the whole melody.'

The premiere of *La Traviata*, on 6 March 1853, was an utter failure. The next morning Verdi wrote to Muzio: '*La Traviata* last night was a fiasco. Is the fault mine or the singers? Time will tell.' The audience at

Fanny Salvini-Donatelli was too plump to play convincingly the consumptive Violetta in *La Traviata* and was greeted with laughter by the first-night audience.

the Fenice did not just hiss or boo. Worse, they laughed during the whole of the last act when Violetta, the former *demi-monde* kept woman, dies of consumption. Fanny Salvini-Donatelli, who performed the part of Violetta, looked healthy and rather fat, a sort of Valkyrie. Every time she coughed, signalling her early demise, the audience was convulsed with laughter. Verdi had been nervous about her, suggesting another singer 'with a beautiful figure', but the management could not get her. He had even received an anonymous letter predicting a disaster if the fat soprano would sing.

He had also failed, under the pressure of time, to prepare the production with his usual care. The singers wore contemporary dress. Dumas had written a 'modern' play and Verdi called it 'a subject from our own time' but the people did not like it. The fiasco of the premiere was repeated the following night. Verdi wrote to his friend Angelo

Mariani, the conductor: 'I am not upset. For my part I do not believe that the last word on *Traviata* was spoken last night. They will see it again and we shall see. . . .'

For more than a year Verdi did nothing about the opera. Ricordi was not permitted to show it around. Then a group of Venetian friends around Antonio Gallo, a violinist, asked Verdi to let them produce *La Traviata* again, not at the Fenice but at the smaller Teatro San Benedetto. There would be plenty of time to rehearse, Piave would be in charge, and the opera would be staged in the style of 1700, in beautiful, historical costumes. After some hesitation, Verdi permitted them to go ahead.

On 6 May 1854 the Venetians heard *La Traviata* again. This time the opera was a sensational success. Verdi, then in Paris, did not even bother to come to Venice. He remarked that 'practically the same audience as before was seeing the same opera'. Perhaps not quite. The singers were excellent, the costumes and sets established the intimate mood of the period, and the music sounded more beautiful than before; or anyway some people thought so. *La Traviata* remains one of the most beloved of Verdi operas. Even people who have no use for *Il Trovatore* ('the story!'), *Don Carlos* ('not enough melody!'), or *Otello* and *Falstaff* (because they cannot understand these subtle masterpieces) love *Traviata*, which has everything – a romantic, scandalous story, a heroine who 'sins' and 'suffers', beautiful people, fascinating sets, Paris society, a heartbroken lover with his noble father, and, above all, a wealth of melody. Francis Toye, the eminent Verdi biographer, knew an aristocratic Frenchwoman who attended every performance she could get to, and often left before the sad ending, shaken with emotion: 'Lovers, especially lovers whose love was illicit, attended it with very much the same spirit as they afterward attended performances of *Tristan und Isolde*. In short, *La Traviata* became the symbol of revolt against current sexual conventions.'

Perhaps, but *La Traviata* also happens to be a masterpiece, with very beautiful music, the creation of an Italian genius who deeply understood human beings and expressed this in melody. It is the old, forever new story of two people who find one another only to lose each other. In operetta it would be the other way around but Verdi wrote drama. He knew that life and love are short and that in the end, there is death.

The costume design for Violetta
at the first La Scala production.

A scene of Parisian high society
in the 1850s – the salon of
Princesse Mathilde.

6
'CURSED OPERAS'

In October 1853 Verdi and Giuseppina went to Paris again. She wanted to get away for a while from the hostile, cold world of Busseto. In Paris she felt much more at home. She spoke good French, she felt she could breathe again, no one bothered them. It was shortly after Louis Napoleon, President of the Second Republic, had proclaimed the Second Empire and took the title Napoleon III. The appointment of Georges Haussmann as the super-architect of the modern city marks the beginning of a new era in Paris, brilliant, ironical and decadent, which Jacques Offenbach described so well in his operetta parodies.

Verdi had a contract with the Opéra but he disliked the house and the management. 'I have a ferocious desire to go home', he wrote to Clarina Maffei. But Giuseppina liked it there, and he did not leave. The Opéra sent him a libretto by Eugène Scribe, the most famous French librettist after his libretti for Meyerbeer's *Robert le Diable* and *Les Huguénots*, and Halévy's *La Juive*. Scribe was a super-craftsman with the reputation of creating *la pièce bien faite*, the well-made play. He was a virtuoso of stage technique and a master architect; the structure of his plays was often impeccable but their content was shallow. He wrote, alone or with others, close on four hundred plays. Scribe knew what could be done on the stage. Alexandre Dumas *fils* once said wistfully that a playwright who had Balzac's knowledge of the human soul and Scribe's stage technique would be a very great dramatist. For opera composers, Scribe had developed a formula for the 'self-activating plot' that could be used in every language (he said). Arias and ballets could be inserted so skilfully that they did not stop the action.

Unfortunately for Scribe, Verdi completely disagreed with him on opera. Verdi was just finding his way, creating human beings who were involved in human problems. He expressed their emotions in melody; he was not too bothered about the fine architecture of the plot. He knew what he had done with *Il Trovatore*, the worst-structured

Augustin Scribe, a popular
French dramatist, proved far less
complaisant than Verdi's Italian
librettists and refused to make
the changes Verdi wanted in
Les Vêpres siciliennes.

libretto imaginable. The moment Verdi began thinking of plot he was in trouble. Scribe on the contrary thought only of plot and created characters to fit it. Verdi was no fool, though; he respected the laws of the stage. Once he wrote to Antonio Somma, the Venetian poet who later created the libretto of *Un Ballo in Maschera*, 'In the theatre long is synonymous with boring, and of all styles being boring is the worst.'

Scribe knew that a libretto for the Paris Opéra must be a 'spectacle', meaning five acts, large choruses, many stage effects, a long ballet, not too early, and many shorter dances, which is exactly what he did for Verdi when he put together a libretto based on a religious massacre in Palermo that had taken place on 30 March 1282 and is known as the Sicilian Vespers. It was not what Verdi wanted. He could not get close to the characters, and he had much trouble with the intonation of the words in the French libretto. He spoke much better French than when he had met Giuseppina in Paris, but speaking was one thing and composing a French text another. Being a perfectionist, he soon got in trouble with everybody at the Opéra, from Louis Crosnier, the *directeur*, to the stagehands. He asked Crosnier to cancel his contract: he had hoped that

M. Scribe would have the goodness to appear from time to time at the rehearsals to watch out for certain troublesome words or lines that are hard to sing ... that he would change everything that attacks the honour of the Italians. ... Here and there I hear words, observations, which if not altogether wounding are at least out of place. I am not used to this and will not endure it. ...

Crosnier refused to cancel the contract. He needed the work of a famous composer during the First Paris Exhibition. The intrigues went on. Verdi was stubborn about major artistic questions but he was flexible enough to make a minor compromise when he could gain a larger artistic success. He knew that at that time the Paris Opéra was still a very important house. He knew its great history – Gluck, Spontini, Cherubini, Mozart, Weber, Rossini and Donizetti had written for the Opéra, and now there were Meyerbeer and Gounod. Berlioz, today considered the greatest composer among his French contemporaries, never made the Opéra because he could not stand the intrigues. (Some of the finest French operas – *Carmen*, Massenet's *Manon*, Debussy's *Pelléas et Mélisande* – were first performed at the Opéra-Comique or the Théâtre-Lyrique, which were smaller, more intimate, and had smaller-scale intrigues.)

Verdi even wrote the obligatory ballet, which he disliked, and agreed not to have it too early. One rule at the Opéra was that the ballet must be given only about an hour after the beginning because the members of the powerful Jockey Club, a group of rich men and influential officials who 'supported' ballerinas, liked to have a pleasant dinner before coming to the Opéra. Richard Wagner later refused to have the ballet in the second act of *Tannhäuser*, defying the Jockey Club. When the members came to the Opéra, the Venusberg ballet and the first act were over. The irate Jockey Club members, who did not like Germans anyway, started a scandal and Wagner withdrew his opera after the third performance, but he never forgot the shock. *Tannhäuser* appeared at the Opéra in 1895, twelve years after Wagner's death, and was a great success.

So Verdi went on with *Les Vêpres siciliennes*, frustrated and unhappy. He always had strong feelings about blending words and music, and the best things he wrote are a complete fusion of words – or rather, syllables – melody and rhythm. So far as he was concerned, there was no argument whether opera should be sung in the original

The frontispiece to the score of *Giovanna de Guzman*, the first Italian version of *Les Vêpres siciliennes*.

91

language. Verdi always believed that his operas should be performed in Italian. He was right: much of the incredible beauty of *Otello* and *Falstaff* is lost in translation, and that goes for the best things in many of his other works too.

Les Vêpres siciliennes, premiered on 13 June 1855, was a success, but Verdi's real feelings are apparent in his letter to Clarina Maffei when he wrote, 'It seems to me that the opera is not going too badly.' The Italian version, *I Vespri siciliani*, was soon performed all over Italy. It has some good music. Verdi was not capable of writing an opera without any good music, though some of his earlier ones contain little. *Vêpres* has a fine overture, some exciting arias and duets. In Italy the opera was originally performed under the title *Giovanna de Guzman*, and the setting was switched to faraway Portugal as the censors would not permit an exciting revolt in Sicily to be glorified on the opera stage.

Verdi remained in Paris that summer, troubled again by his occupational disease, a chronic sore throat, after the rehearsals of his new opera. He was very angry when he learnt that pirated productions of his works were being performed in Paris and elsewhere. He complained to Tito Ricordi, Giovanni's son and now in charge of the publishing house, about copyright, contracts and royalties. He reminded Ricordi, not tactfully but with justification, that the House of Ricordi had made a 'colossal' fortune from Verdi's operas: 'I have never been considered anything but an object, a tool, to be made use of as long as it works. Sad words but true.' He complained about Ricordi's printed editions of his most recent operas, 'done with little care' and full of mistakes. Verdi scholars have long complained about some editions of Verdi's operas, with interpretative markings that had not been in earlier editions, showing the clumsy hands of arrangers. Scholars have found changed notes, altered tempi, and other incongruous detail. The dead composer cannot defend himself against the arranger or editor who feels he ought to follow current trends and to make compromises to changes of taste, often for the worse. Fortunately there is the growing conviction nowadays that a good musician must go back to the composer's original score.

The status of the composer was undergoing a change during Verdi's long life. Haydn, Mozart and Beethoven had often complained about their publishers and were unable to prevent piracy. Contracts were drawn up haphazardly. The operatic world was small. In the days of Gluck, Paris and Vienna were the important places; Mozart added Prague to these. Rossini was performed all over Europe. When he visited Vienna in 1822 the local composers, among them Beethoven and Schubert, were completely eclipsed; after all, it was said, they were always around. (Verdi had learnt in Busseto that the prophet is *nemo in patria*.) Despite his fame, Rossini's operas were not protected by copyright and after the first year or so could be produced by anybody without paying royalties to the composer; no wonder composers had to produce fast – so fast that many cracked under the strain. The orchestral parts existed only in manuscript and were taken by the impresario from one theatre to the next.

Then new printing techniques were introduced. Publishers could now have several complete scores of the same opera and rent them out to houses in different cities. Copyright was established in many countries, and composers were paid royalties. Not always, though: Verdi had problems in collecting royalties in North and South America even after 1850. As copyright laws became more sophisticated, the power gradually switched from the impresario to the publisher. In his early years Verdi dealt with Merelli, Lanari and other impresarios. There was Lumley in London and Verdi's agent, Léon Escudier, in Paris. He did *Il Corsaro* for the publisher Francesco Lucca. But almost all his works had been published by Ricordi since old Giovanni Ricordi had acquired *Nabucco*. (Giovanni started publication only after he was certain that *Nabucco* was a success.) Thanks to Verdi, Ricordi became Italy's most powerful music publisher and it remains one of the leading ones in the world. Until his death Verdi was the emperor at Ricordi's, and Puccini was the crown prince.

Around 1850 composers began writing operas for a certain publisher rather than for a certain opera house. As Verdi got older he no longer did most of his composing in the hectic atmosphere of the opera house, between rehearsals, but worked at home. Some composers considered this method preferable; some liked to be surrounded by the stimulating atmosphere of the opera house. The composer was also expected to act as producer – to supervise the staging, to look after sets and costumes. He had to rehearse the singers and the orchestra, and he was expected to conduct the first three performances. The professional conductor was gradually emerging, but his name was not yet mentioned on the programme.

Verdi did much to improve and strengthen the composer's legal status. He was shrewd and later he was powerful; and he hated to be taken advantage of. He did much of the legal work himself because he did not completely trust his publishers and agents, and they had no real power as yet. He travelled all over Europe to protect his rights. He went twice to London to prevent pirated productions of *Il Trovatore*. He was often frustrated in his efforts because he was a citizen of the small Duchy of Parma, which had no international treaties with France and England. Once he wrote to his lawyer in Busseto: 'It has

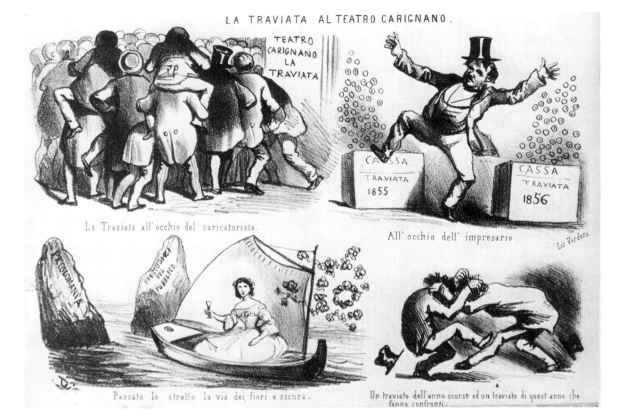

LA TRAVIATA AL TEATRO CARIGNANO.

La Traviata all'occhio del caricaturista.

All'occhio dell'impresario

Passato lo stretto la via dei fiori e sicura.

Un traviato dell'anno scorso ed un traviato di quest'anno che fanno confronti.

Cartoons on the eventual success of *La Traviata*: A crowd battles for seats; the impresario dances for joy at his takings; the opera sails through the rocks of public prejudice to receive garlands of flowers; a *traviato* of this year and of last year confront each other.

OPPOSITE ABOVE The costume design for Jacopo Fiesco in *Simone Boccanegra*.

OPPOSITE The Teatro La Fenice at the time of *Simone Boccanegra* in 1857.

been suggested that I become a citizen of England, France or even Piedmont ... but I wish to remain what I am, a peasant from Le Roncole. I prefer to ask my government to make a treaty with England.' But in Parma they did not worry about Verdi's 'artistic problems'.

Late in December 1855 Verdi and Giuseppina returned from Paris to Sant' Agata. To Clarina Maffei he wrote: 'I walk in the fields from morning to evening, trying to recover, so far without success, from the stomach trouble caused me by *I Vespri siciliani*. Cursed operas!'

He was forty-two, famous and rich; the years in the galley were over but he had to go on with his operas. He was often unhappy with them but even more unhappy without them. In March 1856 he conducted a new production of *La Traviata* at the Fenice in Venice, where he had conducted the disastrous premiere three years earlier. This time it was a great success, Verdi was vindicated and happy, and the directors quickly made him sign a new opera contract; and he was landed again with another cursed opera. *Simone Boccanegra* was just that, the story of a former pirate who becomes Doge of Genoa. Verdi had liked the play, written by his favourite Spanish playwright Gutiérrez. Piave could not cope with it, and the libretto is a mess. The premiere (12 March 1857) was no success. This time the critics liked Verdi's orchestration and his skill with the recitatives. But the public waited for great arias which did not come. Twenty-four years later, after *Aïda*, Giulio Ricordi asked Verdi to revise *Simone Boccanegra*. Arrigo Boito was asked to doctor the libretto but even he was defeated by the task. *Simone Boccanegra* has some fine dramatic music, but modern audiences find it gloomy and unrewarding.

That was bad enough, but what made him agree to a revision of another earlier failure, *Stiffelio*? Now the German evangelical minister was to become a thirteenth-century Crusader named Aroldo. Piave suggested other changes, Verdi would add some new music, and Angelo Mariani, then the leading conductor in Italy, would conduct the festival premiere at the newly opened theatre in Rimini, of all places. The superficially revamped *Aroldo* was no lasting success and is now forgotten. If it proves anything it is that Verdi was lost when he got involved with historical characters who did not interest him. He needed human beings, with passions he could express in music. Like millions of people, he loved mystery, excitement, adventure – and somehow he had the ability to translate them into music no matter how bizarre the story was. He had proved it in *Rigoletto* and *Il Trovatore*. But he was lost in history, and failed with *Vêpres* and *Aroldo*.

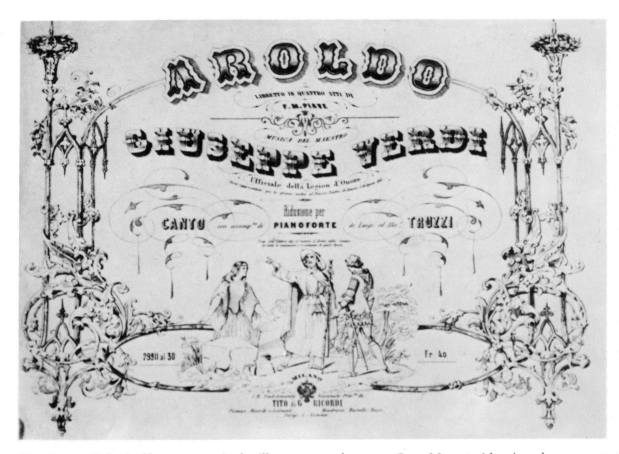

The piano music for Aroldo.

And still more cursed operas. On 2 May 1856 he signed a contract with San Carlo in Naples to deliver an (unspecified) 'grand opera of not less than three acts' for production in January 1858. The contract said that the impresario would have to provide sets, costumes and stage machinery 'worthy of so illustrious a Maestro'. Verdi would have to submit the libretto 'to the Censor of Naples without whose approval the opera cannot be produced'. The payment would be six thousand ducats in three equal instalments.

Once again he was undecided between several ideas. He had read another play by Gutiérrez, he liked Victor Hugo's *Ruy Blas*, and he was thinking, as so often before, of *King Lear*. But in October, with little time left, he accepted another libretto by Scribe, *Gustave III ou Le Bal masqué*. Why Scribe, with whom he had been unhappy in Paris only a while ago? Perhaps because the Scribe libretto had already been made into an opera, in 1833, by Daniel Auber, and there had been no trouble from the censor at the Paris Opéra. Verdi asked the Venetian poet Antonio Somma to translate Scribe's libretto and at the same time condense it from five into three acts. Verdi thought he had a fine title, *La Vendetta in domino*.

96

Scribe's play was based on fact. One night in 1792 King Gustavus III of Sweden was shot by Count Anckarström during a masked ball in Stockholm's opera house. He was married to a Danish princess. Scribe became interested in the situation; he liked the masked ball, which had great possibilities. (In Auber's score, the masked ball takes up 114 pages.) The rest was easy for Scribe. He invented a love-story between the king and the wife of Anckarström, who was promoted to 'the king's best friend'. Love versus honour: there is your conflict. Verdi liked the conflict but (he later told his friend Vincenzo Torelli in Naples) 'the story has the conventional formulas of all operas which always displeased me, and which I now find insufferable'. Then why did he do it? He would have said that he had signed a contract. Giuseppina would have thought it was the money.

Verdi and Somma worked fast, and the libretto and some music were finished early in 1858. They had preserved Scribe's 'well-made play', condensed the action into thirty-six hours; everything was shown, nothing was explained. The masked ball was pushed down-stage, and the dramatic finale would take place in front of it. Verdi hoped to achieve some multi-level effects as in *Il Trovatore*. Of course there were still censorship problems, and the censors were tough in Naples; but Verdi thought a simple change of the setting and of the names (as in *Rigoletto*) might do the trick.

His luck was out, or his timing. On the day he arrived in Naples (14 January 1858), a follower of Mazzini, Felice Orsini, threw a bomb at the carriage in which Napoleon III and Empress Eugénie were on their way to hear Rossini's *Guillaume Tell* at the Opéra. They were unhurt (others were killed), and to commemorate the miracle – which it was – Napoleon summoned his best architect, Charles Garnier, to build an opera house near the site of the attempted assassination, which is where the Opéra stands today. And a year earlier, King Ferdinando of Naples had been attacked during a military review by a soldier jumping at him with his bayonet. The king was only slightly injured; another minor miracle.

Not unreasonably, perhaps, the censors in Naples would not permit the assassination of a king to be shown on the opera stage. They had informed Luigi Alberti, the impresario at San Carlo, but he had not informed Verdi, afraid that Verdi might stop composing. Even after Verdi arrived in Naples with Giuseppina and with Loulou (which he called Lulu, being an individualist), their cocker spaniel, Alberti told them nothing; perhaps *he* was now hoping for a miracle. At last Alberti informed Verdi but Verdi told him not to worry; they would make a few slight changes, names and so on, and all would be well. But Verdi soon realized that there was no chance of saving the production. The censors had demanded that the protagonist became an

ordinary gentleman, the wife a sister, there must be no masked ball, and certainly no murder ... 'And then, and then, and then!!!', he wrote to Vincenzo Luccardi, a friend in Rome; 'As you will suppose, these changes cannot be accepted. Therefore, no more opera. Therefore, the subscribers will not pay two instalments. Therefore, the government will withhold the subsidy. Therefore, the impresario will sue everybody and threatens me with damages of 50,000 ducats. ... What a hell!'

Much money was involved, and in such circumstances people often go and see their lawyers instead of talking to each other and trying to straighten things out. Lawyers do not want things straightened out. They have rent and overheads and greedy families: they want to sue and make money. Under the law of Naples it was forbidden to sue the censor. Thus Alberti and Verdi were soon suing each other. Alberti said he had the right to get Verdi's score but Verdi, no fool, was keeping his score. Then Alberti told his 'house poets' to write quickly a changed libretto that would be accepted by the censor. Verdi had the 'new' libretto presented in court and compared to the one he and Somma had written. Sparing no expense, he had the two libretti printed side by side, and had written his own comments in the margins. They range from the amused to the ironical to the furious. Alberti had not listed the names of his librettists. 'Praise be to the management which doesn't want to blame anyone for this artistic murder,' Verdi commented in the margin. He also made some very wise observations, as in so many of his letters: 'Between sleep and death [*dorme, muori*] there should be some differences musically speaking. Compare the difference between a Neapolitan and a Swedish song.'

Everybody in Naples was delighted with the suit and the scandal. Neapolitans are fond of gossip. Most were on Verdi's side, though not for musical reasons. Verdi was against Alberti, who was 'on the side of the censor'. There were cheers and demonstrations in front of Verdi's hotel. At one point Verdi was threatened with arrest by Alberti. Eventually the suit was settled out of court. Verdi and Giuseppina left Naples, Verdi provocatively carrying the score under his arm. No one knew that he had secretly started negotiations with Cencio Jacovacci in Rome to have *Un Ballo* produced there at the Teatro Apollo.

He also had some problems with the Papal censors in Rome. They said the setting would have to be changed; it could not be Sweden. Verdi suggested 'North or South America and possibly the Caucasus'. At last, *Un Ballo in Maschera* was first heard in Rome, on 17 February 1859. It was a success, and well deserved. The libretto was not confused, and the music was beautiful. Verdi had learnt to treat the orchestra as his beloved voices: the opera has his finest orchestration

OPPOSITE A dramatic moment in *Un Ballo in Maschera*.

A cartoon, believed to represent Wagner, entitled 'Indispensable musical doctrine for the public who wish to enjoy the new style of Verdi's music'.

since he began writing, and points toward his late masterpieces. The characters included Ulrica, the fortune-teller, another great mezzo part (what would mezzo-sopranos be doing without Verdi?), and Oscar, the page, a distant relation of Cherubino (and of Rofrano, the *Rosenkavalier*, later added by Richard Strauss). The opera needs a good orchestra and first-rate singers, and there are problems of staging.

To confuse the censors, Verdi and Somma had moved the place and time to seventeenth-century Boston, a long way from eighteenth-century Stockholm where the whole thing took place. King Gustav of Sweden became the 'colonial governor' of Boston, named 'Riccardo, Conte di Warwick'. The Swedish aristocrats became the conspirators 'Sam' and 'Tom'. Count Anckarström was made 'Renato, a Creole'. It is very funny, especially when put on in Italy, where producers sometimes feature marble staircases and Florentine tapestries not exactly characteristic of seventeenth-century Boston. In the later Paris premiere the setting was Naples, and the Swedish King became the Duke of Olivarez. Covent Garden in 1952 took the action back to Sweden, giving the characters their original names. *Un Ballo in Maschera* should be heard in Sweden, where the details are historically and visually accurate.

Verdi was amused when Muzio told him about the American premiere which he conducted in Boston on 15 March 1861. A Boston paper wrote: 'In Europe the ÉLITE of the Opera HABITUÉS have been accustomed to attend the Opera wearing Dominoes, and have frequently entered upon the stage and united in the CONCLUDING GRAND BAL MASQUÉ.' Poor Muzio had to compose some special dances for the last act, praying that *Il Mio Signor Maestro* would never find out about it. The Boston critics praised the opera but the *grand bal masqué* was said to be a total failure. Verdi would have been pleased.

He stayed in Rome with Giuseppina for a while. They had rented a house ('very ugly', according to her), hired a cook – very important for Verdi, the gourmet – and brought some of their personal servants from Sant' Agata. Verdi was getting used to living in the style of a successful, wealthy man, though he did not overdo it. He was Italy's greatest composer, and a very famous citizen. People shouted *Viva Verdi!* when he appeared in public. And Giuseppina was beginning to think of a new, final part for her. The biographer Franco Abbiati reports that after 1856 her handkerchiefs were embroidered 'G.V.', and she signed some letters with 'Giuseppina Verdi'. Three years earlier, Verdi's friendship with Madame Appiani, one of his Milanese ladies, had ended after Appiani had sent a letter to Paris, by error or intent, addressed to 'Giuseppina Strepponi'. That was Giuseppina's true name but it created complications because the name was unknown to the postman, who only delivered it after some delay. Strepponi was very angry, there was a scene, and Verdi sent Madame Appiani a short letter, 'We are in a great hurry, packing our bags,' – and that was the end of another beautiful friendship.

On 29 August 1859 Verdi and Giuseppina went from Geneva by coach to the small village of Collonges-sous-Salève. The village was then in Savoy and is now in France. The local priest was 'sent for a walk', according to Verdi. The marriage ceremony was performed by Abbé Mermillod, Rector of Notre-Dame in Geneva, who had come with them in the carriage. The Swiss coachman and the bellringer at Collonges were the witnesses; no one else was present. Having lived all these years as husband and wife, they may not have wanted to make much of the ceremony, for which Giuseppina must have been waiting for a long time. Ten years later Verdi wrote to a friend: 'Mermillot suggested holding the wedding at Collange [sic] so that it would be recognized civilly. He could have done it just as well in his Catholic church with only the religious ceremony in mind.' Giuseppina had much admiration for Mermillot. He later became a bishop and in 1890 a cardinal. Giuseppina's feelings had been right, not for the first time.

7
THE PATRIOT

Much has been written about Verdi the political man, but Italians remember him, more accurately, as the patriotic man. Verdi was never a politician or even in politics. He considered politics as a means of achieving the liberation and unification of his homeland. After that had been done, he became openly disgusted by the dirty side of power politics. It has been suggested that Verdi spent periods of his life in retirement, more so as he grew older and the intervals between his operas became longer. But Verdi never retired: that was not in his intellectual make-up. Even when he walked through his corn-fields, the country squire at Sant' Agata, or listened to gossiping friends at home or in Genoa, he was always, though often sub-consciously, thinking of music; he could not help it, even when he did not write a note for months. But next to music, and his affection foɪ Giuseppina and a very few other people, Italy's problems were most important to him. Verdi, the man and the musician, always re-mained the patriot.

He had been born in the great decade that produced the three men who, each in his own way, contributed most to the liberation and unification of Italy. Mazzini, the intellectual prophet who inspired the young with his ideas and writings, was born in 1805; Garibaldi, the fighting hero of Italy's *Risorgimento*, in 1807; Cavour, the wise states-man and architect of modern Italy, in 1810. And Verdi, whose very name had become a symbol of patriotism since the 'Va, pensiero' chorus, was born in 1813. *Risorgimento* means 'resurgence': the rebirth of Italy. In the late 1850s, when the patriotic movement swept the peninsula, the letters 'V.E.R.D.I.' appeared on many walls, an acrostic for 'Vittorio Emanuele Re d'Italia'. (In 1957 there were complaints in the Italian Parliament because members of monarchist university clubs called them 'VERDI' clubs, using the former acrostic to honour 'the young Pretender', Vittorio Emanuele.) Verdi wrote music for Mazzini, gave money to buy rifles for Garibaldi, and, because

of his admiration for Cavour, accepted public office though he disliked it.

In 1813, when Verdi was born, the village of Le Roncole and the town of Busseto (and the Duchy of Parma) had been part of Napoleon's Empire. Two years later, after the Congress of Vienna, Parma with Piacenza and Custozza was made an 'independent' principality under Marie-Louise of Austria, Napoleon's wife and the mother of his only legitimate son, the Duke of Reichstadt ('L'Aiglon'). Marie-Louise was independent so long as she listened to her Austrian 'advisers' who sent regular reports to Metternich in Vienna. In 1831 (when Verdi was not yet eighteen) the Duke of Reichstadt, then a prisoner of Metternich in Vienna, was proclaimed in the Duchy of Modena, near Parma, as 'Napoleon II, King of Italy ... who comes from the blood of the immortal Napoleon'. Bologna, Ferrara and Ravenna joined the revolt in Modena. Marie-Louise had refused to go with her husband into exile on the island of Elba. She was kept 'prisoner' by the revolu-

An Italian patriot scrawls 'Viva Verdi' on a wall in defiance of the Austrian soldiers strolling towards him.

tionaries in Parma and after a few days was permitted to 'escape' to Piacenza, still under Austrian control. In Vienna she was called a 'heroine'. She was also permitted to return to her palace in Parma. Eighteen months after the revolt, the Duke of Reichstadt died in Vienna of tuberculosis at the age of twenty-one. He was buried in Vienna; so was Marie-Louise, a Habsburg Archduchess, in 1847.

The Italian peninsula was then completely split up. The Austrian Emperor was also King of Lombardy-Venetia, crowned in the Duomo of Milan, the capital. When young Verdi became the toast of Milan after *Nabucco* and met the intellectuals and aristocrats, he was often confused. Milan's aristocracy had intermarried with the Austrian nobility. Some were loyal to the House of Savoy in Piedmont and others to the Habsburgs in Vienna. It was said that in some families they had relatives at the Emperor's court and in the Emperor's jail. The confusion began at the very top. The Empress of Austria was Maria Anna Carolina, formerly a Princess of Savoy. King Vittorio Emanuele of Savoy, who became the first King of (united) Italy in 1860, was married to the Archduchess Adelaide Habsburg. In many families loyalties were divided. Verdi had seen the Maffeis, his friends, break up because Clarina was an Italian patriot and Andrea was lukewarm about 'the cause', perhaps even pro-Austrian.

The situation was just as complex elsewhere. The House of Savoy, which did not consider itself 'Italian' around 1848, ruled Sardinia, the region from Nice to Milan including the island of Sardinia. Relatives of the Habsburgs were ruling in Tuscany and Modena. The Papal States were under the absolute power of the Pope. In the impoverished south, the French Bourbons ruled the 'Two Sicilies', the island of Sicily and the region of Naples. The political confusion was confounded by the economic and social chaos. Poverty was widespread and so was ignorance. Millions were illiterate (among them Verdi's parents). Until Manzoni wrote *I Promessi Sposi* there was no common language but a number of regional dialects. Communications were scarce. The people were often exploited by the foreign occupiers. At the Congress of Vienna Metternich had declared that the word 'Italy' was 'only a geographical term'. The use of the word 'Italy' in a patriotic or national sense was considered evidence of revolutionary sentiment by Metternich's bureaucrat-policemen, and by his reactionary followers everywhere.

Metternich's secret police network was well organized. Under the circumstances, merely to speak of 'unification' in Italy took idealism, vision and personal courage. The early pioneers of the Risorgimento – among them many writers and intellectuals – had all that was needed. The early insurrections in Milan (1821) and Modena (1831) were local affairs. When the people of Rome revolted against Pope Gregory XVI in 1831, people elsewhere heard about it much later and probably did not care much. Few knew that the Pope had asked for Austrian troops to suppress the revolt by force. The Vatican also used priests as informers and several hundreds of people were arrested. Many were freed after the amnesty which Pope Pius IX proclaimed after his election in 1846.

Verdi's personal involvement with the national movement began as a teenager when he read Manzoni, who remained the great idol of his life. Verdi's letters after *Nabucco* prove how deeply he was influenced by Giuseppe Mazzini from Genoa who remained a great spiritual force, though he was not good as an organizer and was at his best when he stayed away from the scene of action. Verdi also admired Giuseppe Garibaldi from Nice, the most colourful hero of the movement who dared challenge vast armies with ridiculously small bands of volunteer guerrillas. Verdi saw Garibaldi in Turin, when he was a Deputy, but never talked to him. He had met Mazzini in London when the revolutionary was there in exile in 1847, and again after the glorious Five Days in Milan. Verdi later often regretted that he had not been in Rome when the short-lived Republic had been proclaimed on 9 February 1849, just two weeks after he had conducted there his patriotic opera *La Battaglia di Legnano*. Garibaldi commanded the revolutionary forces; Mazzini directed the politics. The Pope had gone to Gaeta in the south where he was being protected by King Ferdinando of Naples. From there he asked the Austrians, the French and the Spanish to re-take Rome for him. (Several years later Pius IX, once hailed as a reformer, issued his encyclical *Quanta Cura*, condemning freedom of the press and religion, and proclaiming the legal supremacy of Church over State.)

There was much hesitation in France, where many citizens sympathised with the Risorgimento. But eventually the French Assembly authorised Louis Napoleon to send troops to Rome. They surrounded the city which surrendered after a four-week siege. In the end there was fighting in the city streets, even hand-to-hand fighting between the French and the members of Garibaldi's Italian Legion, and stories of Garibaldi's heroic resistance are told even today. Garibaldi retreated in true guerrilla style to San Marino, later to Venice, and eventually went to New York. His failure to keep Rome became one of the inspirations of the Risorgimento, which was kept alive by its failures rather than successes. The Pope returned to Rome and ruled with more power than before. But Garibaldi's sacrifice had not been in vain. The heroic adventure, the resistance of a few brave men against impossible odds, is the stuff ideals are built of. The Roman Republic did for generations of Italians what Massada did once for the Jews and Thermopylae for the Spartans.

This was the end of the heroic epoch. The 1850s were the decade of Count Camillo Cavour. He held several cabinet posts in Turin under King Vittorio Emanuele of Savoy, and eventually became prime minister. He knew that Italy could be unified only as a monarchy under his King, and he skilfully persuaded Italy's republicans (such as Verdi) to support the House of Savoy. To Daniele Manin, the republican hero of Venice, he wrote: 'Convinced that it is necessary to create Italy, the republican party says to the House of Savoy, "Make Italy and I am with you, if not no!"' Cavour persuaded Mazzini. Even Garibaldi, the most ardent republican of all, promised to fight under the King 'to make Italy'.

Cavour was a realistic idealist, and he became a statesman and a great European. His letters prove that he had no admiration for the House of Savoy, but he realized, with some reluctance, that there was no other way of making Italy. Cavour's admirers in Europe often understood this better than his enemies in Italy, both among the republicans and the aristocrats, who considered the anti-clerical nobleman from Turin a traitor to their class. Cavour wanted 'a free Church in a free State', which made him a heretic at the Vatican. He proceeded with patience and statesmanship. Piedmont supported France and England in the Crimean War (1854) against Russia. Cavour slowly built up the army, the finances, and the international organization of Piedmont, which was no longer called 'Sardinia'. At the Congress of Paris, after the Crimean War, 'Italy' was for the first time mentioned officially, by the French Foreign Minister, as a nation and not as a geographical term. Italy was now a fully-fledged ally of France and England. Cavour knew that the French would help Piedmont only if Piedmont were attacked by the Austrians; he also knew that the English would practise benevolent inactivity but would not get involved on 'the Continent of Europe' for the sake of Piedmont.

Some people called Cavour an *intrigant* because he admitted that the end justified the means. He was certainly closer to Talleyrand and Bismarck than to Mazzini and Garibaldi, the romanticists. Cavour understood the meaning of expediency. He made a secret deal with Napoleon III. He was now reasonably sure that French troops would come to the help of Piedmont if it could be arranged that the Austrians invaded Piedmont. It was a dangerous scheme but Cavour thought he would take a chance.

After much diplomatic activity in the chancelleries of Europe (which now seems old-fashioned in these days of terrorism, blackmail and power politics) the Austrians fell into Cavour's trap. He had started mobilizing in Piedmont, which was certain to provoke Vienna. On 23 April 1859 Austria sent an ultimatum to Piedmont demanding complete demobilization or Austria would declare war. The

OPPOSITE Count Camillo Cavour, whose diplomatic skill helped to bring about the unification of Italy.

offensively-worded ultimatum gave Piedmont seventy-two hours. Emperor Franz Joseph, then twenty-nine, had listened to his generals and turned down the warnings of his cautious diplomats. (He apparently learnt little during his long, lonely life. In 1914, when he was eighty-four, he let himself be persuaded to send the ultimatum to Serbia which led to the First World War and the end of the Habsburgs.)

Piedmont rejected the Austrian ultimatum. On 29 April the Austrian troops crossed the Ticino and invaded Piedmont. Emperor Napoleon III came to Piedmont's help with a hundred thousand men. Garibaldi, back from America, had organized his private mini-army of three thousand, trying to cut the Austrian supply-lines leading down from the Brenner Pass through the Adige Valley. The Austrians were defeated at Magenta. The King of Piedmont and the Emperor of France made a glorious entrance into Milan. The Austrians retreated everywhere, and the Italian patriots were delirious. In Sant' Agata Verdi started a subscription, raising money for the wounded. He led the list by giving 550 lire, followed by Giuseppina and his father. His tenant farmer gave five francs. Verdi wrote to Clarina Maffei, '... I confess and say *mea culpa, mea grandissima culpa*, that I was unable to believe that the French would come into Italy and spill their blood for us without the idea of conquest.' He hoped Napoleon III would stick to his task, '... and then I will adore him even more than I have adored George Washington.'

Verdi was kept informed of current events by his conductor friend Mariani in Genoa who wrote almost every day: 'The town of Varese contributed effectively to the defence of Garibaldi's barricades. To the cannon shots of the Austrians, the population replied with cries of '*Viva Italia! Viva Vittorio Emanuele!*' 'It is said that Emperor Napoleon has written a letter to the Emperor of Austria, reproaching him for the infamous manner in which his hired assassins wage war', and Mariani quotes a French soldier wounded at Montebello who saw 'the bodies of some French officers with their eyes gouged out'. Verdi thanked Mariani for the daily report but wrote that they now had the *Gazzetta di Milano* sent to Sant' Agata and had the news 'from nearby'.

After the battle at Solferino on 24 June, when the French and the Piedmontese under Napoleon III defeated the Austrians, under the personal command of their Emperor, Napoleon began to have some second thoughts. Vittorio Emanuele was getting too popular for Napoleon's taste. Back in Paris the clerical party was violently against the war, and so was the Empress Eugénie, a devout Catholic and the daughter of a Spanish aristocrat. Many Frenchmen did not like to see French soldiers getting killed in order to create a strong Italy, right next to the southern border of France. Ominous Prussian troop movements were reported north of the Alps. On 11 July Napoleon and

Franz Joseph signed the 'secret' treaty of Villafranca. Its terms soon became known. Austria and France declared themselves in favour of an Italian Confederation, 'with the Pope as honorary President'. Austria would cede Lombardy to France which in turn would hand it over to Piedmont. But Austria would retain Venetia. The Dukes of Tuscany and Modena would return to their states and proclaim an amnesty. The Pope would be 'asked to make indispensable reforms in the Papal States'. And there would be a general amnesty.

Cavour considered the treaty a tragedy and a case of French treachery. (It was remembered by many that Mazzini had always said Napoleon could not be trusted.) Vittorio Emanuele said he had not even been asked about the treaty with which he was presented; could he fight the Austrians *and* the French? Some said it was too bad about Venetia but at least Piedmont was getting Lombardy. All Italians felt humiliated. Cavour resigned and departed for Geneva. Vittorio Emanuele signed the treaty, adding *'en ce qui me concerne'* ('in so far as it concerns me'). There was widespread depression, and the Italians

Austrian troops being thrown into the canal at Palestro, 31 May 1859.

were divided. The Milanese were happy that the Austrians were gone. But French troops were still in Lombardy, and many said the French were just as bad as the Austrians. In Venice, Parma, Modena, Tuscany there was talk of 'the French betrayal'. Verdi was stunned. 'Isn't Venice Italy too?', he wrote to Clarina Maffei: 'After such a victory, what a result! So much blood for nothing! Poor deluded youth! And even Garibaldi who sacrificed his convictions to fight for the King didn't achieve his goal. . . .'

In August Parma voted to join neighbouring Modena, and on 4 September (a week after Verdi and Giuseppina were married) the men – only the men – voted for representatives to the new Assembly in Parma. Verdi was elected in Busseto. The ballot-boxes were set up in the church of Santa Maria degli Angeli, and Verdi had to go there, whether he liked it or not. Everybody cheered him and he was very embarrassed. He and four others were sent to Turin respectfully to ask Vittorio Emanuele for a union of Parma with Piedmont, after the deposition of the Bourbons. Verdi wanted to see Cavour, whom he had never met and whom he admired. Sir James Hudson, the British Ambassador, arranged the visit and went along to the estate at Leri, near Turin, where Cavour was in temporary retirement. A few days earlier Verdi had received a beautiful letter from Giuseppina in Sant' Agata:

Perhaps when this letter arrives you will be in Turin if you decide to see Cavour and Sir James. What a thing it is to have genius! One goes to pay calls on ministers of state and ambassadors. . . . Yet however worthy your genius of the art which you profess, the talisman that fascinates me and that I adore in you is your character, your heart, your indulgence for the mistakes of others while you are so severe with yourself, your charity, full of modesty and mystery, your proud independence and your boyish simplicity. . . . O my Verdi, I am not worthy of you . . . continue to love me: love me also after death, so that I may present myself to Divine Providence rich with your love and your prayers, O My Redeemer. . . . Good night, my *Pasticcio*. Enjoy yourself but remember that I am at Sant' Agata.

Your Peppina

The visit with Cavour did not go too well. Cavour was not interested in music but he respected Verdi as a political symbol in Italy. Later Verdi wrote a short note to Cavour: 'I had wished for a long time to make the personal acquaintance of the Prometheus of our people. . . . I had the honour of shaking the hand of the great statesman, the first citizen, the man whom every Italian will call the father of his country.' Verdi called himself in the letter 'a simple artist who loves and always has loved his native land'. In his reply, Cavour was grateful for 'the affectionate sympathy of a fellow-citizen who has helped to keep Italy's name honoured in Europe'.

Verdi went back to Sant' Agata and stayed. Everybody said that something was bound to happen soon. Lombardy was handed over to Piedmont but French troops remained there and in Rome. More and more Italians wanted unification of the country north of Rome under Vittorio Emanuele. Mazzini and Garibaldi said that was not enough, the whole peninsula had to be unified, Napoleon wanted the French to stay in Tuscany. Intelligent Italians began to understand that the French wanted a seemingly independent Italy, but not a completely unified one. There was endless debate and discussion. Verdi asked his friend Mariani in Genoa to buy 172 rifles for the town militia in Busseto. Just in case Garibaldi showed up; he might need them.

Cavour was recalled as prime minister on 21 January 1860 by King Vittorio Emanuele. Everybody in northern Italy was pleased. And almost everybody understood that Cavour's problem was not to get the Austrians out of Venice – that would come anyway – but to get the

Verdi leads a delegation to Vittorio Emanuele to ask for the union of Parma with Piedmont, 1859.

Italian troops take the Piazza del Municipio in Perugia, September 1860.

OPPOSITE:ABOVE The encampment of the Piedmontese army outside Milan, 1859, painted by Christiano de Albertis.
BELOW Vittorio Emanuele enters Milan, 1859, painted by M. Bisit.

OVERLEAF La Scala in 1852, painted by Inganni Angelo.

French out of many parts of Italy, from Lombardy to Sicily. Cavour would have to make a deal with Napoleon. The French wanted Savoy, French-speaking and pro-French; no problem. But they also wanted Nice, where people spoke the Ligurian (almost Genoese) dialect. Nice had Genoa's old republican tradition; Genoa was the most republican city in Italy. Mazzini, from Genoa, might be persuaded; but what about Garibaldi, from Nice?

Garibaldi sent an emissary to Vittorio Emanuele who was asked, quite directly, whether the rumours about Nice were true? The King answered, just as directly, that they would give up not only Nice but also Savoy: 'If I can reconcile myself to lose the cradle of my family . . . the General can do the same.' General Garibaldi was furious. But Cavour went ahead and signed another secret treaty with Napoleon. Parma, Modena, Tuscany and the Romagna would be permitted to unite with Piedmont. The Pope, who considered the Romagna *his* territory, excommunicated the King and Cavour. Vittorio Emanuele made a tour of the newly annexed states. He visited Parma and made a short stop in Busseto, where he was presented with a cannon. Verdi

had been asked to write a cantata but had declined. He told the people he had already rejected similar requests from Milan and Turin. He was still a republican at heart although he had made his peace with the monarchy for the sake of a unified Italy. The Bussetani understood. After his marriage and election, Verdi's relations with Busseto had temporarily improved.

Cavour's next problem was Garibaldi. The General said that since Nice and Savoy were lost, he would at least try to bring Sicily and Naples into a unified Italy. His incredible 'expedition of the thousand' remains a truly heroic adventure. He had about a thousand young volunteers, wearing red shirts and carrying old muskets. They also had five cannons. They left Genoa 'secretly' in May. Cavour, who could not help being impressed, gave them some protection by the navy. Garibaldi landed in Sicily and captured Palermo, which had been defended by almost twenty-five thousand Neapolitan troops. Many Sicilian boys, called *piccioli*, 'the little ones', and some Sicilian priests joined Garibaldi. Demonstrating his mastery in guerrilla tactics, he invaded southern Italy. In September he occupied Naples

The meeting of two great Italian patriots: the poet Manzoni meets soldier Garibaldi.

OPPOSITE The opening of the Suez Canal in 1869 in the presence of Emperor Franz Joseph of Austria and Crown Prince Friedrich Wilhelm of Prussia. Verdi's *Aïda* was commissioned to celebrate the opening.

while almost fifty thousand Neapolitan troops retreated to Gaeta. Verdi wrote to Mariani; 'Hurrah for Garibaldi. By God, he is truly a man before whom we should kneel.'

In Turin however feelings were rather mixed. Cavour admired Garibaldi's enormous success but what was he going to do next? He was ruling the southern regions with his republican guerrillas in elegant, dictatorial style, and the chancelleries in Europe were getting concerned. Was Garibaldi going to take orders from Vittorio Emanuele, who represented law and order in Italy? Garibaldi might lead his volunteers against Rome.

In Turin it was decided (and Napoleon was informed) that Vittorio Emanuele would lead the Piedmontese army down south, taking all regions except the Patrimony of St Peter (Rome) that belonged to the Pope. Verdi wrote to Mariani about Garibaldi and General Cialdini of Piedmont: 'Those are composers! What operas! And what finales, to the sound of guns!!'

Italy was united except for Venetia, still under the Austrians. But Garibaldi and his followers were furious at Vittorio Emanuele and Cavour for keeping them out of Rome. The King did not improve matters by deliberately insulting Garibaldi, who had virtually given him southern Italy. Garibaldi had his men assembled for a farewell parade. Vittorio Emanuele did not appear and did not bother to apologize. He did not like the 'republican radicals'. They never forgave him. They went home but their sons and later the sons of their sons remembered the insult. Italian historians believe it was remembered as late as 1946, when the Italians voted for a Republic, deposing the House of Savoy.

Garibaldi turned down all honours, and went back to his farm on the island of Caprera, taking along, symbolically, one bag of seed corn. Millions of people in Italy felt as Giuseppina who wrote to a friend, 'Do you love Giuseppe of Caprera? I hope so', and calls Garibaldi 'the purest and greatest hero since the world was created'.

Cavour decided that elections would be held in January 1861 for Italy's new National Parliament in Turin. The Deputies would be chosen from the less than half a million men who had property or other qualifications. It was not yet the perfect democracy but it was a step towards it. In Busseto a lawyer, Giovanni Minghelli-Vanni, announced his candidacy for the town and the district of Borgo San Donnino. Then Cavour asked Verdi to come to Turin and be a candidate. Cavour wanted Alessandro Manzoni in the Senate and Verdi in the Chamber of Deputies. The two great Italians would give much moral support and prestige to Italy's first elected Parliament.

Verdi told Cavour he was not the right man; he was a musician and a farmer and he had no patience with long speeches. Cavour laughed and quickly convinced Verdi that it was the composer's 'sacred duty' to serve. He could have convinced Verdi of anything; he was, next to Manzoni, Verdi's second Italian hero. Verdi returned to Sant' Agata, announced his candidacy, and wrote to Minghelli-Vanni,

... I have not campaigned, I will not campaign, nor will I take a step to insure my election. I will serve, although at a heavy sacrifice to myself, if I am elected, and you know the reason why I must do so. Nevertheless, I am resolved to resign as soon as I can. ... If you succeed in being elected yourself, and freeing me from this duty, I will not find sufficient words to thank you for such a great service. You would do a favour to the Chamber, a service to yourself, and give the very greatest pleasure to

G. Verdi

Verdi was elected by 339 votes to 206, and went with Giuseppina to Turin for the opening of Parliament on 18 February 1861. Verdi's seat was right up in the second row, among other Cavour followers. Giuseppina told Barezzi in Busseto that she had watched the opening 'in a very good position, armed with my opera glasses'. She rightly considered it another Verdi premiere.

Verdi attended the sessions regularly, always voting with Cavour ('That way I can be absolutely certain of not making a mistake'). On several occasions he tried to sell Cavour some of his favourite projects. The three leading Italian opera houses (Milan, Rome, Naples) should have permanent orchestras and choruses maintained by the government. The conservatories should provide free singing lessons for gifted pupils. Cavour liked his ideas and promised future legislation. Verdi wanted to leave Turin and get back to his fields but Cavour asked him to stay. Verdi was in the Chamber on 18 April 1861 when Garibaldi appeared there and made his dramatic speech, accusing Cavour of having tried to start 'a fratricidal war' between his volunteers and the Piedmontese troops. He shouted that he would 'never grasp the hand of the man who made me a foreigner in Italy'. It was very dramatic, very operatic, but Verdi was bitterly disappointed by this show of disunity. He still admired Garibaldi but now he understood that Cavour was the right man for the future of Italy.

The blow affected Cavour. It was noticed that he looked ill. He told his friends that he had sleepless nights and had often vomited since that day in the Chamber. The doctors, unable to agree what was wrong with him, bled him, and the loss of blood proved to be fatal. Cavour died on the morning of 6 June.

Verdi had gone to Sant' Agata at the end of the session. He was stunned by Cavour's unexpected death. He was convinced that no one in Italy would be able to continue Cavour's work. He wrote to his friend, Opprandino Arrivabene, the Deputy from Mantua, that he did not have the strength to attend Cavour's funeral. Instead, he organized a memorial service in Busseto: 'I cried like a boy. ... Poor Cavour! And poor us. ...'

Verdi remained a member of Parliament for another two years but rarely attended the sessions. He wrote to Piave, 'The 450 Deputies are truly only 449 because Verdi as a Deputy does not exist.' He returned to his cornfields in Sant' Agata and to his music.

Surprisingly, Verdi accepted a commission to write Italy's musical contribution to the London Exhibition though he had earlier turned down similar requests. After Cavour's death he felt under a moral obligation to do it. Meyerbeer had contributed several marches, ending with *Rule Britannia*. Auber wrote an Overture. Sir William Sterndale-Bennet composed an Ode. Verdi's contribution, *Inno delle Nazioni* ('Hymn of Nations') is noteworthy for the text which was by a young Italian poet, Arrigo Boito, who later helped Verdi create his two finest operas, *Otello* and *Falstaff*.

Musically, the *Hymn* is no masterpiece. Patriotism does not usually stimulate the creation of great music, from Beethoven's *Wellington's Victory* to Shostakovitch's *Leningrad Symphony*. In his short cantata for chorus and solo voice, Verdi used several national anthems: England's *God Save the Queen*, France's *Marseillaise*, and Italy's *Mameli's Hymn*. (Actually, both the *Marseillaise* and *Mameli's Hymn* became their countries' anthems only later, but Verdi was often prescient where music was concerned.) Verdi's *Hymn* was a success in London. It was again performed, much later, by Toscanini during the First World War in the arena of Milan, and during the Second World War, in New York's Madison Square Garden.

After the death of Cavour, Verdi no longer took an active part in Italian politics, though he remained involved emotionally and often bitterly to the end of his life. In 1866, during the short war between Austria and Prussia, Italy had a secret alliance with Prussia. The Italian contribution remained shameful: they were beaten at Custozza and again at Lissa where seven Austrian warships defeated fourteen Italian ironclads. Somehow the Italian admiral managed to avoid being aboard his flagship as it was sunk and was later court-martialled. The only cheerful note, so far as Verdi and the Italian people were concerned, was contributed by the astonishing Garibaldi who collected a band of volunteer guerrillas and made a final comeback. Among others, Arrigo Boito and his friend Franco Faccio, later a celebrated conductor, had joined him. Garibaldi captured much of the Trentino region from the Austrians, but after the peace treaty it remained with Austria. It was his last glorious adventure.

The Prussians defeated the Austrians at Sadowa. The treaty forced Austria to cede Venetia to France. After a plebiscite, in which the Venetians voted for union with Italy, the last occupied region became part of the Kingdom of Italy. Verdi felt deeply humiliated by his country's 'national disgrace'. He understood that the heroic days were over. Cavour was dead, Mazzini died in 1872, and Garibaldi ten years later. (The revered Manzoni died in 1873.) Verdi, the last survivor of a great era, felt lost and lonely. His letters often show understanding and foresight in political problems. He was not narrow-minded. He was bitter about the French who had 'betrayed' Italy, but he knew how much France meant to Western civilisation and was worried about Prussian militarism and German expansionism. In 1870 he wrote to his friend Cesare de Sanctis in Naples:

I have lived too long in France not to understand how the French make themselves insufferable by their insolence ... but whoever feels himself to be truly Italian must be above such pinpricks. We must remember that Prussia has declared that 'the sea of Venice and Trieste belongs to Germany'.

Verdi wrote to Arrivabene in September 1870 that 'the European war will not be avoided', and to Clarina Maffei:

France gave liberty and civilisation to the modern world. If she falls, let's not fool ourselves, all our liberty and civilisation will fall too . . . ; in the conquerors' veins flows still the ancient blood of the Goths, these men are monstrously proud, hard, intolerant, contemptuous of everything not German, and rapacious without limit. Men of brains but without heart; a strong race but not civilised.

And then Verdi makes a shattering prophecy: 'We will not avoid a European war and we will be *devoured*. It will not come tomorrow but it will come.' He was right; the war did come seventy years later and Italy was almost devoured. Even with his sense of melodrama, Verdi could not have guessed the monstrous terror that was to come.

8
'IN THE MIDST OF FLAME AND FIRE'

Verdi wrote only two operas during the 1860s, *La Forza del Destino* and *Don Carlos*. Both were relatively unsuccessful when they were first performed and many people in Italy and elsewhere said that Verdi was finished, burnt out. They had reason to regret their gloomy prophesies. The best of Verdi was yet to come. Today both *La Forza* and especially *Don Carlos* are much appreciated by the cognoscenti as stepping-stones to Verdi's ultimate glory.

The pace of Verdi's creative genius had slowed but its depth had increased. He was under no financial pressure; he could take his time, selecting offers and subjects. A few weeks after the death of Cavour, in the summer of 1861, Verdi signed a contract to write an opera for St Petersburg, to be produced in the winter of 1862. He wanted to get away from Italy for a while. Giuseppina, who was 'royally bored' in Sant' Agata, was excited at the thought of seeing Peter the Great's 'window toward Europe', the fascinating Paris of the Far North. Verdi was thinking less of St Petersburg and more of what he was going to do there. He had his usual libretto problem. After suggesting Victor Hugo's revolutionary drama *Ruy Blas* he was informed by the Imperial Theatre that they would prefer something else. No wonder. A lowly valet who loves his queen in seventeenth-century Spain and kills a grandee and himself was not the ideal subject in Tsarist Russia. Verdi decided to use a Spanish drama, by Angel de Saavedra Ramírez de Banquedano, Duke of Rivas, that had been a great success in Madrid in 1835. It was then called *Don Alvaro, o La Fuerza del Sino*, and eventually became *La Forza del Destino* ('The Force of Destiny'). Verdi always had a weakness for the early Romantics and he liked Spanish drama. His new opera went right back to the sinister implausibility of Gutiérrez's *El Trovador*. Verdi was almost fifty but he had not lost his taste for melodrama and he knew he was the only composer who could make it believable, almost true, through the force of his melodies.

The tragedy of *La Forza* (which modern audiences often consider a farce) begins soon after the curtain goes up. Don Alvaro, the tenor, wants to elope with Leonora, whom he loves. They are surprised by the Marquis of Calatrava, Leonora's noble basso father. Don Alvaro, a fine young man, admits that he alone must be blamed for the elopement. He dramatically expresses his regrets to Papa and elegantly throws his gun on the floor. Bang! It goes off and the old nobleman dies, but not before cursing his daughter. Fortunately audiences often do not know what is going on, otherwise there might be laughter in the wrong place.

Afterwards everything goes terribly amiss for poor Don Alvaro, who is persecuted by 'the force of destiny' until the very end. After various side and sub-tragedies nearly everybody dies except Alvaro, who turns religious and is asked by the Padre Guardiano, another imposing basso figure, 'to seek forgiveness'.

A sketch of the soldiers' camp in *La Forza del Destino*, set in eighteenth-century Spain.

123

ABOVE Angel de Saavedra, Duke of Rivas, a Spanish soldier and politician whose play *Don Alvaro* was the basis for *La Forza del Destino*.

Verdi wrote some incredibly beautiful music for the melodramatic nonsense. He was inspired by Spain in the age of Romanticism. He understood the dark passions and expressed them in wonderful melodies. The brilliant overture is often performed on the concert stage. Some of the finest music in *La Forza* is religious in character, in the true sense of the word. Verdi, the agnostic, had no use for the conventional trappings and the pomp of the Catholic Church, but deep in his heart and soul he was a believer, and his music proves it. *La Forza del Destino* has fine prayers, moving choruses, beautiful arias. It even has a new character, taken from the *opera buffa*, the fat, lazy, noisy monk called Fra Melitone. But it has no dramatic unity; the scenes are disconnected; neither Verdi nor poor Piave could make anything out of the Spanish play. Verdi wrote longer melodic phrases than before, and made dramatic use of the orchestra; he was clearly progressing toward his music drama, though there are still numbers and arias, such as Leonora's prayer, 'Pace, pace, mio dio'.

The premiere at St Petersburg's beautiful Imperial Theatre, on 10 November 1862, was a *succès d'estime*. Tsar Alexander II and his court were there, applauding and cheering. The critics were less enthusiastic and some local composers were said to be angry. Verdi

ABOVE and OPPOSITE Verdi in St Petersburg for the premiere of *La Forza*.

125

had been paid twenty-two thousand roubles, while they might get as little as five hundred roubles for an opera. A few months after the premiere the opera was performed in Madrid (where Verdi supervised the production), and at Rome's Teatro Apollo; it was also given in New York at the Academy of Music, and at Her Majesty's Theatre in London. But Verdi knew that something was very wrong, and for several years he permitted no performances of *La Forza* in Italy. (Nearly a hundred years later *La Forza del Destino* became a real drama at the Metropolitan Opera House, New York on the night of 4 March 1960. Leonard Warren [as Don Carlos] suddenly collapsed as he was singing the recitative following 'Urna fatale'. Thomas Schippers, the conductor, ordered the curtain down. After a long, dreadful pause, Rudolf Bing came in front of the curtain to announce that Warren was dead.)

Verdi's next opera was heard five years after the St Petersburg premiere of *La Forza*. *Don Carlos*, a problematic work, is his first real music drama, with very exciting music. Verdi had been inspired by Schiller's *Don Carlos* for a long time. Schiller had written a long, inspiring verse drama for freedom, against tyranny. In the 1860s freedom and tyranny were much on Verdi's mind. Schiller's heroes are two romantic idealists: Don Carlos, son of the autocratic King Philip II of Spain, who wants freedom for the people of Flanders; and his friend Rodrigo, Marquis of Posa, who has the courage to tell his ruler that the Inquisition has made a 'graveyard' of Flanders, and asks Philip for *Gedankenfreiheit*, freedom of thought.

Schiller was an idealist and a first-rate playwright when he invented a love-story between Don Carlos and Elisabeth de Valois, his fiancée who later marries his father, the King. The fourth important character is the Princess of Eboli, the mistress of the King, but very much in love with Don Carlos. The villainous powers are the State (represented by the King) and the Church (personified by the formidable, grim Grand Inquisitor). It seemed just what Verdi needed. Unfortunately, he had been talked into signing a contract with the Paris Opéra, though he hated the place. Again it seems that money was much of the issue. The Opéra would perform *Don Carlos* as the great attraction during the Exposition Universelle. Verdi, who referred to the Opéra sarcastically as *La Grande Boutique*, knew of course that he would have to deliver the usual elements of a 'grand opera spectacle', some ballet music, and a fantastic *auto-da-fé* when Philip and his court come to see the heretics burnt at the stake. It also meant accepting a French-language libretto, which was always problematic.

The libretto was written by François-Joseph Mery and Camille du Locle, who were nearer Scribe than Schiller. In a mistaken-identity

The ballet in the third act of
Don Carlos.

scene, for instance, Carlos meets a veiled lady he believes to be the Queen. He tells her his love – but she is Princess Eboli who loves Carlos and now gets angry with him. And so it goes from bad to worse. In Schiller's fine play the King in the end hands over his own son to the Grand Inquisitor: 'Cardinal, I've done my duty. Now do yours.' The librettists, searching for a less unhappy ending, have a mysterious monk appear – apparently Carlos's grandfather, Emperor Charles v – who takes Carlos to his monastery, saving him from the Inquisition.

Verdi knew he would have problems with the story. He wrote to Escudier, his agent in Paris, 'Composed in the midst of flame and fire, either this opera will be better than the others or a horrible thing.' 'Flame and fire' was a reference to the unhappy war of 1866 being waged that June. He was right. The premiere was, in Verdi's own words, 'not a success'. He was so disappointed that he left the follow-

Il *Trovatore* alla Fenice di Venezia.

ing day, 12 March 1867. He had seen and felt much opposition around him. During the most dramatic scene Empress Eugénie, the devout Spanish Catholic, had provocatively turned her back to the stage as the King tells the Grand Inquisitor, '*tais-toi, prêtre*', 'keep quiet, priest'. At the end of the scene the King apologizes to the Cardinal and completely submits to him, and the Empress faced the stage again. Not much has changed since then. In 1950 when the Metropolitan presented *Don Carlos*, which had not been given there for twenty-eight years, the premiere was picketed by Catholic groups. The pickets told reporters they had not seen the opera but were told that it was 'bad for the Church'.

For the first, but not the last time, some critics accused Verdi of 'imitating Wagner'. That happened four years before Verdi heard Wagner's *Lohengrin*, which is *not* a Wagnerian *Musikdrama*. Some critics had noticed the Wagnerian influence in the scene between King Philip and the Grand Inquisitor when the melody is played by the orchestra. But Verdi had done it sixteen years earlier, in *Rigoletto*, in the scene between the hunchback and Sparafucile. There was more valid criticism. *Don Carlos* was too long, and still is, though Verdi later eliminated the first act at Fontainebleau, and the ballet.

But the excitement and beauty of *Don Carlos* is indisputable. Verdi's genius is particularly strong in moments of terror and fear, passion and darkness. Verdi's *Don Carlos* is closer to El Greco, Velázquez and Goya than to Schiller. The dominant musical colours are black and sinister, only occasionally contrasted by moments of love and friendship. *Don Carlos* will never be a popular success but great conductors, from Beecham and Toscanini to Gui and Karajan have done it because they love the challenge of the great music. Great singers have been tempted by the complexities of their parts. Mezzos, already eternally indebted to Verdi for Azucena and Ulrica (*Un Ballo*), often bring down the house after Eboli's 'O don fatale'.

Verdi became deeply depressed after the failure of *Don Carlos*. Though the Paris Opéra gave it forty-three times, he knew it was not a success. He said nothing about it in public – though he may have told much to Giuseppina – but went into a long stretch of melancholy. He wondered whether he had lost his touch. As always in such moments, he escaped to his wife and his cornfields. His tenant farmers respected him as a first-class farmer though they knew little about him as a composer. When Giuseppina explained to him that she could not stay in the house for days on end while he was outside in the fields, he agreed to rent a second home in Genoa where they would spend the winters. Verdi's friend Mariani found a suitable floor for them at the elegant Palazzo Sauli, surrounded by gardens with cypresses, cedars, palms and magnolias, with a fine view of the port and the sea. Verdi

A cartoon of 1866 shows Vittorio Emanuele (as Manrico) clasping Italy (Leonora) and singing words of encouragement from the third act of *Il Trovatore*. In fact the war of 1866 brought Italian defeats at Custozza and Lissa.

and Giuseppina were then in Paris where Verdi was preparing *Don Carlos* at the Opéra. Mariani sent Giuseppina long letters with details about furnishing and decorating the apartment. Mariani himself had taken the few small attic rooms, above Verdi's floor, being in fact Verdi's sub-tenant. ('I'll pay you six hundred francs rent annually ... it's an honour for me to have my nest under the roof, my Signora Peppina ... to be the guardian of Verdi's house.') Not quite correct, since the ground floor was occupied by the Marchesa Luisa Sauli Pallavicino. Verdi paid 3,700 francs a year.

Verdi wrote to Clarina that 1867 was an 'ill-fated year, like 1840'. His father had died while he was in Paris rehearsing *Don Carlos*. His fatherly friend and benefactor Barezzi died in July. Verdi and Giuseppina were in his bedroom. Barezzi, unable to speak, was wistfully looking at the piano. Verdi understood. He sat down at the piano and played 'Va, pensiero', which Barezzi loved more than anything else he had written. Barezzi was said to murmur '*O, mio Verdi!*', and died. And in December his librettist and friend Piave suffered a stroke. He lived for another eight years but was never able to move or to speak. Verdi could not bear to go and see him but he helped Piave's wife financially and set up a trust fund for Piave's daughter.

Verdi was unable to snap out of his melancholy early in 1868. *Don Carlos* failed in Bordeaux and Brussels. And his father's death had affected him deeply. Had he done enough for his father? He had strong feelings of guilt. At last Giuseppina felt she had to get away from Sant' Agata for a few days. She would buy furniture for the winter apartment in Genoa, and she thought the best shops were in Milan. There Giuseppina visited Clarina Maffei, whom she had never met. The Contessa often went to see Alessandro Manzoni and once took Giuseppina along to meet the great writer, Verdi's idol. Manzoni gave her a picture signed 'To Giuseppe Verdi, a glory of Italy, from a decrepit Lombard writer'. After her return Giuseppina gave Verdi the picture, which he at once hung in his bedroom. When she told him that Manzoni was expecting him in Milan, 'Verdi turned first red, then pale, and began to perspire'. He was reluctant to visit Manzoni; perhaps he was even afraid. He thanked Clarina Maffei and enclosed his own picture, with a long, rhapsodic dedication ending 'You are a saint, Don Alessandro'. Many Italians called Manzoni *sant' uomo*, a holy man.

In the spring of 1868 Verdi went to Milan. He had not been there for twenty years, since the glorious Five Days in 1848. He did not go near La Scala though Clarina Maffei told him that *Don Carlos* had been a great success there a few months earlier, and that some of it was due to a new prima donna, Teresa Stolz from Bohemia. Milan seemed much changed. Verdi regretted that some of the old classical buildings

had been torn down to make space for higher, modern structures, broad avenues, wide piazzas. He liked the new Galleria between La Scala and the Duomo. And at long last he went to see Manzoni.

Verdi never wrote down exactly what happened during the visit, and frustrated biographers were reduced to local 'tradition'. The meeting was said to have taken place in Manzoni's study on the ground floor of his house, the windows looking out on the trees of the back court. The small panelled studio (which may now be visited) has Manzoni's books on the shelves, a desk, tables, two chairs in front of the fireplace. The meeting was strained at first. Both men were ill at ease. Manzoni was always shy with people he did not know, and in such moments he would stutter. Verdi, who had often been un-impressed by the high and the mighty of this world, was overwhelmed by his hero, feeling like a small boy, unable to speak.

After a painful pause Manzoni is said to have broken the silence, saying, 'Verdi, you are a great man.' Verdi, twenty-nine years younger, said, 'But you are a saintly man.' The meeting was short and the conversation perfunctory. Music probably was not discussed. Manzoni often said he knew nothing about music. The only evidence of the meeting is Verdi's letter to Clarina Maffei, written after his return to Sant' Agata: 'What can I say of Manzoni? How can I describe the extraordinary sensation the presence of that saint, as you call him, evoked in me? I would have gone down on my knees before him if we were allowed to worship men. . . .'

And at the same time when Verdi, almost naive in his admiration of the saintly man, would have gone down on his knees, he was involved in another fight with his fellow men at Busseto that shows a different side of his complex character. Essentially Verdi remains a paradox. His relations with the citizens of Busseto had been hostile and later glacial when he had arrived there with Giuseppina Strepponi from Paris. They became almost friendly during the heroic days of the Risorgimento and later when he represented Busseto in the Chamber of Deputies in Turin. They declined again when the Bussetani decided to build a small opera house which they wished to call Teatro Verdi. The people said they wanted to honour their most famous fellow-citizen. Verdi said they wanted to exploit him. Verdi's anger grew worse when he heard that some hoped he might even compose a new opera for the opening of the new house. Some people said, not aloud of course, that there was nothing wrong with 'making a little money out of Verdi'. Had not Busseto done much for him when he was poor and unknown? It was Verdi's duty to contribute a lot of money to the project. In 1865 Verdi wrote a furious letter, probably addressed to Barezzi, who was a member of the Commission for the proposed opera house:

This is more than an inconvenience. This is an insult. ... I know that many, speaking of me, murmur: 'We made him.' The words leaped to my ear the last time I was in Busseto eight or ten days ago. ... But I still can reply, 'Gentlemen, I have received a four-year stipend of twenty-five francs a month, one thousand two hundred francs in all.' Thirty-two years have passed. Let us make an exact account of the principle and interest and I shall pay it off. The moral indebtedness will remain. Yes. But I raise my head and say with pride, 'Gentlemen, I have carried your name with honour into all parts of the world. That is well worth one thousand two hundred francs.' Hard words, but fair. ... I never wish to speak of the matter again, I ask only one thing from you. *Peace*; if you wish, even *oblivion*.

Verdi, often so understanding and wise in matters of life and of his art, still had a peasant's pride and stubbornness. He might give a friend an expensive gold watch and get very angry because a branch of a neighbour's tree was overhanging his property. Years ago he had lent the city ten thousand lire for the repair of a bridge leading to his estate. When the city did not repay the loan, Verdi had a chain put up across the bridge, 'until the loan was paid off'. As the wrangling about the opera house went on, Verdi offered the city the cancellation of the loan as his 'contribution'.

The Teatro Verdi was built and opened on 15 August 1868. It was pitifully small and had, at the most, a hundred and fifty (removable) seats and a tiny stage (where Toscanini once produced *Aïda*, however). It has a certain intimate charm. The opening performance was *Rigoletto*, preceded by the overture, *La Capricciosa*. The programme said that Verdi wrote it at the age of twelve; apparently somebody had kept it. Perhaps Verdi had been unable to burn it. After the overture, the curtain went up, revealing a bust of Verdi surrounded by flowers. But the guest of honour was not in the box which the city had given him for life. Verdi and Giuseppina had left for Genoa two weeks earlier. Later Verdi is said to have received an unpleasant anonymous letter. He got so furious that he sold his box for two thousand lire, adding insult to injury. And he returned on 16 September, exactly a day after the festival season at the Teatro Verdi. Afterwards, relations between the Bussetani and the Verdis came to an end. Giuseppina, that wonderful, wise woman, was no help so far as the town was concerned. She never forgot how they had treated her when she came there as 'Verdi's mistress'. She never forgave them. Only because she loved Verdi did she stay holed up in Sant' Agata, 'in the middle of all these *crétins*', as she wrote to Léon Escudier in Paris.

Rossini died in Paris on 13 November 1868. He was twenty-one years older than Verdi, the last great Italian composer of the previous generation. Verdi had never been close to him, but he felt that his

country should honour the creator of the immortal *Il Barbiere di Siviglia*. In Milan he explained his plan to Giulio Ricordi: a Rossini Mass written by Italy's leading composers which would be performed only once, on the first anniversary of Rossini's death, in Bologna, which Verdi called 'Rossini's musical home'. (Rossini was in fact born in Pesaro, a hundred miles away.) After the memorial performance the score would be sealed and kept in Bologna's Liceo Musico. The Requiem Mass would probably lack artistic unity but it would express Italy's gratitude towards the great composer. It would also prove to the world at large that Italy, two years after the scandalous defeats of Custozza and Lissa, could make better contributions to civilization than by way of generals and admirals.

There was much discussion about Verdi's plan which was generally applauded, though some people were heard to say that he had propagated his own ego. These people had forgotten that Rossini himself had once called himself 'ex-composer and pianist of the fourth class' and Verdi 'illustrious composer and pianist of the fifth class'. There was more criticism when the committee, whose secretary was Giulio Ricordi, asked Verdi to write the final section of the Requiem Mass, *Libera Me*. Verdi wrote it and other Italian composers, now forgotten, contributed the other sections. But the Rossini Mass was never performed. A large chorus was needed. Angelo Mariani, Italy's leading conductor and Verdi's close friend, had been asked to conduct. He told Verdi that the chorus of Bologna's Teatro Communale was not good enough. Mariani had conducted a festival honouring Rossini, in Pesaro, but the specially assembled chorus had been dispersed. There was no money; it was said that the impresario in Bologna refused to have his chorus members used without payment, and the whole project fizzled out ingloriously. Everybody said it was 'a national disaster'. The various contributions were returned to the composers. The anniversary of Rossini's death was ignored. Verdi was very bitter; he felt it was another defeat for Italy. He blamed Mariani for the fiasco. To Clarina Maffei he wrote, 'The Bologna affair is an ugly business for many people, including my distinguished friend Mariani who has not lifted a finger. ...' And to Arrivabene he wrote, 'Mariani has not done what he should have done, both as artist and my friend, perhaps a little piqued because he was not included among the composers. *Vanitas vanitatis*, etc.'

But the available evidence proves that Verdi was unfair. Mariani never wanted to be included among the composers. 'After examination of all the evidence one is forced to the conclusion,' writes Frank Walker, 'that if nothing came of Verdi's project it was principally his fault. If anyone else deserved a rebuke it was surely the unimaginative Milanese committee.' And Walker asks: 'What led Verdi, normally

OPPOSITE Verdi with Rossini.

135

tola, l'*Italiana in Algeri* nello stile buffo; la *Gazza Ladra*, *Otello*, *Mosè*, *Semiramide*, l'*Assedio di Corinto*, *Guglielmo Tell* nel genere serio; il *Conte Ory* nel genere brillante dell'opera francese, sono monumenti eterni che il tempo non valse a distruggere, e che ora risplendono di luce più viva che mai. Qualche concessione al gusto del pubblico, pel quale furono scritte, qualche sfoggio di *fioriture* che ora, per l'imperizia degli odierni cantanti è giudicato abuso, nulla tolgono alla grandezza di quelle opere. Nello stile buffo, Rossini non fu, e probabilmente non sarà mai superato; nel serio può aver avuto dei competitori, ma non è inferiore ad alcuno. Tra la congiura del *Guglielmo Tell* e la congiura degli *Ugonotti* si può rimanere incerti e perplessi, ma non si deve dimenticare che il *Guglielmo Tell* ha aperto la via alle opere del Meyerbeer. Tutti i grandi maestri succeduti al Pesarese furono grandi appunto perchè ebbero un'impronta propria, ma nessuno al pari di Rossini fece progredire la musica teatrale. Questa è la vera ragione per cui il nome del compianto maestro suona tant'alto su quello di tutti gli altri. Rossini nella storia musicale darà il proprio nome ad un intiero periodo musicale, al secolo d'oro dell'arte non solamente italiana ma mondiale.

E infatti egli fu veramente il maestro universale. Ebbe da principio avversari in Francia ed in Germania; ebbe pure detrattori, doloroso a dirsi, più recentemente in Italia; ma le sue opere da cinquant'anni esercitano una specie d'apostolato nel mondo intero. Oltre quelle che son sempre rimaste nel repertorio dei teatri, alcune altre risorgeranno, e fra esse la *Zelmira* e la *Donna del lago*; ma di tutte, anche di quelle che più non reggono alla prova del teatro, qualche pezzo vivrà, perchè in tutte v'è qualche lampo di genio.

Come abbiamo detto fin da principio, sarebbe follia lo scrivere il panegirico dell'artista. La biografia di Rossini venne scritta da molti, ma è spiacevole ch'egli stesso non abbia dettate le proprie memorie. L'autore del *Barbiere* era uomo colto e prosatore un po' fiorito, come la sua musica, ma argutissimo. Egli era in grado di narrare, meglio d'ogni altro, la propria vita, e forse l'Italia avrebbe un bel libro di più e saluterebbe un emulo di Benvenuto Cellini. Ad ogni modo, facciamo voti affinchè almeno l'epistolario del divino maestro non vada perduto. In esso si rivelerà ai posteri un nuovo Rossini. Desideriamo che di queste nostre parole si tenga conto; ed a tal uopo ci rivolgiamo agli amici del maestro ed al Governo, sperando che l'egregio ministro dell'istruzione pubblica prenderà l'iniziativa della pubblicazione di tutti gli scritti letterari del Pesarese.

A nessuno farà meraviglia che la morte di Rossini abbia cagionato la più viva impressione di dolore nell'animo del Verdi, il quale sempre professò un culto di adorazione per l'autore del *Guglielmo Tell* e del *Barbiere*, e fu anche in stretti rapporti di amicizia coll'immortale maestro. Infatti, appena giunta la trista novella, il maestro Verdi diresse a noi da Sant'Agata una sua nobile proposta, intenta ad onorare la memoria dell'illustre trapassato con un monumento artistico, fatto per opera di soli artisti, e a mezzo dell'arte stessa che fè grande il nome di Rossini. La proposta ci sembra degna di chi l'ha iniziata, degna dell'avvenimento, degna del grande a cui si riferisce. Al modo di effettuarla ed alle norme più facili onde ottenerne un grande risultato verremo più tardi. Ciò che fin d'ora guarentisce la riuscita e l'importanza del progetto, è che il maestro Verdi, iniziatore e promotore, prenderà parte alla composizione dello spartito monumentale.

Ecco la lettera di Verdi:

Sant'Agata, 17 Novembre 1868.

Carissimo Ricordi

Ad onorare la memoria di Rossini vorrei che i più distinti maestri italiani (Mercadante a capo, e fosse anche per poche battute) componessero una *Messa da Requiem* da eseguirsi all'anniversario della sua morte.

Vorrei che non solo i compositori, ma tutti gli artisti esecutori, oltre il prestare l'opera loro, offrissero altresì l'obolo per pagare le spese occorrenti.

Vorrei che nissuna mano straniera, nè estranea all'arte, e fosse pur potente quanto si voglia, ci porgesse aiuto. In questo caso io mi ritirerei subito dall'associazione.

La messa dovrebbe essere eseguita nel S. Petronio della città di Bologna che fu la vera patria musicale di Rossini.

Questa messa non dovrebbe essere oggetto nè di curiosità, nè di speculazione; ma appena eseguita, dovrebbe essere suggellata, e posta negli archivi del Liceo musicale di quella città, da cui non dovrebbe esser levata giammai. Forse potrebbe esser fatta eccezione per gli anniversarii di Lui, quando i posteri credessero di celebrarli.

Se io fossi nelle buone grazie del Santo Padre, lo pregherei a voler permettere, almeno per questa sola volta, che le donne prendessero parte all'esecuzione di questa musica, ma non essendolo, converrà trovare persona più di me idonea ad ottenere l'intento.

Sarà bene istituire una Commissione di uomini intelligenti onde regolare l'andamento di quest'esecuzione, e soprattutto per scegliere i compositori, fare la distribuzione dei pezzi, e vegliare sulla forma generale del lavoro.

Questa composizione (per quanto ne possano essere buoni i singoli pezzi) mancherà necessariamente d'unità musicale; ma se difetterà da questo lato, varrà nonostante a dimostrare, come in noi tutti sia grande la venerazione per quell'uomo, di cui tutto il mondo piange ora la perdita.

Addio e credimi

Aff.º G. VERDI.

the embodiment of fairness and justice, to make such wildly misleading statements about Mariani in his letters to his friends? There is something mysterious about the episode.' There were such mysteries in Verdi's life, and one of the saddest is the way he later broke with Angelo Mariani.

While Verdi had been in Milan, promoting his idea of the Rossini Mass, Giulio Ricordi urged him to revise *La Forza del Destino* for a new production at La Scala. Verdi had never liked old Giovanni Ricordi, Giulio's grandfather, and he was often bitter about Giulio's father, Tito; but he had a paternal affection for the young, enthusiastic Giulio, then twenty-eight, a good writer and minor composer who considered Verdi the greatest Italian genius. Giulio so hated Wagner that he attacked his music even after acquiring some of Wagner's works from Lucca, after Wagner's death. His judgment was not always sound – he rejected Bizet, Leoncavallo, and Mascagni, among others – but publishers are only human, and Ricordi did much to make Verdi write his late operas and he early recognized the great gifts of Verdi's 'crown prince', Puccini.

Now, late in 1868, Ricordi explained to Verdi that La Scala was in serious trouble and needed him. Verdi had not set foot there since he had walked out angrily twenty-four years earlier. He said he had no use for La Scala, where they had treated him so badly. Ricordi explained that La Scala had had a couple of bad seasons. Now the Austrians, who had generously subsidized La Scala – giving the Milanese what the Milanese liked best, opera – were gone. The new Italian government was poor and had refused to continue the annual subsidy. Ricordi said that Teresa Stolz, that fascinating soprano from Bohemia, and Mario Tiberini, an excellent tenor, would sing in the new production of *La Forza del Destino*. Even the Mayor of Milan, who was the chairman of La Scala's board of directors, talked to Verdi at Ricordi's request. At last Verdi gave in. He added several numbers, changed the sequence of scenes, replaced the former prelude with the beautiful overture, and personally directed the production. The premiere of the revised opera, on 27 February 1869, was a very great success. People loved the arias, duets, the religious scenes. The Milanese were delighted to have Italy's greatest composer back at Italy's greatest opera house. Now the problem was to keep him there.

OPPOSITE The publication of Verdi's letter to Ricordi suggesting that Italy's leading composers should contribute to a requiem mass in memory of Rossini.

9
LA STOLZ, FEMME FATALE

Teresa Stolz – the Italians called her 'La Stolz' – became, perhaps un-
willingly, the *femme fatale* in Verdi's life. The Stolz enigma gave rise to
a large literature by sensationalist gossip-writers and inventors of
apocryphal stories, such as Gino Monaldi, who disregarded facts
which did not fit their theories. But even Verdi's more respected
biographers have guessed, argued and disagreed about his relations
with Teresa Stolz. The mystery has not been solved and it looks as
though it never will be. There are hints and hearsay, speculation and
deductions – but no real evidence. For the *dramatis personae* happened
to be civilized people. They said little and wrote less about their very
private lives. None of them had the bad taste to write 'memoirs',
telling it all. And thus Italians will go on happily guessing about Verdi
and Teresa Stolz just as the Viennese do about Emperor Franz Joseph
and Katharina Schratt.

Teresa Stolz was born in 1834; she was nineteen years younger than
Giuseppina Strepponi, also a soprano. She came from Elbekosteletz
in Bohemia, and was sometimes called Teresina Stolzova (*Stolz* is
the German for 'proud'). It was a musical family; five of her eight
brothers and sisters became professional musicians, among them her
twin sisters Fanny and Lidia who later lived with Luigi Ricci, the
Italian composer. They were identical twins and he is said to have
fallen in love with both of them at first sight. Much better than the
story of *Così fan tutte* or anything Hofmannsthal thought up for
Richard Strauss. Ricci later married Lidia but lived with both sisters,
and each had a child by him. Unfortunately the end is not out of
Hofmannsthal: poor Ricci went insane and died of paralysis in Prague
in 1859.

Teresa herself studied there under Giovanni Battista Gordigiani but
showed little promise and was told to give up any hope of a career as
singer. She went back home, but she must have had determination

OPPOSITE The costume design
for Aïda which was worn by
Teresa Stolz (above).

because she returned to study privately and her voice became strong and promising. For a while she joined her twin sisters in Trieste and appeared there in a concert in 1856, when she was twenty-two. (Giuseppina Strepponi also made her debut in Trieste, at the age of twenty.) Teresa continued her studies and the next year made her debut on the opera stage in Tiflis. Later she sang at Odessa and Constantinople, remote outposts of the Italian opera repertory. She was dreaming of La Scala but the closest she got to it was Nice, where she had 'a stupendous success' in *Il Trovatore* in 1863. She was now twenty-nine. There had been malicious references to the *prima donna assoluta* from Tiflis but a few months later she was a sensation in *Norma* in Nice, sang in *Ernani* in Grenada and was engaged for the season in Bologna, where she appeared under Angelo Mariani, then still Verdi's friend, in *Ernani*. Obviously Mariani, who later became her lover, did not 'discover' her as some sources claim. And just as obviously, she was a very good singer and became a great 'Verdi soprano' – and, eventually, Verdi's first Aïda.

After 1864 Teresa Stolz sang in the leading Italian houses, but rarely under Mariani though the celebrated love-affair was said to have started some time after they met in Bologna. Her first appearance at La Scala was in November 1865 in Verdi's *Giovanna d'Arco*. Her dream had come true, at last. During the years that followed she sang under Mariani in *Don Carlos* and *Un Ballo in Maschera*. Coached by Mariani, the lady from Bohemia was becoming the leading Verdi soprano in Italy. Verdi always wanted to know how the productions of his operas were going and he must have known of her long before he met her personally. They met either during the rehearsals for the revised *La Forza del Destino*, in which she sang Leonora and Verdi coached the singers, or possibly a few months earlier in Genoa, as some writers believe, where Mariani may have introduced her to Verdi and Giuseppina. Teresa was deeply impressed: here was the Maestro who had written her most successful parts. Prima donnas often think of their 'parts' rather than the operas in which they appear. It has been suggested that Verdi wrote *Aïda* for Teresa Stolz, but he was not that kind of composer. He never wrote an opera for a singer or a conductor. In his younger years he wrote because he suffered when he was not writing, and because he needed the money. Later he wrote compelled by his genius. He had certain singers in mind; but he knew they were here today, gone tomorrow.

Teresa Stolz has been described by her contemporaries as being tall and statuesque, and very attractive. On the stage she had presence, which is something an artist either has or has not; it cannot be acquired. And Angelo Mariani, a glamorous star conductor (one of the earliest, followed a generation later by Artur Nikisch), was dark, handsome,

The conductor Angelo Mariani was a close friend of Verdi and the lover of Teresa Stolz.

and fascinating, with burning eyes and elegant gestures and – what is more important – a man who knew his music. Verdi respected Mariani as a musician. Women found him irresistible; nor could Mariani, beautiful and weak, resist, and he was always involved with them. Among them was another Teresa, the beautiful and perhaps somewhat wild (some biographers call her 'highly eccentric') Teresa Pallavicino Negrotto. Mariani's affair with her went on before, and also after, that with Teresa Stolz. Giuseppina Verdi, who could be very Victorian, commented in a letter to friends in Genoa that Mariani gave 'the most sentimental and philanthropic colouring imaginable' to the 'story' – meaning the affair with Mme Pallavicino Negrotto. The Italian columnists and gossip-writers were delighted when they discovered Mariani's affair with Teresa Stolz. The glamorous conductor and the beautiful prima donna – it could not have been better.

Giuseppina's first mention of Teresa Stolz is dated 11 April 1868, when she had heard the *diva* in *Don Carlos* at La Scala: 'The ovations to Signora Stolz give me pleasure, being homage to real and very distinct merit.' These are the words of a once-famous singer, sure of her judgment and free of all emotion. At that time Verdi had not met Teresa Stolz. After the revised *La Forza* premiere in February 1869 which Verdi attended with Giuseppina – young Franco Faccio conducted – Verdi was heard to say that La Stolz and Tiberini, the tenor, had been 'sublime'. Still Giuseppina had nothing to worry about. Teresa Stolz wrote to a friend that she was not really that good (which is a rare admission for a prima donna) and that 'both Maestro Verdi and his kind wife have been indulgent to me'.

An extraordinary letter exists which Giuseppina wrote from Genoa to Verdi on 3 February 1869. He was then in Milan, rehearsing *La Forza del Destino*. Giuseppina wrote that she had thought it over carefully and would not come to Milan:

Thus I shall spare you from having to come mysteriously to the station, at night, to slip me out like a bundle of contraband goods. I have thought about your profound silence before you left Genoa ... and my presentiments counsel me to decline the offer you make me – to attend a few rehearsals of *La Forza del Destino*. I sense that this invitation is forced and I think it a wise decision to leave you in peace and stay where I am. If I don't amuse myself [here in Genoa] at any rate I will not be exposing myself to further and useless bitter experiences, and you, on the other hand, will be completely *à ton aise*.

Then comes the gist of the letter:

When, last spring, my heart gave me the courage to present myself to la Maffei and Manzoni ... I did not think of the strange and bitter consequence with which I am faced, of being repudiated. ... May God forgive you the most acute and humiliating wound you have dealt me. For Giuditta and Clarina who write (I don't know why and for what end) you will find some pretext to justify my refusal.

A very bitter letter, but most biographers agree that the subject of Giuseppina's bitterness is not Teresa Stolz; there is no mention of her. No, it is 'la Maffei', Verdi's old friend. And one remembers that Verdi, after all the important events in his life, always commented on them to Clarina Maffei. There was no affair; certainly not. But she was very important to him, and Giuseppina was wounded. Possibly Giuseppina never got over the fact that for ten interminable years she had lived with Verdi without being married. Did she not realize that all that time Clarina Maffei was living with Carlo Tenca without being married?

In the end Giuseppina *did* go to Milan for the premiere of *La Forza*, but in many letters to Clarina Maffei one detects a note of rancour, almost of depression. Late in September 1871 Teresa Stolz was asked to come to Sant' Agata to study the title role in *Aïda* with Verdi. She stayed three weeks. Four days after she had left Giuseppina wrote to her, for the first time:

I want to embrace you again because I love you, esteem you and am attracted by your frank, sincere and elevated character, in no way tainted by the backstage atmosphere. I blushed a little in spite of my *venerable* age, in reading the praises you shower upon me. ... I don't deserve them at all but one part I do not disclaim and that is, of being a firm and loyal friend ... which occurs very, very seldom.

Some Verdi scholars believe that by that time Verdi had become very attracted to Teresa as a woman, and that Giuseppina had decided that since she could not fight them, she would join them. Among Italian biographers there are two schools of thought concerning the relationship between Verdi and Teresa Stolz. Carlo Gatti and his followers claim that Verdi had a love-affair with Teresa Stolz which caused him to break off his friendship with Angelo Mariani. It is generally agreed that Teresa broke with Mariani immediately after her first visit to Sant' Agata. The school of Alessandro Luzio consider this an 'odious legend'. They claim it was Giuseppina, not Verdi, who induced Teresa to break off with Mariani. After her visit to Sant' Agata Teresa wrote to Mariani that from now on theirs would be 'a simple friendship as between fellow-artists'. She also asked him to return some of her savings, which he did, though after some delay. Verdi, always strict in money matters, considered this inexcusable. Everybody agrees that *if* there was something between Verdi and Teresa Stolz, it started with *Aïda*.

Giulio Ricordi was not the only one who wanted Verdi to write a new opera. Among the interested parties was Camille du Locle, who had worked with Verdi on the libretto of *Don Carlos* for the Opéra. Verdi made it quite clear to him that he would never write for the *Grande Boutique* again:

In your opera houses there are too many connoisseurs! Each one must apply his standards and his taste, according to a system, without considering the individuality and character of the composer. Each one must give an opinion, voice a doubt, and the composer who lives for a while in such an atmosphere of doubt soon loses his confidence. He ends by correcting and adjusting or, more exactly, by spoiling his work. ... No one denies that Rossini had genius! But there hovers in *Guillaume Tell* the fatal atmosphere of the Opéra. The musical flow is not so free and confident as in the *Barbiere*. ... If an opera is an inspiration, there is one idea to it, and everything must conform to that. In Italy it can be done, at least I can always do it – but not in Paris.

... I am no composer for Paris. My artistic ideas are very different from yours. I believe in *inspiration*; you believe in *construction*. I want the essence of art, in whatever form it may take; not the compromise, the artifice, or the system that you prefer. Am I wrong? Am I right? Be that as it may, I am entitled to say that my ideas are different from yours. ...

But du Locle understood and admired the difficult composer, and did not give up, even after such a letter. He knew Verdi would never write for the Opéra again, but what about the Opéra-Comique, the second opera house in Paris, which had recently gained distinction with the success of Ambroise Thomas's *Mignon*? During the winter of 1869–70 du Locle had made a journey up the Nile with Auguste-Édouard Mariette ('Mariette Bey'), a noted French Egyptologist. Mariette had written a short-story and given it to the Khedive, suggesting that it be made into an opera that would commemorate the opening of the Suez Canal. In fact the Suez Canal had already been in operation since November 1869, with ships of many nations going through. But Ismail Pasha, the Khedive, thought it was a splendid idea. He had travelled in Europe and liked music and opera; in fact, the new opera house in Cairo had just been completed. Some experts believe that the idea had actually come from the Khedive, who gave it to Mariette who in turn suggested that his friend du Locle should write the scenario. Mariette thought they should get 'one of the best composers' for the music, either Gounod, Wagner or Verdi. Du Locle said it could only be Verdi, though he had not asked him about it. Looking back now, his choice seems absolutely right.

Du Locle sent a four-page sketch and Verdi liked it: 'It is well done, with a magnificent *mise en scène*.' The premiere was to take place in Cairo in 1871; it would be an opera of 'vast proportions', which was as close as Verdi could bring himself to using the expression 'grand opera'. But this time he was not going to use a French text; he had learnt a lesson, after all. Du Locle would write the complete outline and an Italian poet would write the text which Verdi would set to music. Verdi had less than a year to finish the work, but that did not bother him. As late as June 1870, when du Locle had sent his outline, no Italian text existed. Only six months left; but Verdi was thinking a lot about the as yet unwritten opera. He had also settled the business details. The Khedive would deposit the enormous sum of 150,000 gold francs at the Rothschild Bank in Paris, a lot of money for only the

The procession of ships through the Suez Canal on its opening in November 1869.

Egyptian premiere. Afterwards the world rights belonged to Verdi, and there would be the real premiere, so far as Verdi was concerned, at La Scala, just a few weeks later. Piave was at home, paralysed. Verdi hired Antonio Ghislanzoni from Lecco, a former baritone who had switched to writing and eventually turned out eighty librettos as well as plays, novels and poetry. He also edited the *Gazzetta Musicale* for Ricordi and had worked with Verdi on the revision of *La Forza del Destino*.

Ghislanzoni was invited to Sant' Agata. He did not even bother to discuss money. He was an amiable, kind-hearted eccentric and Verdi liked him. Verdi wrote the *Aïda* libretto almost alone, asking Ghislanzoni for a few verses here, an aria there. He accepted some sound suggestions from the poet. But in *Aïda* Verdi approached the methods of Wagner, who did everything himself, the text, the music, the stage-directions.

Verdi settled all business details himself, almost secretly; he was growing fond of having secrets. Only after everything was decided did he tell Giulio Ricordi. The publisher was delighted. The Cairo

145

ZAMBELLI. INC.

A caricature of Ghislanzoni who collaborated with Verdi in the libretto of *Aïda*.

premiere would have worldwide publicity. The House of Ricordi could make a fortune on *Aïda*, and it did.

Incredibly, Verdi wrote much of the text and most of the music in only four months, between August and November 1870, at a time when he was depressed by the Franco-Prussian War and was trying to escape into work from the grim realities of life. On 2 September the Prussians defeated the French at Sedan, capturing Emperor Napoleon III. Two days later, in Paris, the Second Empire was at an end and the Third Republic proclaimed. Ex-Empress Eugénie escaped into the apartment of her dentist, an American, and later reached England on a private yacht. The first siege of Paris began on 19 September. Verdi was miserable. To Clarina Maffei he wrote:

The disaster for France desolates my heart as it must yours. ... Old Attila stopped his march before the majesty of the old world: but this new one is about to bombard the capital of the modern world. ... Poor Paris! that I saw so merry, so lovely and splendid last April. ... I see everything very black, but even so I haven't told you half the troubles I fear.

Work was the only possible therapy, often interrupted by more sad news about the siege of Paris. Verdi had the score ready for delivery early in December 1870, fulfilling his contract. He never bothered to show or even mention the Suez Canal, but that was not a condition of the contract. The most dramatic scene in *Aïda* takes place on the bank of the Nile.

The sets and costumes were ready in Paris, where they had been made, but owing to the siege they could not be sent to Cairo. The contract gave Verdi the right to produce his opera outside Egypt if Cairo failed to perform it by July 1871. The Egyptians asked Verdi to consider the siege an 'Act of God'. He promised to wait. Verdi had written to Mariette in Cairo, asking the Egyptologist about customs and dress and other local detail. There was no reply: Mariette was in Paris during the siege.

His work on *Aïda* finished, Verdi abandoned himself to another depression, brought on by the events in Paris. In January 1871 the German Empire had been proclaimed in Versailles. A few weeks later Paris capitulated. The indomitable Garibaldi, no longer able to fight in Italy, went to France to fight for the Republic. The French Government reluctantly let him assemble a few thousand guerrillas, and he won some minor victories; but the French wanted neither him nor his talk of *liberté*, and Garibaldi went back to his island of Caprera, more disappointed than ever. In March the Paris Commune was set up against the 'spirit of Versailles'. Paris was a republican stronghold. The French Government assembled 130,000 troops – *French* troops – around the capital and the second siege began. It was enough to break the heart of a lifelong republican like Verdi, but things went from bad to worse. In May Paris was captured, and once again Frenchmen were killing Frenchmen. Verdi wrote to his friend Vincenzo Luccardi, the painter, in Rome:

A French balloon passes over the Prussian camp during the siege of Paris, October 1870. The costumes and scenery for the Cairo performance of *Aïda* were trapped inside the city.

Paris pushed both good and evil to the extremes, and these are the results. The same thing will happen to us if we don't learn to control ourselves. You have an example before your eyes. Your priests' refusal to compromise over the dogma of *infallibility* is causing a schism in Germany. Your priests are certainly priests but they are not Christians. . . .

Verdi was referring to the Vatican Council the previous year, at which Pope Pius IX, the erstwhile progressive, had proclaimed the dogma of papal infallibility. Two months later Vittorio Emanuele's ambassador had informed the Pope that the Patrimony of St Peter must be occupied by the King's troops 'to prevent a revolution in Rome'. The Pope declared that the King and his crowd were 'whited sepulchres and vipers', and that the King would not enter Rome; prudently adding that this statement was *not* infallible. It was not. The King's troops occupied Rome, and the Pope, after blessing his tiny army and giving prayers, went into the Vatican. The Papal State no longer existed. Italy was truly united.

The Cairo premiere of *Aïda* was scheduled for 24 December 1871; the Italian premiere at La Scala for six weeks later. There were to be different productions, different casts, different conductors. Verdi said he was not going to Cairo for the first night, though he promised to coach the singers and work with the conductor before they left for Cairo. Officially it was stated that Verdi was reluctant to make the long voyage and that he wanted to avoid the publicity. The gossip around La Scala was that he wanted to work with La Stolz, who was singing the title role in Milan.

The Cairo premiere was more a social than a musical event although the leading European music critics had been invited. They knew that the *real* premiere was being prepared by Verdi himself at La Scala. It was widely reported that the Khedive had the ladies of his harem seated in three boxes on the first tier. Some critics were more interested in them than in the members of the cast. Verdi's comments are not known but he certainly was not surprised. This was exactly why he had never even considered attending the Cairo premiere. At the time he was completely involved with the Scala production. He wrote an overture to replace the beautifully lyrical prelude but then retained it after all. He added Aïda's 'O cieli azzurri', the introduction to 'O patria mia', now known as the 'Nile aria' – very difficult, and very beautiful if well sung. He kept revising and asked Ghislanzoni for patience. 'The only thing I'm looking for is success,' he once said. He would settle for nothing less. He rehearsed the singers in his apartment in the Palazzo Sauli in Genoa. The new aria 'O patria mia' was a real test for Teresa Stolz. It has since made life miserable for generations of sopranos.

Early in 1872 they all went from Genoa to Milan, but Giuseppina did not enjoy the visit. To her friend Nina Ravina in Genoa she wrote, two weeks before the premiere:

I have been only once to La Scala and I don't think I shall go again except for *Aïda*. In Milan there is much noise and movement. ... I long for the silence and calm of my solitude at Genoa and Sant' Agata. Nothing re-awakens in me any desire to amuse myself, in the usual sense of the word. Verdi is well, working hard, in good humour; he pays visits to some of his old acquaintances and continues to love Milan. *Tant mieux*.

One senses a note of resignation. Giuseppina, who had often complained she was 'royally bored' in Sant' Agata, now wanted to be back there. She put up a brave front but could not always conceal her worries. Writing to Nina Ravina again:

There is always some part of our unhappiness of which we must accuse ourselves, but there is too another large part which we owe to destiny and to the goodness of men. In saying with Montebruno [Don Francesco Montebruno, the Genoese priest who was Giuseppina's confessor] 'patience!' I add 'courage!' to continue the struggle. About this I would have a whole volume of things to say, some of them already discussed between us, during those intimate evenings spent together in my room in Genoa.

Nina Ravina, who was married, had fallen in love with the Spanish painter Serafino de Avendaño, a friend of Mariani. She and Giuseppina had talked about their intimate problems, but they were surprisingly reticent and nothing is known of what was discussed 'during those intimate evenings'. There has been speculation whether Giuseppina was complaining about Verdi's 'old acquaintances' (Clarina Maffei) or the new one, Teresa.

Giuseppina was not happy when she attended the triumphant *Aïda* premiere on 8 February. Verdi took thirty-two calls. Franco Faccio, Boito's friend, conducted, and did well under Verdi's stern control. (Not much is known about the conductor of the Cairo premiere, Giovanni Bottesini.) Verdi was pleased with Maria Waldmann (Amneris), Giuseppe Fancelli (Radames), and particularly, according to Scala gossip, with Teresa Stolz as Aïda. At La Scala *Aïda* remains Verdi's most popular opera, followed by *Rigoletto*, *La Traviata*, and *Falstaff*. But some critics still wrote about Verdi trying to 'imitate' Wagner. Verdi told Ricordi bitterly, 'A fine result after thirty-five years [of composing], to be called an imitator!'

The critics were wrong. Verdi did not imitate Wagner's principle of 'endless melody', though he must have known the score of *Tristan*, first performed seven years earlier. But Verdi had used recitatives as early as 1844 in *Ernani*. Ever since then he had slowly evolved his *own* music drama, though unlike Wagner he never bothered to propagate aesthetic principles and musical theories. Once he wrote to his friend, Cesare de Sanctis in Naples, that he was nobody's disciple:

I am what I am. . . . There is no Italian music, nor German, nor Turkish . . . but there is MUSIC!! Don't harass me with these definitions. It is useless. I write as I please and as I feel. I detest all schools because they all lead to conventionalism. . . . I love beautiful music when it is really beautiful, no matter who wrote it. 'Progress of Art!' More meaningless words! Art is a thing that moves by itself. If the author is a man of genius, he will make art progress without seeking or wishing to do so. . . .

Some critics at that time did not understand the fundamental difference between Verdi's and Wagner's conception of the music drama. Verdi wrote principally for the voice. In *Aïda* the great climaxes are expressed vocally. After the short prelude which, at its

A caricature of the conductor Franco Faccio.

best, can sound as though it were sung by human voices, the curtain
goes up and the dramatic situation and the character of Radames are
beautifully and completely explained by the great aria, 'Celeste Aïda'.
The trio that follows develops the inner conflict of Radames, torn
between two women who love him. Aïda is completely revealed in her
moving prayer, 'Pietà, pietà'. Everything is dramatically shown
through the human voice. On the other hand, Wagner in his great
masterpieces uses the voices as extensions of the orchestra. Isolde's
farewell is seen on the stage but the *Liebestod* really takes place in the
orchestra. Some of the best modern conductors conduct the music
that way, treating the singers in *Tristan* as glorified adjuncts, which
does not please the singers but is faithful to Wagner's intentions.

Aïda remains Verdi's most popular work, and one of the two or
three most frequently performed operas all over the world. Some

Designs for the props of *Aïda*.

people prefer the melodious, moving beauty of *La Traviata* to the harrowing tragedy of *Otello*; many do not fully appreciate the wonderful wisdom and irony of *Falstaff*. But everybody loves *Aïda* – neophytes who have never heard an opera before as well as highbrow aesthetes. Like *Carmen*, the only comparable work, *Aïda* has something for everyone, and everything for many: convincing characters involved in passions that everyone can understand; an exciting story with one of Verdi's favourite conflicts, love versus patriotism; exotic scenery, intimate love scenes, the sinister court of the priests, high treason and tragedy, even ballet and grandiose mass parades; and an incredibly beautiful third act in which the inner tension never lets up. *Aïda* begins and ends with some of the finest lyrical music Verdi wrote.

Aïda is very grand, though certainly not 'grand opera' in the Parisian style. On the contrary. Verdi used the elements of Meyerbeer's grand opera – chorus scenes, parades, ballets, pomp and pageantry – in order to carry the story forward. In essence *Aïda* is a simple love story, one of the oldest in the world: a man between two women. The man is weak, and the two women, each in her own way, are strong. The miracle is that Verdi's melodic invention makes this absolutely clear even to people who know little about music. When he writes a triumphal scene – better than any written by the virtuoso practitioners of the conventional grand opera – the impact is not created by visual splendour but by the intimately human tragedy. This sounds like a paradox, but it is not. With several hundred people on the stage during the triumphal return of Radames, Verdi manages to focus the audience's rapt attention on the very intimate moment when Aïda recognizes her father, the King of Ethiopia, among the prisoners. Much is happening on the crowded stage, but people cannot help watching Aïda, who suffers as only a woman in love can suffer while Radames is forced to join hands with Amneris. The very private emotions of the protagonists always dominate the pageantry.

Verdi knew the quality of Aïda. After the premiere at La Scala he personally supervised a production in Parma because he was a Parmigiano and loved the place. Faccio and the soloists from La Scala were there and, naturally, Scala gossip said that he was in Parma because Teresa Stolz was too. He did not go to Padua for the new *Aïda* but 'supervised the production by mail', as the biographers claim, though it is hard to imagine how. Questions and answers in letters can never replace the composer's authority during rehearsals. There were productions elsewhere (*Aïda* was performed in New York in 1873 and in London in 1876, with Adelina Patti) and Verdi was furious when he heard that conductors and singers were taking liberties with his music. He told Ricordi that *Aïda* must be withdrawn if any changes were made.

Meanwhile life in Sant' Agata was not as cheerful as one might have expected after Verdi's greatest success. His friends were in no doubt that he was attracted (fascinated, maybe even infatuated?) by Teresa Stolz, and not only because she happened to be a fine Aïda. She was thirty-eight, an interesting *femme entre deux ages*, with great sexual attraction. Verdi was fifty-eight, sure of his genius, a healthy, good-looking man whom any woman would respect and many would love. No one knew this better than his wife. Radames in *Aïda*, the man between two women, and now Verdi, between her and. . . . She was watching Verdi. He was always in high spirits when Teresa appeared, no matter how irritable he had been in the morning with her alone. Giuseppina was a woman, and wise; once she, too, had been a prima donna. Now she was nineteen years older than Teresa; and she had learnt that men never change, not even her beloved *Pasticcio*. Why did he go back to Milan – alone, not taking her along – because he wanted 'to watch another *Aïda* performance'. Once she wrote to Clarina Maffei (whom she disliked, as we now know), 'If this goes on, Verdi might as well get a reduced season ticket for Milan.'

, She noticed other things. Verdi was interested in Teresa's private problems, of which she had told him. He questioned his friend Giuseppe Piroli about some of Teresa's financial difficulties under Austrian law. When Teresa sang Aïda in Parma, she would write frequent letters to Verdi in Sant' Agata, telling the 'dearest Maestro' how things went and often adding gossip. Many of her letters have survived, and they prove nothing. But Giuseppina did not like it, and one day she read some of the letters while Verdi was away. Once she was so angry that she made a pencil note on the left upper corner of a letter dated 15 August 1872: 'Sixteen letters!! in such a short time!! what activity!!' She put the letter back where it had been. Did Verdi see her pencilled remark, and how did he react to it? One of Teresa's letters is signed 'Aïda'. The signature, which is unremarkable since she *was* Verdi's favourite Aïda, is followed by two pencilled exclamation-marks. Were they later added by Giuseppina, and did Verdi see them? Yet these were certainly not love letters. Teresa is always respectful, often sending her kindest regards to 'Signora Peppina', always telling the 'dearest Maestro' how the performances went. ('How is dear Signora Peppina? I can just see her rambling about that delicious garden. . . . Please give her my kindest regards.') What did 'Signora Peppina' say when Verdi gave her Teresa's 'kindest regards'?

Teresa loved theatrical gossip and sometimes she could be amusing though malicious. From the middle of November 1872 until April 1873 Verdi and Giuseppina were in Naples, for *Don Carlos* and *Aïda* at the San Carlo. Teresa Stolz sang in both operas. After Verdi returned with his wife to Sant' Agata, he wrote to his friend de Sanctis in Naples about various matters, adding a postscript, 'Peppina is well but very sad'. Giuseppina herself added a piece of paper on which she had written:

I am curious to know whether the gossip circulating about that matter, of which you told me there is so much talk at Naples, has reached the ears of la S. . . .
If you should by chance mention this stupid and infamous tittle-tattle, and learn something about it, it will suffice if, when you reply, you write on a piece of paper: She knows that.

The words 'She knows that' are written in English. Verdi knew no English; the small piece of paper was probably added after he had given her his letter to post. We know nothing about the 'stupid and infamous tittle-tattle'. But Peppina's note to de Sanctis proves that she was deeply worried. Yet she was too wise to attack Teresa, and perhaps there was no reason; perhaps (and probably) Giuseppina's fears were unjustified. She would often ask Teresa to spend a few days with them at Sant' Agata. Would she do that if she knew that something serious was going on? But why was she never disturbed about Verdi's correspondence with Maria Waldmann, the Viennese mezzo who sang the part of Amneris and who was younger and more beautiful than Teresa? Because Giuseppina knew that Waldmann would soon be marrying Conte Galeazzo Massari and retiring from the stage? Paradoxically she wrote her most truthful letters to Verdi's 'old acquaintance', Clarina Maffei. On 5 March 1874 she wrote:

Happy you who believe, possess and deserve to possess the affection of your old and new friends! I – and I tell you this in profound discouragement – I no longer believe in anything or anybody, almost. I have suffered so many and such cruel disillusions as to become disgusted with life. You will say that everyone has to tread the thorny path of disappointment, but that only means to say that, stronger than I, others have retained some hope and some little faith in the future. Instead of which, now, when anyone tells me they love me, I laugh. . . . Even my religious enthusiasm has vanished and I scarcely even believe in God, when I look at the marvels of creation!

The letter has been variously interpreted. It was probably written during a deep depression, when one should not write letters. But something must have been very wrong, with Giuseppina, or with Verdi, or with both of them. Characteristically, Giuseppina would not put down names even when she was very low and bitter. In May, shortly before Verdi conducted the *Requiem Mass* for Manzoni, Giuseppina wrote to her sister, 'I never have a day's peace and with the noise outside and

The soprano Teresa Stolz whose exact relationship with Verdi remains a mystery.

the chatter inside I go to bed so worn out that every day I seem to grow older by a year!' By August she seems to have got over her depression. She invited Stolz to Sant' Agata. She intervened in an angry dispute between Verdi and Tito Ricordi over what Giuseppina called 'irregularities' in the accounts; 'I don't know what they would be called in legal terms.' Verdi thought that he had not received all that was due to him. Ever since he had kept the ledgers in Barezzi's wine shop, Verdi had known all about accounts. When he discovered that 'irregularities were being committed, wounding him materially and morally', as Giuseppina wrote, he refused to talk to his publishers and left the matter to his wife, who handled it with poise and determination. 'I promised loyally and sincerely to act for you, and I did so,' she wrote to Giulio; 'With my heart full of anguish but with the same loyalty and sincerity, I believe it my duty to warn you that I cannot, at least for the moment, allow myself to touch on this unhappy subject further.'

An admirable blend of softness and toughness, and after some months of unpleasant haggling Ricordi paid Verdi an extra fifty thousand lire, but Verdi was still angry. ('There has been no reconciliation, in the moral sense of the word. . . . A financial settlement has been reached, no more.') A little later the *Rivista Indipendente* in Florence began printing a series of articles about 'certain intimacies of Signora Stolz, both with Maestro Mariani, and now with Verdi . . .'. Subsequent articles, written in an openly sensationalist style, reported that in Teresa Stolz's hotel room in Paris

the amorous couple [Verdi and Stolz] stretched themselves out, that is to say, did not stretch themselves out but accommodated themselves, made themselves comfortable, sat themselves, on a soft sofa. What strange things they did on that sofa, what contests took place, what disputes, why they became so agitated, we don't know, to tell the truth, because we were not in the room and the door was shut. . . .

This was obviously highly irresponsible journalism, but it might have poisoned the atmosphere between the protagonists. Apparently Teresa Stolz was upset and wrote to Sant' Agata, angry and embarrassed. On 15 September Giuseppina replied in one of her truly fine letters:

Calm down again if you are angry. . . . That you love us I know, or rather we know, we believe it, and are glad to believe it, and are confident that over you we shall never suffer disillusionment. For you we shall be the same as long as we live. So, my dear Teresa, the fear of *being in the way*, because you saw me in a tinge of sadness, is a fear to set aside. . . . With us, you will never be in the way, as long as you and I remain the honest and loyal persons we are. And with that and a kiss I close this paragraph.

Once again Peppina had shown wisdom. Though she was probably deeply upset – and how could one blame her? – she had disarmed Teresa Stolz. But the story is not finished yet. Among Giuseppina's letters is one to Verdi, dated 21 April 1876:

'It didn't seem to me a fitting day for you to pay a call on a lady who is neither your daughter, nor your sister, nor your wife!' The observation slipped out and I perceived at once that you were annoyed. Your irritation hurt me. For the lady is neither sick nor about to give a performance, and you could go twenty-four hours without seeing her, especially since I myself had taken the trouble of asking her personally how she was. . . .
I don't know if there is or isn't anything in it. . . . I do know that since 1872 there have been on your part [erased : 'febrile'] periods of assiduity and attention that could not be taken by any woman in a sense more flattering.

Costume designs for *Aïda*: left to right, Radames, dancing girl, Amonasro,
standard-bearer.

[erased: 'I know that I have never failed to show cordiality and courtesy to this person.'] I know that I have always been disposed to love her frankly and sincerely.

You know how you repaid me! With harsh, violent, biting words! You cannot control yourself. . . .

If there is anything in it. . . . Let's get this over. [erased: 'if you find this person so seductive.'] Be frank and say so, without making me suffer the humiliation of this excessive deference of yours.

If there is nothing in it . . . Be more calm in your attentions [erased: 'don't be so agitated'], be natural and less exclusive. Think sometimes that I, your wife, despising past gossip, am living at this very moment *à trois*, and that I have the right to ask, if not for your caresses, at least for your consideration. Is that too much?

How calm and gay I was the first twenty days! And that was because you were cordial. . . .

The letter has the ring of truth. The dates and details are correct. It was in 1872, at the time of *Aïda*, that Verdi became deeply attracted by Teresa Stolz. The letter proves that Giuseppina tried for years to cope with a difficult situation. It also proves – and this is the most important conclusion – that after four years she was not certain whether there was 'anything in it' between Verdi and La Stolz. If Verdi's wife was not certain at that time, how can the writers and biographers claim to be certain after half a century though they have uncovered no new evidence?

It is not known, for instance, what Verdi replied. 'With harsh, violent, biting words?' Or not at all? When Giuseppina wrote her rather desperate letter in 1876 she was sixty-one, Verdi was sixty-three, and Stolz only forty-two. Frank Walker, whose *The Man Verdi* is the most thorough, most completely objective documentation of the composer to date, writes: 'A person of undoubted integrity told me that Giulio Ricordi had told him personally that there was a time when Giuseppina said to Verdi: "Either this woman leaves the house or I leave it", and received the reply: "This woman stays or I blow my brains out".' This is only 'hearsay' but it is corroborated in a letter written by Luigi Illica, Puccini's librettist, to the wife of Mascagni. It provides food for thought, though no conclusion can be drawn.

It does not seem pure accident that several weeks after Giuseppina wrote that long, startling letter to Verdi, Teresa Stolz went to Russia where she sang for the next six months, though the respected *Gazzetta Musicale* had announced her retirement on 2 July. Verdi told Clarina Maffei 'she could not refuse', explaining that Stolz had been offered 'a hundred and forty thousand francs in gold', a fortune for a singer about to retire. But money was probably not the sole reason. Teresa wanted to get away for a while from Italy where there was so much talk.

On 16 December Giuseppina sent Teresa Stolz a Christmas letter: 'Here is Christmas. The Man-God appears to redeem humanity and to teach by his example the greatest of virtues: that of not only forgiving offenses but also of loving the offender.' This can be taken literally as a homily; or it may be a veiled allusion. It is well known that Giuseppina, an extremely discreet woman since her early youth, would often make such allusions in her letters, which would be understood only by those in the know. She kept writing more letters to Stolz in Russia. The following year Giuseppina wrote to a friend, 'I thank God a thousand times that I went, though with some trepidation, to such a Father'. She refers to Don Montebruno, her confessor in Genoa. He probably knew a great deal, and so did Nina Ravina, Giuseppina's friend. Some of the letters she wrote to Nina still exist but have not been published.

Teresa Stolz did not thank Giuseppina for her Christmas greetings. After returning from Russia, in March 1877, she announced her retirement from the stage. After receiving another letter from Giuseppina, Teresa wrote on 19 March: 'May God keep you always in perfect health, happy and beloved by your friends, among whom I flatter myself I too have a tiny place. ... Accept an affectionate kiss from your poor Teresa who loves you very much and begs you to love her a little in return.' A web of subtle lies? That would not tie in with Stolz's character. She was not subtle, like Giuseppina, but rather direct, and her letters are rarely brilliant and often gossipy. The following year she wrote to Verdi and Giuseppina, sending her wishes for St Joseph's Day (19 March), an important holiday in Italy:

I am not a woman of empty phrases and compliments, so I express myself badly, but I would like to find words eloquent enough to express all the affection I feel for you both. You are for me persons absolutely to be revered. Every word is to me an oracle, so you can imagine all my good wishes for your happiness.

And in June, Verdi wrote to Clarina Maffei:

Let me know what our distinguished friend Signora Teresa is doing. It's a century since I heard anything of her. Since the Mass at Bologna I haven't received a word from her! I can quite understand how, living in a great city, in fine apartments, paying and receiving calls, going to theatres and concerts, as I often read in the papers, she doesn't think any more about the old Maestro. ...

The year was 1878. Verdi would soon be sixty-five, which is not old, certainly not for a genius who did not know himself that he was still going to create *Otello* and *Falstaff*. But when he wrote that letter to Clarina he may have been thinking of Teresa Stolz and the past and perhaps feeling a little like 'the old Maestro'. One senses a touch of resignation. Men have these moods, some sooner, some later, knowing that resignation is regret rather than wisdom. What happened, had happened; but now it was all over.

Teresa Stolz never married. She was now in her middle forties, still very attractive, famous and wealthy, and men were always interested in her. But perhaps she compared them subconsciously to the 'dearest Maestro', and the comparison was not flattering to any of her admirers.

Gatti mentions a photograph which Giuseppina gave Verdi on her sixty-third birthday, inscribed 'To my Verdi, with my former affection and veneration! Peppina.' Gatti and other biographers have long wondered about Giuseppina's meaning. Her subtlety is known. What did she mean by 'former'? That her affection had gone, or that her affection was now again as strong as in the early days? And to make matters even more complicated for posterity, Giuseppina wrote to Verdi on 21 April 1879:

Don't work too hard, my dear *Pasticcio*, and consider however little is left, it will always be more than the heirs deserve. . . . I salute, I kiss and I embrace you. I wish you a good appetite [Verdi was then in Paris and, a true connoisseur, he liked French cuisine] and I hope to see you arrive soon, very soon because I still love you with an insane affection, and sometimes when I am in a bad mood it is a sort of *loving fever*, unknown to doctors. . . . What stupid things I have written. I'll be seeing you soon then.

Peppina

That year Teresa Stolz sang for the last time in public, in the *Requiem*. Verdi was conducting. She lived quietly afterwards in Milan but she would often come to Sant' Agata, or to Genoa to celebrate the New Year with Verdi and Giuseppina. They were friends now. Whatever had been was overcome. One cannot help being moved when one reads Giuseppina's short note to Teresa Stolz, on 24 December 1886, while Verdi was preparing *Otello*: 'Verdi is well and it is with a joy full of tenderness that I say it!'

Late in 1872, after *Aïda* and before seriously starting work on the *Requiem*, Verdi and Giuseppina had gone to Naples where *Aïda* was to be produced. Then Mme Stolz became ill, the rehearsals were postponed and Verdi had nothing to do. In Sant' Agata he would have walked through his fields; in Naples, he had the idea of writing a string quartet. He knew the great classical string quartets; he kept their scores by his bedside at Sant' Agata because they taught him lucid, economical writing. So, he sat down and wrote his *String Quartet in E Minor*, his first and last. (Debussy and Ravel are other composers who wrote only one string quartet.) 'The Verdi,' as chamber musicians call it with reverential familiarity, is considered by some writers to be 'of little importance' because Verdi did not want to have it published for several years. For him it was something of an experiment, almost a private undertaking. Only after Giulio Ricordi told him that many people wanted to try it did he permit his quartet to be published. Chamber musicians, a very demanding group of enthusiasts, now consider it a minor masterpiece. It is beautifully thought-out and beautifully finished. And it is, interestingly, Verdi's only non-vocal composition, although he treats the four parts of the quartet very much as human voices.

He had carefully studied the masterpieces of Haydn, Mozart and Beethoven, and when, nearing sixty, he started to write his own quartet he knew exactly how to go about it. The Verdi *Quartet* is a mini-opera: what else would one expect? Like the *Requiem*, which came a year later, the *Quartet* is full of drama and melody. Verdians will find his quartet a gold-mine of Verdi melodies. Stylistically, it is late Verdi, with long melodic phrases and tender love themes, and always beautifully structured. For a moment the 'popular' Verdi appears, in the Trio of the Scherzo, 'sung' by the baritone (the cello), with pizzicato accompaniment by the other three players. There are several bars in the first movement which anticipate *Otello*, composed fifteen years later. And the fugue in the last movement seems the distilled essence of the marvellous fugue in *Falstaff*, 'The whole world is a joke,' which Verdi composed some eighteen years later.

10
THE REQUIEM AND WAGNER

Alessandro Manzoni died, aged eighty-nine, on 22 May 1873. His pompous funeral was attended by princes, ministers and many dignitaries, and all Milan was watching the bier drawn by six horses. Verdi was not there. He told Ricordi he was too moved. To Clarina Maffei he wrote: 'With him ends the purest, holiest, greatest of our glories. I have read many papers. No one speaks fittingly of him. Many words but none deeply felt. There is no lack of gibes, even at him! What a bad lot we are!' Manzoni, not a 'good' Catholic in the Church's sense, was called 'a born revolutionary' by the Jesuits in Milan. Pius IX publicly ignored the death of a great Italian.

A few days later Verdi went to the cemetery in Milan and stood at the grave, alone. Then he sent Giulio Ricordi to the Mayor of Milan with a proposal: Verdi would write a requiem mass for Manzoni which would be performed on the first anniversary of Manzoni's death, probably at a church in Milan. Verdi would pay for the printing of the music. The city of Milan would finance the performance. The *Requiem* would remain Verdi's property.

The Mayor agreed. Verdi is said to have started work on the *Requiem* in the summer in Paris where he had gone with Giuseppina, but many Verdi scholars believe that he had been thinking of it long before the death of Manzoni, perhaps after the fiasco of the Rossini *Requiem* which had been jointly composed by him and several others but was never performed. Verdi made it clear that this must not happen again. He had deep feelings about Manzoni; Verdi would create his memorial in music all by himself. If the *Requiem* were successful, it would be performed like an opera in the theatre or concert hall. Each performance would remind people of Manzoni. The idea was beautiful and so was the execution. Today, many music lovers who have never heard of Manzoni, know him through Verdi's *Requiem*.

Verdi started with the final section, *Libera Me*, which he had written

OPPOSITE The first performance of Verdi's *Requiem*, at the Church of San Marco in Milan on 22 May 1874, marked the first anniversary of the death of the great poet and novelist Alessandro Manzoni, for whom it was written.

for the Rossini *Requiem*, but he revised it so thoroughly that it is almost a new piece. The Manzoni *Requiem* (today generally known as the 'Verdi Requiem') has the dramatic unity and musical maturity of Verdi's late operatic masterpieces. The *Requiem* is a sort of opera, though the singers wear no costumes. It has one of the greatest 'libretti' of all – the powerful text from the Roman Catholic liturgy. Verdi, true to style, wrote the *Requiem* for the human voice. All emotions are expressed by the four solo voices (soprano, mezzo, tenor, basso), the chorus, and the *super-voice* of the orchestra.

Verdi knew the earlier requiems by Mozart, Cherubini and Berlioz which had been written to be performed principally in the church, usually on All Souls' Day, 2 November, though they could be sung at a funeral too. A requiem is a prayer of the living for the dead. Verdi's *Requiem* ends with a prayer for eternal peace and perpetual light – but not for the dead. Verdi felt that the dead have no need of our prayers. We, the living, must pray for ourselves: that is Verdi's message. He knew how to dramatize his message musically; he did not mind shocking his audiences so they would be certain to receive his message. After an almost ecclesiastical, quiet beginning with *Requiem* and *Kyrie*, Verdi shocks us with the terrific violence of *Dies Irae* – the vision of The Last Judgment as seen by Thomas of Celano, a friend of St Francis of Assisi. The middle sections, *Domine Jesu*, *Sanctus*, *Agnus Dei* and *Lux Aeterna*, are again almost ecclestiastical in style. In the final section Verdi, the unsurpassed master of the musical climax, throws the performers (and the listeners) once more into terror. Then comes the supreme message. The soprano sings, angel-like and alone, 'Libera me, Domine': 'Free me, Lord, from eternal death on that terrifying day when the heavens and earth are shattered.' She is praying for herself – and for all of us. Once more the *Dies Irae* is heard in all its terror. Then comes the finale, a fugue sung by the chorus, closing with *Libera Me*.

Verdi's *Requiem* was not written for the Roman Catholic Church, yet it is the work of a deeply religious man who is suffering for his fellow men, and who believes in God. No one understood this better than Giuseppina, who had often been perturbed by Verdi's agnosticism, but who in her letters turns out to be a somewhat enlightened Catholic, certainly not an orthodox one. On 3 September 1872 Giuseppina writes to Clarina Maffei: 'For some virtuous people a belief in God is necessary. Others, equally perfect, while observing strictly every precept of the highest moral code, are happier believing nothing. Manzoni and Verdi! These two men give me food for thought. . . .'

Giuseppina knew that many Italians who loved opera and were 'good' Catholics had uneasy feelings about Verdi. His operas had

OPPOSITE The first page of the *Requiem* manuscript with a dedication to Teresa Stolz.

166

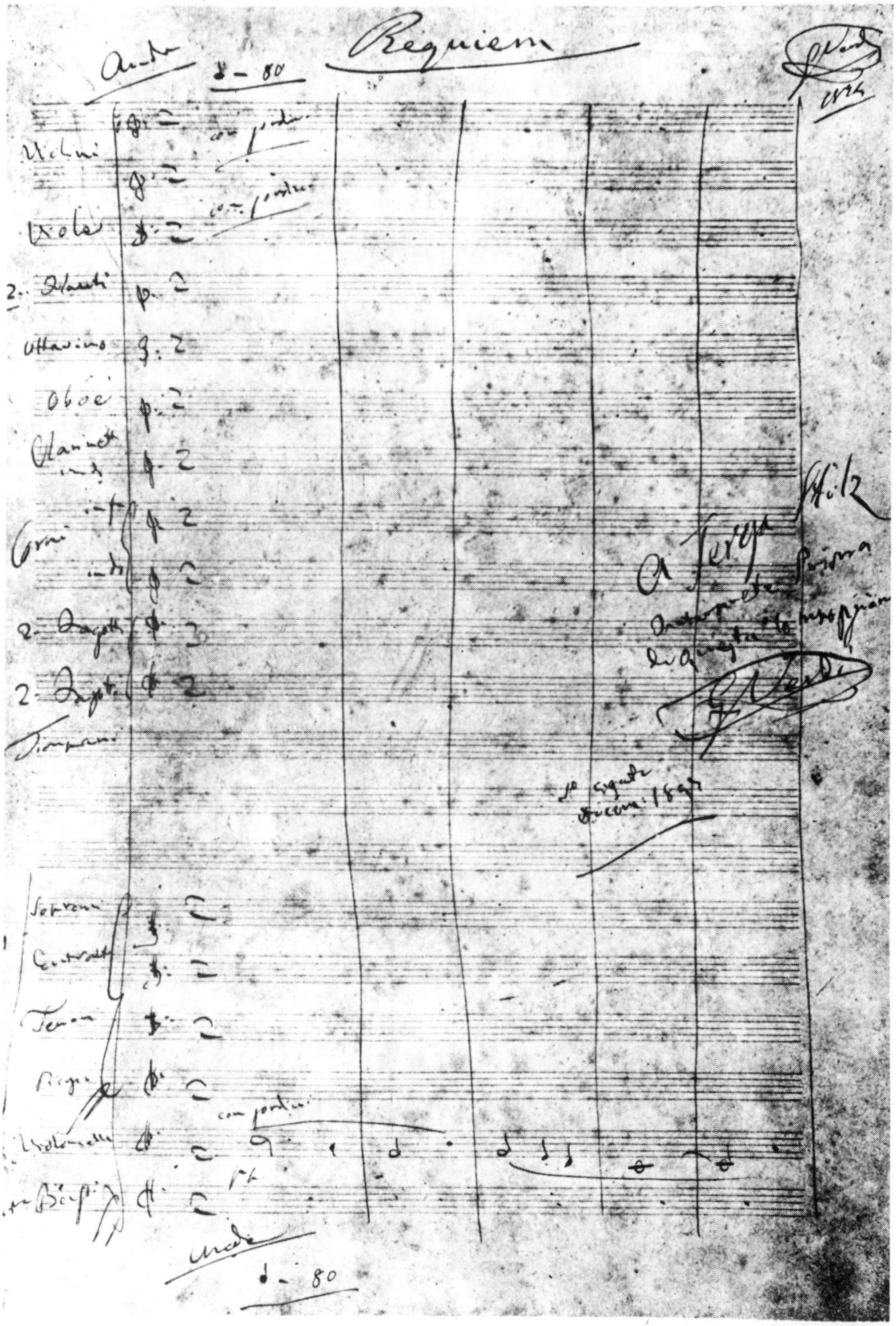
Requiem
Oboe

condoned, sometimes even glorified, adultery, rape, murder, debauchery, suicide. They knew it was all make-believe melodrama but many did not like it. Also, Verdi had for many years lived with Giuseppina 'in sin'. Yet after the *Requiem* Giuseppina, who was then suffering (this was the time of the rumours about Teresa Stolz) wrote to a friend; 'I say that a man like Verdi must write like Verdi, that is, according to how he feels and interprets the text. I would have simply rejected a Mass by Verdi that had been modelled on A, B, or C!! Perhaps I am talking nonsense. . . .' She was not, but she could not change the official position of the Church.

After the memorial premiere of the *Requiem* which Verdi conducted on 22 May 1874, exactly one year after the death of Manzoni, at the Church of San Marco in Milan which he had selected for its acoustics and size, he conducted three more performances at La Scala. There was 'wild applause' and Verdi repeated three sections. Later he conducted seven performances in Paris at the Opéra-Comique. The *Requiem* was everywhere a spectacular success. Many people enjoyed it as they had enjoyed *Aïda* two years before; some thought it was even more exciting. Manzoni, wherever he was, must have been pleased and, perhaps, amused. Italian Catholics had known the text of the *Requiem*, ever since they had been children and this increased the popularity of what, in the opinion of the Church, should have been a religious service; there was talk of 'sacrilege' in Church circles. Small opera houses made alterations, some even replacing the (expensive) orchestra with several pianos. Verdi asked Ricordi to prevent unauthorized changes, and to be strict about it.

Ricordi and Escudier, Verdi's French agent, knew they were on to a good thing. They arranged a tour of the *Requiem* for the spring of 1875. Teresa Stolz and Maria Waldmann, who had sung Aïda and Amneris in the earlier Scala premiere, were two of the soloists, and Verdi conducted. In London there was a chorus of twelve hundred singers in the Royal Albert Hall. In Vienna the *Requiem* was performed at the recently opened Court Opera, and Verdi also conducted a performance of *Aïda*. He was awarded the Franz Joseph Order by the Emperor. Seemingly the Court had decided to overlook Verdi's activities on behalf of the anti-Habsburg Risorgimento. It was only sixteen years since the last Austrian troops had left Italy.

The Church delayed passing judgment until 1903, two years after Verdi's death, when Pope Pius x issued the encyclical *Motu proprio*, defining the Church's requirements for ecclesiastical music and thus excluding, though never specifically naming, Verdi's *Requiem Mass* and his published *Sacred Pieces*: 'The theatrical style which was in the greatest vogue especially in Italy during the last century . . is by its very nature diametrically opposed to Gregorian Chant and classic

OPPOSITE A caricature on the first performance of the *Requiem*. Verdi, who conducted, is shown with the soloists Teresa Stolz, Maria Waldmann (right), Capponi and Maini.

polyphony, the most important law of all good sacred music.' Verdi had violated the true ecclesiastical spirit both with the unorthodox message of his *Requiem* and with the dramatic character of his music. Paragraph twenty-three of the encyclical says that 'music is merely a part of the liturgy and its humble handmaid'. Not for Verdi. As a result, we now have the most dramatic, most beautiful requiem mass of all those written before or since.

Some Italians continue to be bothered by the thought that Verdi, the greatest Italian at the time of his death, was not a good Catholic. In 1940 Ferruccio Botti, in his essay *Verdi e la religione*, tried to prove that Verdi was *au fond* really a member of the Church. Unfortunately the author conveniently ignored evidence which did not support his thesis and relied on letters said to have been written by Giuseppina Strepponi which were in fact fabricated by Lorenzo Alpino, for just that purpose. In his essays on *Verdian Forgeries*, in the *Music Review*, Cambridge, Frank Walker presented irrefutable evidence that Alpino had 'fabricated' eight letters supposedly written by Giuseppina to Don Francesco Montebruno, her confessor, and to Monsignore Salvatore Magnasco, the Archbishop of Genoa, concerning Verdi's religious feelings and his possible relations with Teresa Stolz. The letters were intended to prove that Verdi was a good Catholic, and that he had not had an affair with Mme Stolz. Botti underestimated the intelligence of his readers.

The 'feud' between Verdi and Wagner created much excitement while the two composers were alive and an enormous amount of post-humous comment. The feud was waged not between the protagonists but between their admirers. During the late nineteenth century, to be for Verdi meant to be against Wagner, and vice versa. In elevated musical circles it was considered incompatible to admire them both. Even today, there are Wagnerians who have no use for Verdi and, more regrettably, Verdians, a more mature, more civilized group, who take a dim view of Wagner's work.

Both are wrong. There are as many similarities as differences between the two musical giants. Each evolved his own idea of music drama. Each is the beginning and the end; nothing greater has been created in their particular fields. The emotional power of *Tristan und Isolde* and the romantic beauty of *Die Meistersinger* are unsurpassed – as are the drama of *Otello* and the irony and tenderness of *Falstaff*. Verdi and Wagner are not mutually exclusive. They are complementary. The operatic form conceived by Monteverdi and developed by Gluck and Mozart was gloriously perfected by Verdi. The monumental symphonies of the Classical and Romantic composers were reflected in the emotional power and orchestral sweep of Wagner,

who created super-symphonies, with the help of the stage, using singers with very strong voices. Wagner's *Musikdrama*, his 'total theatre', must not be compared to *Poppea, Don Giovanni, Otello*.

Tristan and *Götterdämmerung* are enormous symphonic works. The physical action on the stage is always dominated by the psychological action of the orchestra. Wagner understood this well when he created his 'invisible' orchestra in Bayreuth, acoustically the ideal orchestra. What the people believe they *see* happening on the stage, actually takes place, emotionally and spiritually, in the orchestra pit. Wagner, the accomplished craftsman, conjured the illusion of the stage with the reality of the music.

On the other hand Verdi always began with human beings on the

A lithograph by G. Popperik shows Wagner and his friends at a musical evening. Wagner sits in the centre holding a book. At the far left are his wife Cosima and their son Siegfried. Cosima's father, Franz Liszt, plays the piano and the singer Albert Niemann leans over him. Sitting to the right of the window is the conductor Hermann Levi.

stage, more exactly with human beings *singing*. Their voices would express, through melody or vocal lines, simple and complex emotions. Verdi's melodies were written for the voices, Wagner's leitmotivs for the orchestra. It would be possible to listen to Verdi singers without orchestra. Wagner singers would be totally lost without the orchestra. It all seems so simple, yet there was much ignorance among musicians while Verdi and Wagner were alive and 'competing'. Both had become quite sure of what they were doing. Verdi was popular even outside Italy, but he never created the wild controversies which Wagner inspired. Wagner was a polemical man, almost always opposed to somebody or something. Verdi never cared about schools, theories, aesthetics. Verdi knew that Wagner had a strong following among the younger intellectuals in Italy. Verdi had little following in Germany. Being only human, Verdi was often hurt, though he did not admit it.

Both reached their artistic maturity at about the same time, having been born the same year, 1813. *Meistersinger*, in 1868, was followed by *Aïda*, in 1871. *Parsifal* came in 1882 and *Otello* in 1887. It was a stirring time for opera-goers. Communications were slow, and Europe was larger than it seems today, but both composers had much publicity and each was aware of what the other was doing. Wagner was never accused of imitating Verdi even when he wrote arias, in *Tannhäuser*, and monologues, in *Meistersinger*, that might have been done by Verdi. Verdi was often accused of imitating Wagner, after *Don Carlos* in 1867. Italy's young poets and composers, among them Arrigo Boito, were wild Wagnerians in the early 1860s. They called Verdi, after *Rigoletto* and *La Traviata*, a 'hurdy-gurdy' composer. According to Franz Werfel, 'Wagner was in the habit of playing the aria of Father Germont, from *La Traviata*, on the piano as proof of the decline of Italian opera.' But what did Wagner feel about the prelude to the last act of *Traviata*? Did he ever admit to himself that it might be as good, better even, than the prelude to his *Lohengrin*? Hardly.

Verdi heard the *Tannhäuser* overture in Paris in 1865, *Lohengrin* in Bologna in 1870, and the whole of *Tannhäuser* in Vienna in 1875; but apparently no other Wagner opera, though he must have been familiar with the scores of Wagner's later works. He never mentions them, except in a passing remark. Wagner, always interested in the musical stage, never took the trouble to listen to *Don Carlos* or *Aïda*. If he did, he never said a word about it. Very strange because he wrote about almost everything, and his papers, letters, manuscripts and notes were quickly collected by the people around him and preserved with German thoroughness. Yet in all his writings there are almost no references to Verdi. In an early letter Wagner briefly mentions the opera *Hernani* by 'Verdy'; no comment, two spelling mistakes in two words.

172

Wagner, growing more megalomaniac with age and fame, would shrug off 'the Italian peasant' in Parma who wrote 'bad' operas. Wagner was quite outspoken about other composers, often negatively. He attacked Meyerbeer as a composer and as a Jew but he did not hesitate to learn something from Meyerbeer's style, from *Rienzi* to *Meistersinger*, though he would never admit this. Verdi was 'far away', so far as Wagner was concerned, though not much farther than Meyerbeer in Paris. No one in Germany admitted that Verdi was slowly developing his own music drama; there was only *Musikdrama*, and that was Wagner's. Verdi never bothered Wagner, but Wagner's presence was very strong in Verdi's mind. He became quite bitter about him and admitted Wagner's greatness only after the German composer's death. Unlike other composers of the epoch, Verdi never went to Bayreuth; he never even considered going there. The two men were aware of their own genius and also of each other's, but they avoided each other.

On 2 November 1875 Wagner and Cosima went to a performance of Verdi's *Requiem*, conducted by their friend Hans Richter in Vienna. Wagner had no comment for posterity but Frau Cosima referred to 'Spontini's expression for Italian musicians'. Spontini had once said that Italian musicians were *cochons* ('pigs'). Spontini later returned to die in the small village of Maiolati where he was born; he was noted for such angry outbursts and arrogant statements. Cosima's remark, however, fits in well with her character.

Verdi heard *Lohengrin* in Bologna in November 1871 (after he had finished the score of *Aïda*). He had never heard a Wagner opera before, and followed the performance with a voice-and-piano reduction of the score, making notes. The score has been preserved, showing 114 remarks, 78 of them rather adverse. He summed it up later: 'Mediocre impression. The music is beautiful when it is clear and expresses an idea. . . . Beautiful effects with the instruments. Abuse of held notes with consequent heaviness. Mediocre performance. Much verve but without poetry or delicacy. In the difficult points always bad.' Mariani, the conductor of the performance, later admitted it had been 'poor', partly owing to Verdi's presence in the house which seemed to terrify the artists.

Verdi did not try to keep Wagner's works out of Italy's opera houses (as has been insinuated), but he was worried by the fascination that Wagner's theories held for young Italian poets and musicians. Verdi perceived that *Tristan* and the *Ring* were metaphysical poems turned into music. Unfortunately, Verdi never heard a performance of *Die Meistersinger*, the only true *opera* among Wagner's late works. Verdi understood that Wagner's theories of the *Gesamtkunstwerk* and 'endless melody' were nothing but an excuse for breaking up the classic

form of the lyric theatre. When Verdi said, 'Opera is opera and symphony is symphony', he stated the truth in one sentence more precisely than Wagner did in all his writings. On another occasion Verdi wrote, 'Do you think that under this sun and this sky I could have composed *Tristan* and the *Ring*?' One cannot put it more clearly. Wagner created *Weltanschauung* and dialectics. Verdi created drama and melody.

The critics were no help. They had called the young Verdi naive and later they called the old Verdi an imitator. Some wrote that the old Verdi was really a 'new' Verdi, because he had used leitmotivs in *Otello*, pointing out that the 'kiss' theme from the love duet is used again in the last act. Verdi had used recurrent themes much earlier, in *Rigoletto*, before anyone was conscious of leitmotivs. The controversies bothered the old maestro. He was Verdi, he had always been Verdi. Whether one prefers the elemental power of the storm that starts *Die Walküre* or the storm that starts *Otello* is simply a matter of taste.

Verdi, so wise in musical matters, understood that Siegmund and Sieglinde, Tristan and Isolde are not really people but symbols made to look like human or heroic characters. On the other hand, Otello and Desdemona, Iago and Falstaff are completely human. Tristan and Isolde are not logically drawn into a tragedy; they get involved in a cosmic catastrophe, created by the dramatically doubtful device of drinking a love-potion. Otello and Desdemona love each other until they are caught in the tragedy of jealousy. Their tender love, reflected in the wonderful duet at the end of the first act, is destroyed by the evil Iago, who is no symbol but real.

The repeated comparisons with Wagner made Verdi quite unhappy. Neither his followers nor the Italian Wagnerians would leave him alone and resentment built up. The situation became personal and ugly when Angelo Mariani, who had lived several years with Teresa Stolz, was rumoured to have 'gone over to Wagner to take revenge on Verdi who had stolen his beloved Teresa'. The newspapers were full of such gossip. Verdi had turned down Mariani who wanted to conduct *Aïda* (according to the gossip), and Mariani paid him back by conducting *Lohengrin*. Unfortunately the gossip was strong enough to break up a friendship.

It was known that Wagner had dispatched Hans von Bülow as his emissary to Bologna for the first *Lohengrin* performances, 'to advise Mariani'. Mariani later denied this: 'Perhaps the Maestro knows nothing of this trick that Bülow and Lucca tried to play on me.' (Lucca, a former employee and later a competitor of Ricordi, was Wagner's publisher in Italy.) Two years before Bülow had publicly expressed his scorn for Verdi. Verdi knew this. He also knew, naturally, that Bülow was Wagner's trusted friend, had conducted the

OPPOSITE Wagner with his son Siegfried in 1880.

first *Tristan* (1865) and the first *Meistersinger* (1868), and that the following year Bülow's wife, Cosima, had run away with Wagner.

Francesco Lucca, a Cremonese and a fine music engraver before he set up his own publishing house, was exploiting the intrigues between the Verdians and the Wagnerians for all they were worth. His wife Giovannina, whom the faithful Muzio called 'an enormous and most formidable woman', was the real head of the firm. Young Verdi had sold his half-share in *Nabucco* to Lucca. Impresario Merelli had sold his to Ricordi. There was a long lawsuit between Lucca and Ricordi. At one point, Muzio reports, the formidable Giovannina had invaded 'Signor Maestro's' (that is, Verdi's) apartment and made a terrible scene, weeping and shouting. Later the Luccas acquired three early Verdi operas, not from the composer but through the impresarios: *Attila, Alzira, Il Corsaro*. They lost money on Verdi. His later successes were all published by Ricordi. Lucca tried to fight the power of Ricordi by acquiring Halévy's *La Juive*, Gounod's *Faust*, Meyerbeer's *L'Africaine*. When Giovannina managed to get *Lohengrin*, the Luccas had a trump card. *Lohengrin* was a sensational success under Mariani, who irritated Verdi and the Verdians by calling the composer 'the mighty Wagner'. Bülow had high praise for his colleague Mariani. Later the mighty Wagner sent Mariani his portrait with the words, '*Evviva Mariani!*' This did not exactly endear Mariani to Verdi.

Bülow happened to be in Milan when Verdi conducted the *Requiem* on the anniversary of Manzoni's death. Afterwards Bülow sent letters to the newspapers stating; 'Hans von Bülow did not attend the show presented yesterday in the Church of San Marco. Hans von Bülow must not be counted among the foreigners gathered in Milan to hear Verdi's sacred music.' Before the premiere of the 'show', Bülow wrote to friends in Germany who quickly copied his letter and sent it to their Wagnerian friends in Italy;

Verdi, the omnipotent corruptor of artistic taste in Italy, hopes to sweep away the last remnants of Rossini's immortality, which inconveniences him. His latest opera, in ecclesiastical dress, will, after the first fictitious compliment to the memory of the poet, Alessandro Manzoni, be exposed to the world's admiration for three evenings. After that, it will go, accompanied by the trained [*dressierte*] soloists, to Paris, the aesthetic Rome of the Italians.

Bülow used the word 'trained' in the German sense of training (*dressieren*) circus animals. He also wrote that 'A hasty, stolen glance at this emanation from *Il Trovatore* and *Traviata* took away any desire to attend this festival.' Bülow's letter was not only tactless but also stupid since he had not even bothered to hear the *Requiem* or read it carefully. Later Brahms looked at the score and said, 'Bülow has blundered, since this could be done only by a *genius*.' Brahms disliked Wagner and Bülow but his judgment turned out to be right.

In 1892, seventeen years later, Bülow wrote a public letter to Verdi in which he called himself 'a contrite sinner who wants to confess'. He wrote that he had studied *Aïda*, the *Requiem*, and *Otello*. He concludes, 'Illustrious Master, I admire and love you.'

Verdi wrote back that Bülow must not have a sense of guilt. Why should he not have said what he felt twenty years earlier? 'If the artists of the North and the South have different tendencies, let them be *different*! Everybody should maintain the natural characteristics of his own nation, as Wagner so rightly said.' But Verdi, no fool, sent copies of Bülow's letter and his own reply to Ricordi, 'just for the record', in case there would be any more sniping.

Verdi believed in self-discipline and hard work, and in good taste. He did not care for theories or systems, he knew only good and bad music. There was much mediocre music in between and Verdi admitted that he did not always know the boundary-lines. He believed in inspiration rather than reflection: 'Art devoid of spontaneity, naturalness and simplicity ceases to be art.' The artist, he said, must know the technique that gives him the tools to develop his art. A composer must be able to write counterpoint and fugues. Verdi had no patience with young composers who trained themselves in melody, hoping to follow in the footsteps of Bellini, or in harmony, following Meyerbeer. 'A young man beginning to write music,' Verdi once wrote to his friend Arrivabene, 'should never think about being a melodist or futurist or any other of the devils created by this kind of pedantry. Melody and harmony must only be means to make music in the hands of the artist. If the day comes when we cease to talk about melody or harmony, about Italian or German schools, of past and future – then perhaps the kingdom of art will be established.'

'To make music' was Verdi's alpha and omega. He did not want to be an intellectual artist, like Wagner, but an instinctive one. He knew that German music was basically instrumental; the symphony and the string quartet were 'German' inventions. (He did not bother much about the difference between 'German' and 'Austrian'.) Italian music was vocal, and the opera was an Italian invention. He once wrote to Boito that he considered Palestrina *'in primis et ante omnes'* the source of Italian music. He thought that Monteverdi's part-writing was 'poor'. He found his great idols – Shakespeare, Dante, Michelangelo, Schiller – outside music. He knew too much about music to have too many musical gods. He revered Beethoven but he considered his workmanship in the last movement of the Ninth Symphony 'poor'. He thought Bach's B minor Mass dry and dull in places. He admired

Bellini's long, sweeping melodies but thought little of his instrumentation. He thought Rossini's *Il Barbiere di Siviglia* the best comic opera ever written. He admired much about Meyerbeer, and he loved the fourth act of *Les Huguénots*. He saluted Berlioz, 'whom I love as a man and respect as an artist'.

After Verdi read that Wagner had died in Venice, in 1883, he wrote to Giulio Ricordi: 'Sad sad sad. Vagner is dead! When I read of it yesterday in the paper, I was, I tell you, stunned. Let's not talk of it. ... A great personality has disappeared! A name that leaves a most powerful mark on the History of the Art!' Verdi was so upset that he misspelt Wagner's name. He scratched out the word *potente* ('powerful') and wrote *potentissima* ('most powerful'). Giuseppina's comment,

Caricatures of the rival composers: RIGHT Verdi conducts the *Requiem*, from *Mondo Aristico* 1874; OPPOSITE Wagner conducts the music of the future, *c.* 1870.

Dies irae !!!

in a letter of 3 March 1883, was different: 'Verdi never knew or even saw Wagner. ... This great individual, now departed, was never afflicted with the petty itch of vanity, but devoured by an incandescent, measureless pride, like Satan or Lucifer, the most beautiful of fallen angels!'

'Time will tell,' was one of Verdi's favourite expressions. Time has told. In 1941 Paul Henry Lang wrote in his standard work, *Music in Western Civilization*:

Wagner's attempt at the final solution of the problem of the lyric drama was unsuccessful; he retarded and almost strangled opera. But the opera's real home again came to the rescue ... in Verdi, the unimpaired triumph of the three-hundred-year-old music drama, proclaiming the glory of the human voice, of human drama.

Being more human than Wagner, he [Verdi] is much nearer to us and to our faculty of understanding and enjoyment. Wagner drew ideals; Verdi, men.

11
BELOVED TYRANT

———

Artistic creation is always personal, sometimes autobiographical. Some artists get more deeply involved than others. Goethe and Wagner, enthusiastic extroverts who were sure of their immortality, conveniently arranged the sources for their future biographers. Others, such as Pushkin and Dostoevsky, told everything about themselves in their manuscripts. And a few, among them Verdi, are congenital introverts who jealously protect their inner life. Scholars are reduced to clues, deductions and conclusions which often fail to penetrate the mystery.

Posthumous analysis does not solve the complex enigma of Giuseppe Verdi. He is a man of many contradictions, gracious toward casual acquaintances and often cruel towards the ones he loved, as though guilty of loving them. Generous in some cases and stingy in others. Thanks to some admiring biographers, the image of the lovable, fragile old gentleman has emerged, wearing his battered felt hat, and surveying the world as a big joke, as in *Falstaff – tutto nel mundo è burla*. For some reason, the best-known pictures of Verdi are made from portraits painted by Boldoni and Tivoli, when Verdi was in his seventies, looking like one of the father figures in one of his early operas. Another frequently reproduced photograph shows Verdi with the felt hat (worn in his native Parma) and rolled-up umbrella, elegant and frail. No wonder: it was taken in 1899, when he was eighty-six, two years before he died. Most pictures seem to convey the idea that Verdi was always an old man. But he was young too, and very much so; and the earlier pictures show a dashing, attractive man whom the women could and probably did pursue, more complex and problematical than the 'venerable veteran' from Sant' Agata.

Genius has prerogatives and privileges that lesser mortals may not enjoy. The way Wagner acted in his financial affairs would make a fine study in criminal law. But Wagner was a genius and, rightly or

OPPOSITE Verdi with Francesco Tamagno, the tenor who first sang the role of Otello.

wrongly, we like to think of him as a latterday Hans Sachs, wise and ironical, and not as a crook who cheated his best friends. Verdi is even more difficult because he is, basically, a nice man. The Freudians' problems with him begin with his relationship with his father, which seems to have affected his whole life. Many letters, written by and to Verdi, prove it. Carlo Giuseppe Verdi is often described in a quick, almost embarrassed way, as though he were a shadowy figure, not around much. But he was very much around, often more than his son liked, and he lived to the age of eighty-three, when Verdi was fifty-four. He died when Verdi was in Paris, preparing the premiere of *Don Carlos*, early in 1867. Verdi was distraught and for several days did not come to the theatre. What did Verdi feel in those days. Remorse? Guilt, mingled with relief? Plain relief?

We do not know. But we know something, though not much, about his father, an illiterate, cunning peasant, bigoted, always in league with the local village priest in Le Roncole. We do not know how he treated his wife. For fifteen years he was secretary and treasurer of the small parish church. When the small boy, then called Peppino, was seven, his father made him serve as acolyte at mass. According to an apocryphal story, the boy became so absorbed by the sounds of the organ that he did not hear the priest asking for the water and wine. The priest kicked the little boy, who fell down (according to one version) or shouted 'God damn you!' and ran out of the church (in another version). Verdi told the story, in various versions, in his later years, perhaps to account for his life-long anti-clericalism. About that there is no doubt; nor that he was however a deeply religious man, otherwise he could not have written his moving *Requiem*. Like millions of other men in Italy, Verdi *believed* but had no use for priests and church ritual. He would accompany Giuseppina on her way to mass, and at the entrance to the church he would turn around and go home, and the poor woman had to go in alone while the Bussetani stared and whispered.

Verdi was on the side of the anti-clericalists in 1855 when the Piedmontese Parliament was discussing a bill that would reduce the salaries of bishops, and in effect tax church property, which was completely exempted. In Piedmont the Jesuits controlled lower education. Church censorship affected newspapers and books. The Church was powerful, the number of priests was large. Little Piedmont had forty-one bishops and archbishops, all well paid. (The archbishop of Turin got twice as much money as the archbishop of Paris.) The total income of the Church was one-thirteenth of the entire national revenue. When Cavour wanted to reduce the influence of the Church to a 'tolerable', sensible level his troubles started in his own family: one of his elder brothers, a conservative Marchese, angrily attacked the bill and Cavour in Parliament. Eventually the bill became law. It made Piedmont a modern state and set a precedent for Italy. Cavour had achieved a great deal despite his untimely death.

Verdi never overcame his distrust of priests. He knew they had been the advisers of his father, who had tried to take advantage of his unusually gifted son. When Verdi's father bought a spinet for the boy and with the help of the local priest arranged for him to play the organ in Le Roncole, he started on a campaign to exploit his son which lasted many years. When Verdi at the age of eighteen studied music with Provesi in Busseto, his father wanted him to come home and work in the shop and in the field, to help support the family. Without the support of Antonio Barezzi Verdi would never have been sent to continue his studies in Milan.

In 1842, when Verdi was twenty-eight and had just bought the small farm in Le Roncole, he set up his parents as caretakers. Verdi had the peasant's healthy belief in the value of the soil. Four years later, when he had more money, he bought a much larger farm in the small village of Sant' Agata, giving up the small farm in Le Roncole as part of the purchase price. Later Verdi sent instructions from Paris to his father about payments; the money would come from Ricordi in Milan. His parents would live in a small house on the farm while Verdi, and Giuseppina, would rent the Palazzo Cavalli in Busseto. His father was delighted, and dictated to Muzio a letter to Verdi, 'Your mother is very happy to be in the country ... and I hope you will once come to live with us and enjoy your beautiful possessions. ...' He told Muzio that he was 'a father lucky and happy about a son that honours me and the region', *il suo paese*. The *paese*, old Verdi felt, was far more important than he was. Verdi was a credit to his home, his parents – what more could one wish?

It did not last long. When Verdi came home with Giuseppina Strepponi, his parents were said 'to speak against her, either directly or by innuendo'. Verdi wrote to his friend Dr Angelo Carrara, notary in Busseto, a letter which, one may assume, Carrara was to show around:

I have learnt that my father goes about saying that I made him the administrator of my properties or that I have leased them to him. ... I should like to repeat, for my own peace of mind, that I will not consent to either of these proposals. *I intend to separate from my father* [my own italics] both in my domestic and family affairs. Finally, I repeat what I said to you yesterday: as regards the world, Carlo Verdi must be one thing and Giuseppe Verdi another.

Things got even worse after Verdi had installed his parents on a farm at Vidalenzo, a certain distance away, perhaps just far enough to guarantee him 'peace of mind'. His father caused more trouble. Eventually Verdi went to see the notary and had a legal document drawn up, 'The Minutiae of the Compromise between Giuseppe and Carlo Verdi', which clearly stated what he was going to do and, by inference, what he would not do. Verdi would pay his parents an annual pension, they would have a home, and he would provide them with transport ('a suitable horse'). Afterwards, his parents were not invited to Sant' Agata. Verdi might have relented but Giuseppina would not forgive them.

Verdi did what he thought was fair for his parents, but even after his mother's death he wanted nothing to do with his father, then old and lonely. Verdi always considered Angelo Barezzi his true father. He always called him 'dearest father-in-law' long after he had married Strepponi, and many years after the death of his first wife, Margherita. Léon Escudier once came to Sant' Agata to bring Verdi the Cross of the Légion d'Honneur which the composer had been awarded by the French Government. Barezzi happened to be there. Escudier later wrote: 'For Father Antonio, Verdi is a demi-god. . . . He never speaks of him or his works without tears coming to his eyes. . . . At dinner, Father Antonio led the conversation, and Verdi was the subject of it, much to the great despair of the Maestro who tired of the struggle and finally gave up trying to silence Barezzi.'

After dinner Escudier handed Verdi the decoration. Verdi tried to hide his emotion but 'Father Antonio threw his arms around him and started crying'. Later the old man 'borrowed the decoration to show it all over Busseto, and promised to bring it back next day'.

Giuseppina was very fond of Barezzi. When the old man died, half a year after Verdi's father, whose death she had almost ignored, she wrote to a friend:

He is dead – dead in our arms. Farewell, beloved old man! Our sorrow, our benedictions, our affections will follow you beyond the tomb. The memory of your goodness, of all you did for Verdi, will be forgotten only when we, in our turn, close our eyes. . . . Weep with us and pray for the soul of this man whom we loved so much.

And a few months earlier, after the death of Verdi's father, Giuseppina had written: 'despite the fact that we were antipodes in our way of thinking, I feel the keenest regrets. . . . Poor old man? May God have mercy on him!' Which is not quite the same thing.

People have analysed Verdi's 'hatred' of his father from the way he portrayed King Philip in *Don Carlos*. Some have gone further, even suggesting 'the physical and spiritual fathers' in Verdi's operas – Church, State, Establishment, Authority generally. This is far-fetched. Verdi was instinctively on the side of the underdog, in his operas and politically. In *Nabucco* it was the Israelites, in *I Masnadieri* Carlo Moor, in *Don Carlos* the Prince and his friend Rodrigo; his heart belonged to Aïda, the 'slave', not to Amneris, the king's daughter. Many Verdi heroes rebel against law and order – Ernani, Rigoletto, Manrico, Violetta, even Falstaff. It has been said that Verdi was often hurt when he was young – by his father, by his rejection by the Conservatory authorities in Milan, by the death of his two children and young wife. Could it be that all his life he remained afraid of being hurt again, and that he often fought back instinctively, out of fear, against those he loved? In his *Carteggi Verdiani* Alessandro Luzio published excerpts from Giuseppina's letters, written in 1867. Extracts can often be misleading when quoted out of context, but Giuseppina's feelings are not:

July 1 ... [Verdi] is so worked up against the servants and against me that I don't know with what words and in what tone of voice I am to speak to him so as not to offend him. Alas! How things will end I don't know, for his mood becomes continually more unquiet and wrathful. To possess such sovereign qualities and to have a character at times so harsh and difficult! July 2 ... A row this evening, about an open window, and because I tried to calm him down. He got into a fury, saying he will dismiss all servants, and that I take their part when they don't do what they ought to do, rather than his part, when he makes 'just observations'. But my God! The poor devils need someone to watch over their interests a bit. They are poor and they are not bad, considering the generally corrupt majority of servants. God grant that he may calm down for I suffer very much from it, and I may lose my head. ...

This is still Verdi, the gentle, often wise man from his *paese* in Parma. He was torn – as so many of us are – by the eternal dilemma of Goethe's Faust, *'Zwei Seelen wohnen, ach!, in meiner Brust'* ('Two souls, alas!, dwell within my breast'). In August Verdi wrote from Turin to his agent Paolo Marenghi at Sant' Agata,

I leave tomorrow for Paris and I repeat once again the orders given, to see if for once I can't make myself understood and obeyed: 1. You will watch over the horses and the coachman in whom I have little confidence in the matter of orders. Let him exercise the horses every two days, without going to Busseto. 2. You will tell Guerino that he was wrong to hand over the key of the engine, that now he must clean it and lock it up until further orders. 3. You will repeat to the gardener what I said to him. The garden closed: no one must enter, nor must the people in the house go out, except the coachman for the short time needed to exercise the horses. If anyone goes out, he can stay out for always. ... Take note that I am not joking. Henceforth I intend to be master in my own house.

Certainly this is not a 'typical' Verdi letter, and admiring biographers ignore such letters. He probably had reason to be irritated, he wanted to keep a strict regime at home, he was in charge and made it clear to Giuseppina as much as to the servants. But the tough side of Verdi's character is as much part of the man as the greatness of the composer. Sometimes Giuseppina was so upset that she confided her distress to her diary, in French, which the (snooping) servants did not understand. On 1 January 1868 she writes;

I wanted to have a *pied-à-terre* in a district near the sea [in Genoa]. ... I never wanted anything splendid but only a little nest in which to pass the rigorous winter months which are so gloomy in the country. ... He has given me a very beautiful present [the splendid apartment in Palazzo Sauli] for he is a *grand-seigneur* and generous. I was touched by that, as by all he does for me, without ostentation and without reproaches.
January 3 ... We played billiards, as we almost always do recently. He is busy playing the carpenter, the locksmith, and the piano. He found nothing of which to complain and grumble. ... Why isn't he always like that, instead of finding fault no matter what I do, while what I do is always done with the same intention: to make his life comfortable, pleasant and serene?!
January 4 ... Alas! The clouds have reappeared! Last night ... Mariani burst out against Genoa and praised to the skies Bologna and its inhabitants. I took part in the conversation, giving my opinions in terms I thought fitting. ... But for a long time, it now seems, I am speaking badly, and out of season. Verdi gets irritated by my voice, which seems to him either too soft or too shrill, and I ask myself what can be the *juste milieu* to suit him! In the morning he approached me, in the presence of Corticelli and Maddalena. I played billiards badly, and as he said something to me brusquely I replied, 'Didn't you sleep well?' Afterwards I asked, 'What did I do wrong last night to merit your observations?' He replied, 'It's the way you say it. ...' But, in God's name, have I at my age to speak and contain myself like a young girl? ... If, when something is wrong and doesn't suit him, he would tell me so with a little less brusqueness! ...

Many women will sympathize with Giuseppina; in many households all over the world such discussions take place every day. Reading Giuseppina's letters and diaries with a sense of detachment one feels that she was often hurt by his 'brusqueness', his lack of concern for her and everybody else, when he was in his difficult, creative moods, and by his often undisguised interest in other women. She loved him always though, with his imperfections, because she truly loved him. One evening in Sant' Agata many years later, after Verdi had played for her and Giulio Ricordi a few passages from *Otello*, on which he was then working, she smiled and said to Ricordi, in Milanese dialect, '*L'e ancamo bravo, el me Verdi!*', which roughly translated means, 'He is still

OPPOSITE Giuseppina Strepponi in middle age.

The domestic staff at Sant' Agata who often suffered from Verdi's temper.

first-rate, my Verdi!' She understood his Faustian complexity, the twin souls in his breast. In 1872 she wrote to a friend in Naples:

Everyone agrees that nature endowed Verdi with the divine fire of genius; he is a paragon of honesty, he understands and feels the most delicate sentiments. Yet this *rascal* claims, with a calm obstinacy that infuriates me, to be, not an outright atheist, but a very doubtful believer. . . .

Somehow Giuseppina, who did so much for Verdi, managed to keep her life apart from his. She had made him understand that she had a right to live her own life, and he respected her for it. She had her friends, mostly women, and he had his. She was not happy that he always confided in Clarina Maffei, often writing to her though he did not see her for twenty years; then one day Giuseppina asked Maffei to come to Sant' Agata, as a surprise for Verdi. 'He received me like a sister,' Clarina later told a friend; 'He gazed at me in astonishment; then he blurted out exclamations and embraced me. . . .' Giuseppina even thanked Clarina for coming: 'Thank you for this appearance which has warmed my heart.'

In 1866 Verdi and Giuseppina took Maria Filomena into their home in Sant' Agata. She was a grandchild of his father's youngest brother. Her father had just died. They called her Maria – she was seven years old – and later adopted and educated her. Verdi was fond of Maria and later thought of her as his daughter. At nineteen Maria married Alberto Carrara, the son of Verdi's friend and lawyer, one of the few Bussetani who was received in Sant' Agata. The wedding took place in the small chapel that Verdi had built in his house next to the winter herbarium. Verdi was delighted that Maria had married a man of his *paese* who was 'serious and honest'. The following year he wrote to friends that Maria had a beautiful baby: 'I can't describe the joy of everyone, especially of Peppina and the Carrara family.'

Verdi's house in Sant' Agata is still the private property of his descendants, the family Carrara Verdi. A large house which he called 'the hut' and the local people called 'the palace', though it is neither, but a comfortable manor house, surrounded by a private park. Moss grows on the stone benches, and the trunks of the old trees which Verdi loved are intertwined with ivy. Every time he finished an opera he planted another tree – a plane tree after *Rigoletto*, an oak commemorating *Il Trovatore*, the willow for *La Traviata* – which was the way he celebrated; the peasant paying tribute to the great composer.

Verdi requested in his will that nothing be changed in the house or in his grounds. His bedroom-study is still as he left it, spacious and high-ceilinged: 'Four walls protect me against the sun and bad weather.' The heavy lace curtains at the windows give it the strange half-dimness that the writer Franz Werfel, an enthusiastic Verdian, once called 'sunny darkness'. Verdi's bed is to one side, under a lace canopy; across from it is the large black piano on which he first played the wonderful music of his late works, which he composed mostly in Sant' Agata. (Much of his earlier music he wrote at the opera house itself, while rehearsing, surrounded by noise and excitement.)

The sense of order and method in Sant' Agata shows that Verdi was as meticulous in his daily habits as in his financial affairs and in his composing. One can see his small shaving mirror; two chairs given to Verdi by the Khedive of Egypt after the premiere of *Aïda*; the white gloves he used to wear at the opera house; several busts of his great hero, Alessandro Manzoni. Tacked to some places were slips of paper on which Verdi had written things he had heard and wanted to remember. The one above his working table said: '*Un Tedesco che sa sa*

troppo – Un Russo che sa è un pericoloso', 'A German who knows, knows too much – a Russian who knows is a dangerous man.'

Verdi kept a small standing bookcase about four feet high by his bed. On the top shelf he placed the works that he read frequently; he never changed them. They are still there: pocket scores of the string quartets of Haydn, Mozart, Beethoven; Shakespeare's complete works, translated by Giulio Carcano; the complete works of Dante; Schiller's plays, translated by Verdi's friend Andrea Maffei. These were Verdi's heroes all his life. On the second shelf he kept Milton's *Paradise Lost*; the works of Byron, translated by Carlo Rusconi; the Holy Bible in the King James version; French and Italian dictionaries. No opera scores, not even his own.

OPPOSITE Verdi in the garden of Sant' Agata. He planted a tree to commemorate each opera.

192

12
THE MARIANI MYSTERY

The strangest event in Verdi's complex emotional life was the break with Angelo Mariani – the only close friend whom Verdi respected for his knowledge of music, though he was often irritated by Mariani's vanity, gossiping, and unreliability. Mariani, born in Ravenna in 1821 (eight years younger than Verdi), had begun as a violinist, switched to conducting in Messina, when he was twenty-three, and soon enthralled the music world when he conducted some very good productions of early Verdi operas at the Teatro Re and the Teatro Carcano in Milan (not yet at La Scala). Around 1850, when he was in his late twenties, he was already internationally famous – a greater achievement than nowadays when a gifted young conductor is helped by recordings, radio and television.

Verdi probably first met Mariani in Milan, around 1846. His earliest known letter to him is dated 7 March 1853, after the Venice premiere of *La Traviata*, when he informed Mariani (and some others) of the fiasco. Mariani's earliest letter is dated 25 September, the same year, when he asked 'to revive *La Traviata* with the honour which such a stupendous work demands'. The letter is already addressed, 'My Verdi'. They met again in Rimini in 1858, when Mariani, already the leading conductor in Italy, conducted *Aroldo*, a now forgotten Verdi opera. The following year Verdi invited Mariani for several weeks to Sant' Agata, a rare privilege reserved only for very close friends. Verdi was amused by Mariani and agreed with Rossini's description: 'the handsome Angelo of the huge black eyes'.

More than two hundred letters from Mariani to Verdi exist, proving Mariani's absolute devotion. He was often confused in his letters, but always loyal in his feelings. He worshipped Verdi. His letters are often badly written; he was not an intellectual; not many star conductors are. He was a fine musician and a true Italian patriot. Music and Italy were the two subjects that brought the two men together. Verdi sometimes called Mariani '*Testa Falsa*' ('Wrong Head') when he

OPPOSITE Angelo Mariani.

became irritated by Mariani's lack of judgment; occasionally he called him *'Buona Testa'* ('Good Head'). Verdi managed to express much meaning in a nickname. Mariani was famous but was always delighted to meet people who were even more famous. In the 1850s when Verdi was collecting the autographs of famous men (he did not realise then that one day he would be the most famous of them all) he asked Mariani to send him some autographs from his trips to England, France and elsewhere. In the spring of 1859 Mariani in Genoa kept Verdi, in Sant' Agata, informed about how the war against the Austrians was going: 'The cheers of the people near the port can be heard from here! What enthusiasm! What a beautiful festal day!' The letters were often addressed to the 'Illustrious Maestro, Friend of My Heart'.

Later Verdi became severe with Mariani who was said to be taking liberties with his scores and was not always careful about selecting the right singers. Mariani always admitted that he had been wrong and would be deeply depressed for a few days. Once he wrote: 'Oh, Don Peppino! Don't be angry anymore with your poor Wrong Head. Write to me, for I really need a letter from you. . . .'

Mariani first mentions Teresa Stolz in his letters in the summer of 1865 from Cesena: 'La Stolz, the prima donna, did very well indeed, and so did Pandolfini, the baritone.' Two years later he conducted *Don Carlos* in Bologna, with Teresa Stolz as Elizabeth. The noted music critic Filippo Filippi wrote: 'The success was immense, the performance phenomenal. The greatest credit for this marvellous achievement is due to Mariani, for whom no praise can be sufficient. . . . From the orchestra his genius (it really is genius) sparkles; one would say that through richness of colour, through fire, through the magic of sonority, he creates another *Don Carlos* within the *Don Carlos* of Verdi. . . .'

This was an anathema to the composer, for whom there existed only one *Don Carlos*, namely Verdi's. Still, he had to admit that Mariani's performances of *Ernani*, *Un Ballo in Maschera*, and *Don Carlos* established exceptionally high standards. Verdi heard much praise of Mariani, and of Teresa Stolz whom he did not then know and who was having an affair with Mariani. Soon Verdi again got upset with Mariani, who had conducted *La Forza del Destino*. Verdi complained to Ricordi that Mariani had completely changed the character of the overture 'by having the brasses boom out'. Celebrated conductors have taken worse liberties with the score but Verdi reasserted that there was only one creator, and that was the composer. The conductor, no matter how famous, had no right to 're-create' the music.

The fiasco of the Rossini *Requiem*, for which Verdi quite unfairly blamed Mariani, created the first tensions between the two men. The

correspondence proves that Verdi was cold and tough toward Mariani, who was suffering. By that time Verdi had met Teresa Stolz and had become interested in the attractive prima donna. As we have seen, Giuseppina was watching from the sidelines, and she did not like it. She wished that Mariani would marry Stolz but she knew that he was always having affairs and did not want to marry. By August 1870 Giuseppina wrote to Clarina Maffei, 'Mariani has not married and will not marry la Stolz – this at least is our opinion.' In another letter Giuseppina calls Mariani 'his own worst enemy, despite self-love'. Clearly Giuseppina did not like Mariani. Perhaps she did not understand that Mariani needed women to prove and assert himself. He was already sick, and he may have sensed that his sickness was more serious than his doctors had told him. He may have known he did not have much time left. Verdi and Giuseppina knew that Mariani did not feel well but attributed it to the conductor's 'hypochondria', especially after a surgeon in Bologna saw no reason to operate, mentioned 'glandular irritation', and recommended cold shower baths.

As we have seen, the relationship between the two men deteriorated further during the preparations for *Aïda*. When Mariani heard that Verdi was working on the score for a premiere in Cairo, he wrote to him: 'If you are staging *Aïda* in Cairo, if you permit me, I would like to come with you, to see the East again. Afterwards we could go to

The cast of *Don Carlos* at Bologna in 1861, when Teresa Stolz (left) played Elizabeth and Mariani (centre) conducted.

Constantinople and from there return by way of Vienna. Why not? One lives only once.' Mariani did not suggest that Verdi might let him conduct *Aïda*. He did not know that Verdi had already decided that his pupil Muzio would conduct the premiere. Verdi later sent Mariani a short note:

You wrote to me once before that you wanted to accompany me to Cairo. I replied I wasn't going. If I had thought fit to send you in my place I should have asked you. If I do not do so, that is proof that I did not think you fit and that I have entrusted the task to someone else.

When the production of *Aïda* had to be postponed because the sets and costumes were in Paris, then under siege, all plans had to be changed. Muzio was no longer available. Verdi decided that Teresa Stolz would sing the premiere – in Milan, where he would coach her, and Verdi put pressure on Mariani to conduct the Cairo premiere. When Mariani, very reluctantly, turned it down because of his health Verdi was furious. So far as he was concerned, their friendship was over. Verdi and Giuseppina invited Stolz to come to Sant' Agata, to study *Aïda*, and shortly afterwards she broke off with Mariani. The gossip was that she had done it under the influence of Giuseppina and Verdi and that Verdi had wanted Mariani to go to Cairo to separate him from Teresa. But the affair might have finished anyway. Teresa was becoming very unhappy about Mariani's erratic ways.

Mariani did not improve matters when he let himself be persuaded to conduct the first Wagner opera in Italy. The premiere of *Lohengrin* was announced for 1 November 1870, in Bologna.

A thick file of letters and documents exists about the complicated affair. Some biographers have claimed Mariani's decision was 'an act of revenge'. The documents do not prove it. But Mariani was pursued by bad luck. He happened to be at the Bologna railway station on the very afternoon Verdi arrived there, alone. Verdi wanted to hear a performance of *Lohengrin* and he wanted to remain incognito. Mariani later wrote:

Yesterday afternoon, between two and three, I was at the station, summoned there by an old friend in the retinue of the Russian Grand Duke Michael. I saw Signor Luigi Monti, Ricordi's agent. I asked him what he was doing there. He replied he was waiting for someone who had not arrived.
Hardly had he said these words when, a few yards away, I saw the Maestro. I went towards him, greeted him and tried to relieve him of his travelling bag. He would not allow me to take it. I understood that he was not pleased that I had seen his arrival. I gave him my word of honour that no living soul would learn of it. He went away, and I remained at the station.

That was the last time the two former friends spoke to each other.

A few weeks later, while Verdi was in Genoa with the singers for *Aïda*, coaching them at his apartment, the newspapers reported that Mariani was seriously ill. Verdi wrote to his friend Arrivabene: 'Mariani is very ill. I hope he recovers and I wish him well but ... his conduct toward me ... I'll say no more.' Mariani summoned up his strength and a year after *Lohengrin*, on 7 November 1872, conducted the first Italian performance of *Tannhäuser*, in Bologna. There was much opposition the first night, but later performances went better though *Tannhäuser* was never a great success. By the end of the year Mariani was so ill that he spent much time in bed in his small attic flat. At that point Verdi and Giuseppina tried to get Mariani out of the Palazzo Sauli. There was much bitterness all around. Teresa Stolz wrote: 'So the illustrious personage is not thinking of looking for an apartment? He probably believes he is himself the proprietor of the house.' It was all very sad and depressing since everybody knew that Mariani was soon going to die. He wanted to go to Bologna but Pietro Loreta, the surgeon who had earlier suggested a regime of cold shower baths, now knew the truth and wanted no more to do with Mariani, who had cancer of the bladder and daily haemorrhages.

No one took care of Mariani during the final days of his life. No doctor came to give him something to alleviate the pain. On 4 June he wrote to a friend: 'The pain I suffer is so great that truly I no longer have the strength to bear it. You can imagine the state I am in, without any comfort. ... I dare not call in other surgeons because I know it would be useless and they would kill me. ... I must die alone, like a dog, and alone I shall die. ...'

And alone he died, on 13 June 1873. Teresa Stolz was singing *Aïda* in Ancona. She had not bothered to visit Mariani while he was still alive and she did not attend his funeral. Neither did Verdi and Giuseppina. Verdi's only comment was that Mariani's death was 'a loss for art'. Yet once upon a time Verdi had written to Mariani, '*bell' uomo, amami*' ('beautiful man, love me').

Some biographers have speculated that Verdi may in the intimacy of his heart have written the Alessandro Manzoni *Requiem* for another 'A.M.' (Angelo Mariani). Back in 1865 Mariani wrote to Verdi from Venice, during an outbreak of cholera, that he hoped Verdi might one day write his requiem: 'I would be completely happy to die so that Italy and all the world might have such a gift from you.' But there is no evidence that Verdi had any guilt feelings after Mariani's death, or that he was thinking of his former friend when he wrote the *Requiem*.

13
AT LAST: BOITO

Fifteen years went by between *Aïda* and *Otello*, and for a long time Verdi seemed determined never to compose an opera again. To Clarina Maffei he wrote; 'Are you serious about my moral obligation to compose? No, you're joking since you know as well as I that the account is settled.' In the 1870s Verdi used his powerful influence to reform the organization and improve the technical standards of the leading opera houses in Italy. Though few people were admitted to Sant' Agata, it never became an ivory tower, and he remained in touch with the musical world. He was getting worried about the low standards of the theatres. He advised the Mayor of Naples 'to put through the reforms demanded by the needs of art today', for 'the careless and ignorant manner of putting on operas in recent years is no longer possible'. He wrote to a friend in Rome that 'modern opera has very different requirements from that of the past', and went on:

to achieve success, a good ensemble is absolutely necessary. Consequently, the direction should be entrusted to only two men, who must be capable and energetic. One of them should direct all musical matters: singers, chorus, orchestra, etc. The other should look after scenic matters: costumes, property, scenery, production, etc. These two men must decide everything and assume all the responsibility. Only then will there be hope of a good performance and of success. ...

Verdi himself assumed dictatorial powers in the production of his late works, directing both musical and scenic matters. In his early years there had been musical anarchy at La Scala and most other houses. As we have already seen, Verdi often complained about sloppy orchestra playing. Instrumentalists and standards of playing improved only after the works of Wagner began to be performed in Italy's opera houses. Conductors realized that these works could not be put on with orchestras playing as badly as during the *Rigoletto* years. Verdi never publicly admitted his 'debt' to Wagner but he knew it when he wrote the complex scores of *Otello* and *Falstaff*. There was a new generation

OPPOSITE Verdi with Arrigo Boito, poet and composer.

199

of conductors – Mariani, Faccio, Edoardo Mascheroni and later Arturo Toscanini – who had musical authority and demanded absolute discipline. They admired Verdi and learnt from him to communicate their enthusiasm to the artists, not only to the leading singers but also to the chorus and the orchestra.

After *Aïda* Verdi often went to Milan, spending more and more time there. Sant' Agata remained the home of 'the peasant from Parma', as he still called himself. Milan was the home of the world-famous composer; specifically, the Teatro alla Scala. Ten of his thirty-two operas were first performed there. (Venice came next, with five.) La Scala remained the burial-ground of his worst failure and the battle-field of his greatest victories. It produced his first four operas and his last three. In his later years, La Scala was truly his own *Festspielhaus* where his word was law, much as Wagner's was at Bayreuth. Verdi was no longer upset about the arrogant claims of the Milanese who called La Scala *'el prim teater del mund'*, the first house on earth. He knew that the Viennese and the Parisians had made similar claims about *their* houses, and he would say, 'So many first houses, and no second', a remark later attributed to Toscanini.

Verdi had himself conducted his early and middle operas but in his later years he left conducting to the professionals. So did Wagner, who gave his full attention to the stage at Bayreuth but used the best conductors he could get. Verdi asked the Scala management to remove the proscenium boxes because he hated the sight of 'horrible tailcoats and white ties among Egyptian, Assyrian and Druid costumes'. The curtain was moved out in front of the footlights, where it belongs. Verdi objected to the orchestra sitting on the same level as the audience – he was particularly bothered 'by the windmill arms of the conductor jutting into the air' – and the orchestra pit was introduced. Verdi admitted that it was Wagner's idea and 'excellent'. In our day he would have thought the same of those celebrated conductors who sit or stand high enough to ensure that they are seen by everybody in the house. No modern composer has the authority to tell them to get back into the pit where they belong.

Verdi's *Nabucco* had been lit by candles. *Aïda* was lit by gas, which replaced candles in the early 1870s. Twenty years later Verdi saw his *Falstaff* lit by electricity. To a certain extent, modern lighting affected the work of the composer. In earlier eras the house lights could not be dimmed and the auditorium remained brightly lit, a place to see and be seen. There was much coming and going and loud talk, except during the important arias. Singers would talk to one another on the stage, just when the much disliked *diva* was trying her runs and trills. During the boring recitatives the people in the boxes would gossip and gamble, drink and flirt.

When the auditorium could be dimmed, the social set no longer went to the opera because one was not being seen, and the auditorium was at last taken over by opera-lovers who would listen even between the great arias, thus paving the way for the music drama, both Wagner's and Verdi's. Verdi was strict about production details but often surprisingly lenient when dealing with singers. Toscanini, who at the age of nineteen played the cello in the Scala orchestra during the world premiere of *Otello* under Franco Faccio, later said that Verdi let singers get away with such liberties that he would have 'boiled them in oil', according to Marcia Davenport. Toscanini often thought of 'poor' Verdi, who suffered so much with the singers. In 1898, the young Toscanini conducted *Falstaff* and received a telegram from Verdi, 'Thanks thanks thanks', which was high praise.

Verdi had many problems with Victor Maurel, the excellent French bass-baritone whom he had admired as Amonasro in *Aïda* and as La Scala's first Simone Boccanegra. Maurel was a great singer-actor. Lilli Lehmann wrote that Maurel left her 'speechless for hours' after Valentine's death scene in Gounod's *Faust*. After a *Boccanegra* rehearsal at the Scala, Verdi was so impressed that he was heard to tell Maurel, 'If God gives me health, I'll write *Iago* for you'. That was a tactical error. Maurel and his 'very intelligent wife', as Giuseppina called her with her fine sense of irony, soon told everybody that Verdi's new opera would be called *Iago*, certainly not *Otello*. Once Verdi asked Francesco Tamagno, who was the first Otello, whether Maurel would make a good Iago. Tamagno is said to have replied, 'Yes, he would make a good Iago on the stage too'. If that is true, Tamagno was cleverer than he was reputed to be. After Verdi had written *Falstaff* (doubtless thinking of Maurel), Maurel in a megalomaniac moment demanded 'exclusive rights' to the part. Verdi was old and no longer exploded. He merely said to Maurel, 'Do you realize that I could burn the score of *Falstaff*?' That left Maurel speechless, for a change.

Tamagno also created problems. He was a great tenor, vain, without subtlety, and the part of Otello demands a subtle artist. Verdi took him with all his shortcomings because there was no better singer for the part. But Verdi must have had some second thoughts when he went out on the balcony of his hotel suite in Milan after the premiere of *Otello*, followed by Tamagno who stepped forward, glanced at the large crowd in the street below and sang, 'Esultate!', which is Otello's first, very difficult entrance. The crowd went wild.

Verdi found his gloomy forebodings about the future of opera confirmed when La Scala was rented in 1896 by Edoardo Sonzogno, the Milan music publisher who two years previously had opened the Teatro Lirico Internazionale. Sonzogno performed only works by the

composers on his list, among them Mascagni but never Verdi. After two years no impresario wanted La Scala, which remained closed for a year. Then a group of Milanese citizens, among them Boito, took over. They hired Giulio Gatti-Casazza as business director and Arturo Toscanini as musical director and reorganized the house, generally following Verdi's earlier ideas. Toscanini immediately introduced *his* reforms, which challenged and infuriated many artists and many citizens. A production of *Norma* was cancelled after the dress-rehearsal because Toscanini decided the soprano was not good enough. No more encores. After four fine seasons Toscanini left La Scala, for the first but not for the last time, after refusing an encore despite public demand.

Among the opera projects which Verdi planned for many years but never finished, *King Lear* is the most important. Early in 1850, after *Luisa Miller* and before *Rigoletto*, Verdi sent an outline of *King Lear* to Cammarano. He felt that Shakespeare's drama was so big and complex that it would be almost impossible to turn it into an opera, but he thought the difficulties were not 'insurmountable'. He would reduce

Three designs for La Scala productions of Verdi's operas: *Rigoletto* (opposite above) *Simone Boccanegra* (opposite) and *Il Trovatore*.

the principal parts to five: Lear, Cordelia, the Fool, Edmund, Edgar. Verdi sensed instinctively that Shakespeare's magnificent flow of language, the mad scene, the storm scene were virtually music already, which only needed to be written down.

Three years later, after the world-wide success of *Rigoletto*, Verdi again returned to *King Lear*, on this occasion with the poet Antonio Somma. This time Verdi had a complete libretto. They worked on it and revised much of it during the following three years. The correspondence between Verdi and Somma concerning *King Lear* is the most interesting with any of his librettists – though, ironically, it deals with a libretto that was never set to music. Much of Verdi's advice to Somma is sound. Keep it short, he would write to Somma: If you are long-winded, you will bore them. Some scenes might be compressed to recitatives, as in *Rigoletto* and *Macbeth*, but even these recitatives seemed too long to him and 'boring'. Verdi wanted 'brevity, clarity, truth'. But Somma was no Boito, otherwise we might now have Verdi's *King Lear*. Only Boito managed to translate Shakespeare into 'brevity, clarity, truth', and to envelop it in an aura of poetry.

In 1856 Verdi again thought of *King Lear*, hoping to have the opera produced at the Teatro San Carlo in Naples. He needed a large stage. Only La Scala and Naples had such stages, but in those days Verdi would not even consider La Scala. Before writing a note Verdi wanted to be certain of having a production and of getting the cast he needed. He was assured that the management could get Maria Piccolomini, who had been a great Violetta in *La Traviata*. Verdi signed a contract with the San Carlo for 'a grand opera of not less than three acts, to be produced in January 1858'. Much as Verdi liked the idea of *King Lear*, he refused to be tied down, and the title of the 'grand opera' was not stated in the contract. When the management could not get Mme Piccolomini, Verdi would not have anybody else for the part of Cordelia and finally wrote *Un Ballo in Maschera* instead.

The subject came up again in 1867 when Verdi was asked to compose a *very* grand opera for the Opéra in Paris, but then Verdi decided on *Don Carlos*, with the great *auto-da-fé* scene. Once more *King Lear* was mentioned as a possibility when Verdi and Boito at last got together, in 1875, since both agreed that if they did collaborate it would have to be Shakespeare. But then they did *Otello* and finally *Falstaff*, and who would want to quarrel with their decisions?

Toward the end of his life in 1896, when Verdi was eighty-three, he offered the entire material on *King Lear* to Pietro Mascagni, who was then famous for *Cavalleria Rusticana*, produced six years earlier. Mascagni was not a Ricordi client. Puccini, whose *La Bohème* was premiered in 1896, was, after Verdi, the second most important

An engraving by M. Levaster of the performance in Paris of *Aïda*, 1880.

Ricordi composer. But Verdi must have thought that Mascagni would be closer to *King Lear*. This was later confirmed when Puccini admitted, after *Madame Butterfly*, that he had been thinking of *King Lear* but 'had been afraid of Shakespeare'. Mascagni was somewhat overwhelmed by Verdi's offer and asked the old Maestro why he had not composed the music.

'Verdi,' Mascagni later recalled 'closed his eyes for an instant – perhaps to remember, perhaps to forget. Then he replied, softly and slowly, "The scene in which King Lear finds himself on the heath terrified me".'

For a composer to find his ideal librettist is even rarer than for a man to find his ideal wife. Among the forty-two thousand operas written (though not all preserved), very few are the ideal marriage of poetry and music. Gluck found Calzabigi. Mozart, who studied Gluck 'because Gluck was trying to forget that he was a musician', found Lorenzo da Ponte. On 13 October 1781 Mozart wrote to his father, 'The best thing of all is when a good composer who understands the stage and is talented enough to make sound suggestions, meets an able poet, that true phoenix.' The best opera composers respected the laws of the stage and worked closely with their librettists, possibly thinking of Mozart's dictum that 'in opera the poetry must be altogether the obedient daughter of music'. Verdi proved it in his earlier successes which he achieved, despite imperfect libretti, through his music. Only toward the end of his magnificent career did he find the 'true phoenix', Arrigo Boito. But the early relationship between the two men was so problematic that their final collaboration seems almost miraculous.

Boito, born in Padua in 1842, was twenty-nine years younger, from another generation and another world. His Italian father, a minor painter, spent most of his wife's money. Josephine Radolinska was a Polish countess. Arrigo Boito grew up as a charming young upper-class man, witty and gifted, arrogant and precocious. He and his best friend, Franco Faccio, who was to become one of Italy's best conductors, studied at the Milan Conservatory (where Verdi had not been admitted) and became the leaders and unofficial spokesmen of a group of young 'modernist' poets and musicians. Boito first met Verdi in Paris in 1862, when he was twenty. Verdi had agreed to write something for the London Exhibition, and decided to do a cantata for solo, chorus and orchestra. Boito and Faccio had come to him with a letter of introduction from Clarina Maffei. Verdi liked young Boito and asked him to write the text for *Inno delle Nazioni*. On 29 March Verdi wrote to Boito:

In thanking you for the fine work written for me, I should like to offer you, as a token of my esteem, this modest watch. Accept it in the friendly spirit in which it is offered. May it recall to you my name, and the value of time. My regards to Faccio, and Glory and Fortune to you both!

Though Verdi probably put no deeper meaning into the words 'the value of time', they seem prophetic in various ways. Time remained Boito's problem all his life. He worked for years on his two operas, *Mefistofele* and *Nerone*. And it took a long time until the two men understood each other. Later Verdi wrote to Clarina Maffei that Boito and Faccio 'are accused of being very warm admirers of Wagner. No harm in that, as long as admiration doesn't degenerate into imitation. . . .'

Faccio's opera *I Profughi Fiamminghi* had a modest success at La Scala late in 1863. At the following banquet in his honour, Boito got up and recited his ode, *All' Arte italiana*, in which he deplored the sad state of Italian music since the days of 'the holy harmonies of Pergolesi and Marcello', hoping that 'perhaps the man is already born who will restore art in its purity, on the altar now defiled like the wall of a brothel'. The ode was later published. Verdi took it as a personal insult. He wrote to Clarina Maffei: 'If Faccio is destined to restore art, on the altar now defiled with the filth of the brothel, so much the better for him and for the public.' And when Tito Ricordi tried to

A cartoon of 1892 shows Boito seeking inspiration for *Nerone*, the opera he never completed.

Arrigo Boito viaggia, a spese del Governo, attraverso i Conservatori del Regno... forse per presentarci presto *Nerone* musico, sotto un aspetto originale, scoperto lungo il suo viaggio.

excuse young Boito's silly language, Verdi said, 'If I too, among others, have soiled the altar, as Boito says, let him clean it and I shall be the first to come and light a candle.'

Young and exuberant, Boito wrote articles for the *Giornale della Società del Quartetto*. The society's aim was to introduce the great chamber music works, especially the string quartets by Haydn, Mozart and Beethoven, in Milan where they were almost unknown. Boito was always certain of his convictions and able to express them enthusiastically: 'Beethoven, a solar intelligence, a nature almost divine, amphibian of sky and earth, is Mendelssohn and Schumann in one. Bach comes up to his chest, Haydn to his knee, Wagner to the ankle of his foot.'

Boito's *Mefistofele* had its premiere at La Scala on 5 March 1868. It was a disaster. It lasted six hours, the singers were terrible, people hissed and whistled, and though Boito himself conducted he was unable to hold the performance together. After two more performances, the opera disappeared. The day after the premiere Verdi wrote to his friend Arrivabene, 'I am and shall be an enthusiastic admirer of the futurists on condition that they produce some music no matter what the system, as long as it is music.' The 'futurists' were Boito and his friends, the 'modernists', also called the 'Germanist claque'.

Boito attended several *Lohengrin* performances, under Mariani, in Bologna. Possibly at the suggestion of Giovannina Lucca, who handled Wagner in Italy, Wagner wrote a letter, 'to an Italian friend', which began, 'May I take advantage of your knowledge of German to ask you to give my thanks to your honoured countrymen in your mother tongue.' Verdi knew of Wagner's letter and, later, that Boito had translated *Rienzi*, *Tristan* and other Wagneriana into Italian. Boito happened to attend the *Lohengrin* performance in Bologna when Verdi had refused to show himself to his admirers. Later the young man and the old man met at the railway station: 'The conversation turned on the difficulty of sleeping in a railway carriage.' It will be recalled that Verdi and Mariani, his former friend, had also met at the station only a few hours earlier, for the last time.

And it was in Bologna, in 1875, seven years after the disastrous premiere, that *Mefistofele* was a success. It is now performed all over the world and is considered a near-masterpiece, though it will never be popular. Boito also wrote poetry, including *Re Orso* and *Libro dei Versi*, under his own name; but when he did something for money, he used the anagram 'Tobia Gorrio'. Under this pseudonym he wrote the libretto for *La Gioconda*, with music by Amilcare Ponchielli, together with various other things. Meanwhile he was trying to work on his second opera *Nerone* but could not get it finished. He had not learnt

209

'the value of time'. Verdi heard a performance of *Mefistofele* in 1877 and wrote to Arrivabene:

It is difficult to say whether Boito will be able to give Italy any master-pieces. He has much talent, aspires to originality but succeeds only in being strange. He lacks spontaneity and he lacks invention; many musical qualities. With these tendencies one can succeed more or less well in a subject as strange and theatrical as *Mefistofele*, but less easily in *Nerone*.

Verdi's knowledge of music and his prescience remain admirable; his statements almost always withstand the test of time. He was right about *Mefistofele*, and he was also right about *Nerone*. The opera was performed in its unfinished form in 1924, six years after Boito's death, at La Scala under Toscanini. It had no success.

In 1872, when Verdi's *Aïda* was a tremendous success at La Scala, Boito's friend Franco Faccio had been forgiven his early sins. Faccio conducted the glorious Milan premiere, with Teresa Stolz. But Boito was still out in the cold. Giuseppina, Verdi's mouthpiece, wrote to Faccio that she and Verdi considered him 'a true friend'. Not a word about Boito.

Verdi did not know that Boito had changed. The brash young man had learnt fast, the hard way; the debacle of *Mefistofele* had taught him that it is easier to write about a fiasco as a critic, making fun of it and showing off one's brilliance to the readers, than to be personally in-volved in it, as composer and conductor. Though only in his mid-thirties, Boito had matured. He was not proud of his earlier excesses. He had some serious second thoughts about 'the mighty Wagner', he had admired *Aïda* and the *Requiem*, and he was almost personally concerned about the silence of Verdi, whom he now considered Italy's greatest composer and one of the very great composers of all times. Boito was a lonely man. He had few friends, and women did not interest him very much until he fell madly in love with Eleonora Duse, after the opening night of *Otello*. Boito was an incurable hero-worshipper who was happy only when he had someone to look up to. He had worshipped Beethoven, Mendelssohn, Wagner, and probably himself too; but now he worshipped Verdi.

It is not quite certain who managed to bring Verdi and Boito together. Certainly Clarina Maffei had something to do with it. She knew both of them, and with a woman's intuition she sensed that they could do great things together. Verdi's former librettists, Somma and Piave, were dead; there was no one good enough for him – except Boito. Giulio Ricordi agreed; he had always considered Boito a poet rather than a composer. Faccio too was a member of the conspiracy. He loved his friend Boito and he admired the Maestro. When *Mefisto-*

fele was performed in Genoa in March 1879, Boito came to pay a call on Verdi. It was probably – and hopefully – arranged by Giulio Ricordi, but nothing came of it. Giulio had written to Verdi, years before:

> Boito would consider himself the happiest, the most *fortunate* of men if he could write the libretto of *Nerone* for you. And he would renounce at once, and with pleasure, the idea of writing the music . . . in all consc[ient]iousness I may send a word of recommendation of this young man, endowed with talents of a truly superior nature, and deserving of good fortune.

In June 1879 Verdi came to Milan to conduct a benefit performance of his *Requiem*, for the victims of a recent flood disaster. Teresa Stolz and Maria Waldmann would both sing, for the last time in public. The concert brought in thirty-seven thousand lire, a small fortune, Verdi was cheered everywhere and, after the performance, the orchestra of La Scala under Faccio played a serenade for him in the Via Manzoni, underneath the balcony of the Albergo Milano – the overture to *Nabucco* and the prelude to the last act of *La Traviata*. Verdi, sixty-four, was certainly not 'forgotten'. Some cynics said it had all been organized by Ricordi but even they had to admit that the cheering crowds could not have been laid on. At a dinner – which Verdi, Giuseppina, Faccio and Ricordi attended – Ricordi seems to have turned the conversation, as though by chance, to Shakespeare and to Boito. Ricordi later told his biographer, Giuseppe Adami: 'At the mention of Shakespeare's *Othello* I saw Verdi fix his eyes on me, with suspicion, but with interest too. He had certainly understood. He had certainly reacted. I believed the time was ripe.'

It was a fine conspiracy, Italian-style, and Contessa Maffei was in it, though she was not present. She knew that Verdi had been thinking about Shakespeare and *Othello* for a long time. Three years earlier, on 20 September 1876, he had written her an interesting letter. He had just seen a comedy by a young protégé, Achille Torelli, in Genoa. It was called *Color del Tempo* and Verdi wrote:

> There are great qualities in [the play] . . . but at bottom there is little in it. To copy the truth may be a good thing but to invent the truth is better, much better.
> There seems to be a contradiction in these three words, *invent the truth*, but just ask Papa. It may be that he, Papa, might have found himself with some Falstaff but he would have difficulty finding any scoundrel as scoundrelly as Iago . . . and yet they are true. . . . To copy the truth is a fine thing, but it is photography, not painting.

'Papa' was Shakespeare to Verdi, who was reading him and Dante in the late 1870s when he was unconsciously trying to find a subject momentous enough to make him write another opera. After *Aïda*, it could not be just another subject. It would have to be something very important, something out of the ordinary. Clarina Maffei knew that he had been thinking of Falstaff as the protagonist of a lyrical comedy. Maybe, he thought, he would try to write a comic opera almost as good as Rossini's admired *Barbiere*. And there was always *King Lear*. And now the evil Iago, invented and 'better' than the truth.

There must have been much talking and whispering between Ricordi, Faccio, Clarina and, no doubt, Giuseppina, who was in on the conspiracy. The next day Faccio brought Boito to see Verdi. Faccio later said that Verdi had been 'cool' and Boito had been 'humble'. Both knew that Verdi had not forgotten the 'insult' sixteen years ago. It was a short visit. Verdi said if Boito would show him the plan of a libretto, he would read it. Boito and Faccio left. Boito returned three days later with the outline. Had he really done it in seventy-two hours, or had he been working on it before? Verdi told him to go ahead but was not very encouraging. In a letter to Ricordi, Verdi wrote: 'I read Boito's sketch of *Otello* and found it good. "Write the libretto," I told him. "It will come in handy for yourself, for me, or for someone else."' Verdi was careful not to commit himself. He discouraged Ricordi from bringing Boito to Sant' Agata. But Ricordi knew that Verdi was interested when the composer began to refer to *Otello* as 'the chocolate project', a reference to the colour of Otello's skin. Verdi, as we know, took a childish pleasure in playing with secrets as he grew older.

Boito began working on the libretto with passionate dedication. He was suffering from facial neuralgia and a painful toothache but he was obsessed by his task. Ricordi became impatient and warned Boito that he must not be late. Boito apologized for the delay and sent long explanations, which were passed on to Verdi by Ricordi. Verdi did nothing yet Ricordi was confident that Verdi was waiting for 'the chocolate'. But what impressed Verdi more than anything was a letter which Boito wrote to Ricordi and which was sent on to Sant' Agata:

I am working as hard as I can but until yesterday afternoon the abscess that torments me had not burst, and with that inferno in my mouth I could not work. I think only of completing my work as best I can. No other undertaking in all my life has caused me the agitation experienced in these months of intellectual and physical struggle.

For the rest, whatever happens, even if Verdi won't have me as collaborator any more, I shall finish the work as best I can so that he may have proof that I, though physically tormented, have dedicated to him, with all the affection he inspires in me, four months of my time. By that I would not wish, heaven forbid, to claim any material reward, either from him or from you, if the thing doesn't turn out well. It would be enough for me to have given Verdi proof that I am much more truly devoted to him than he believes.

Ricordi passed on this letter to Verdi, with no comment; it seems to have made a deep impression on the composer. Verdi did not answer but Giuseppina did, writing on 7 November to Ricordi: 'I don't know Boito well but I believe I have divined his character. A nervous nature, highly excitable. When overcome with admiration capable of limitless enthusiasm, and perhaps also sometimes, by contrast, of excessive antipathies.' She also informed Ricordi, 'Between ourselves, what Boito has so far written of the African seems to please Verdi, and is very well done', and she asked him: 'Don't even tell Verdi that I have written to you on the subject. I believe that is the best way to avoid arousing in his mind even the slightest pressure. ... It's in the wide open spaces that certain men are destined to meet and to understand one another.'

Giuseppina knew her Verdi, and she was wise, accurately predicting what eventually happened. But not at once. Almost five years passed before Verdi took up the 'chocolate' project. On 15 August 1880 Verdi wrote directly to Boito – the first letter of their collaboration – demanding changes. It was the beginning of an immensely laborious undertaking. The score and all the revisions, a thick pile of manuscripts, is now kept at the Casa Ricordi in Milan. *Otello* contains more changes than any other of his works. Verdi liked Boito's libretto and even grew to admire it. But would he be able to do justice to 'Papa'? He had suffered while composing *Macbeth* and now he was apprehensive at the very thought of Shakespeare's *Othello*. He was also a realist. In Italy, he knew, public taste was changing in dramatic and musical matters. Was it the right time for another opera based on Shakespeare? The risks were enormous. If Verdi should fail, the hyenas would tear him to pieces. It seemed much safer to do nothing, resting on one's laurels.

Giulio Ricordi was a businessman and he grew restless. If he could not have a new Verdi, maybe he could get a revised Verdi. Late in 1880 he sent to Verdi a thick parcel with the score of *Simone Boccanegra*, not much of a success when it was first heard in 1857 though it contained fine music. Giulio knew it was the fault of the libretto. Verdi wrote to say he had received the parcel: 'If you come to Sant' Agata in a year or two, you will find it intact, just as you sent it. I detest all useless things.' But Giulio knew him. Verdi opened the parcel and looked at the score; after a while he knew that something was wrong with the second act and asked, 'Who could revise it?' Ricordi had his answer ready: Boito would be available and happy to do anything that Verdi suggested.

Piave's libretto was a mishmash of improbable happenings and unlikely situations. Boito agreed to revise *Simone Boccanegra* provided

Verdi with friends in the garden of Sant'Agata. From left to right, Signora Carrara (his adopted daughter), Teresa Stolz, a sister of Giuseppina Strepponi, Campanari, Verdi, Guilio Ricordi, Giuchitta Ricordi, Methicowitz.

his name was not used. Verdi compared the old libretto to a shaky table: 'by putting a leg in order it might be made to stand firmly on the floor.' Boito did more than fix a leg. Too much in the opera takes place before the curtain goes up, or off-stage, and has to be explained. The revision was a considerable success. Verdi and Boito concentrated on the scenes with beautiful music and Verdi wrote some new music for the Council Chamber scene and elsewhere. It was still an uneven work but it had been much worse. The Scala provided a marvellous cast, with Francesco Tamagno, Edouard de Reszke, and Victor Maurel as a magnificent Boccanegra. The performance, on 24 March 1881, was an unqualified success. Two months later La Scala performed a shortened version of *Mefistofele* which was a triumph. Verdi sent Boito a telegram: 'Delighted with your success. I send my cordial congratulations. Let's have *Nerone* soon.'

After *Simone Boccanegra* everybody agreed that Verdi was as good as ever. All he needed now was Boito's libretto of *Otello*. But there were many problems left. Verdi thought Otello's part was too long; and what about the big ensemble in the third act? 'Get busy on the finale, and make it a well-developed piece, a piece on a big scale, I should say. The theatre demands it; but more than the theatre, the colossal power of the drama demands it.' Verdi was a composer able to make 'intelligent suggestions' (in the sense of Mozart's famous letter to his father), and Boito was more than an able poet. The correspondence concerning *Otello* reads like a textbook for opera-writing. Verdi still remained elusive but there were signs that he was beginning to think of a production. He corresponded with his friend Domenico Morelli, a painter from Naples, about the character of Iago. From the very beginning Iago had interested Verdi more than any other character, and no wonder: in Iago Shakespeare had 'invented the truth', as Verdi said. Morelli had painted several of Shakespeare's characters in *Othello* in a realistic manner, but never Iago because he was not sure how Iago should look. Morelli saw him as a small, cunning, contemptible conspirator. Verdi disagreed: 'If I were an actor and had to play Iago, I would want to have rather a thin, long face, a high forehead slipping off to the back ... manners distracted, nonchalant, flippant, uttering good or evil almost with levity. ...'

He had come a long way toward the 'chocolate' project but as the years went by he still did not compose a line. Giulio Ricordi, getting impatient and frustrated, no longer interfered directly. At Christmastime he would send Verdi a less than subtle reminder – a *panettone*, the traditional Milanese Christmas cake, with a small chocolate boy on top.

Richard Wagner died early in 1883, and later that year Carlo Tenca,

Clarina Maffei's friend of many years. Verdi wrote her a melancholy letter:

I will not say to you that one stupid word 'courage'. A word that has always angered me when addressed to me. We need more than courage. Comfort you will find only in the strength of your soul. ... Now the years are beginning to pile up and I think that life is the most stupid of all things and, even worse, useless. What are we doing? What have we done? What will we do? After considering all, the answer is humiliating and very sad: NOTHING. *Addio, mia cara* Clarina ...

Verdi's letter did not help Clarina very much. She sensed that he needed help himself. Much has been written about Verdi's dark moods during these years when he was rich and famous and apparently in good health, but it is all speculation. He felt he was getting old as he saw people whom he had respected dying off around him. Garibaldi died on the island of Caprera, and was given the state burial which he had not wanted. Victor Hugo died in Paris, and was buried at the Panthéon.

The Vienna Court Opera wanted to produce *Don Carlos* and asked Verdi to shorten his opera. Verdi agreed; he had nothing else to do, he was fond of *Don Carlos*, which had not been a success at the Paris Opéra, sixteen years ago, and he hoped to improve it. He did not want to bother Boito who was struggling with the *Otello* libretto, and did the cutting himself. The ballet and the entire first act in Fontainebleau went. Verdi added a new prelude to the former third act, shifted around some scenes and made other changes, but he knew he had not succeeded. Vienna did not perform it but La Scala did, in January 1884. The revised *Don Carlos* was not a real success. Verdi went back to Genoa in a black mood. Verdi and Giuseppina had left the large apartment at the Palazzo Sauli, perhaps troubled by the memory of Mariani's death in the attic above, and had taken an even larger one at the Palazzo Doria-Pamphily. It contained some twenty rooms and had a large terrace. In March Boito passed through, on his way to Naples where *Mefistofele* was to be performed, and Verdi asked for other minor changes in the *Otello* libretto. On 20 March Boito wrote to Ricordi:

I have good news for you, but for charity's sake don't tell anyone, don't tell even your family, don't tell even yourself: I fear I have already committed an indiscretion. The Maestro is writing, indeed he has already written, a good part of the opening of the first act and seems to be working with fervour.

A few weeks later an incident occurred which almost ruined the carefully nursed 'chocolate' project. After the successful first performance of *Mefistofele* in Naples, there had been a banquet in honour

OTELLO

ATTO QUARTO — A SOLO DI CONTRABASSI.

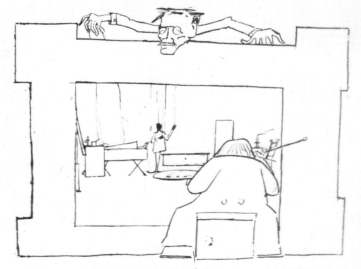

Ultimo tocco di Verdi e Boito al quadrofinale in cornice dell'*Otello*.

Boito holds the canvas of *Otello* as Verdi adds the finishing touches, February 1887.

of Boito. A local newspaper wrote, 'With regard to *Iago*, Boito said that he had taken up this theme against his own will but that, once the libretto was finished, he had regretted not being able to set it to music himself'. Anyone in the inner circle familiar with the new relationship between the poet and the composer must have known that Boito had been badly misquoted. But Verdi immediately remembered the earlier 'brothel' incident and he was shocked. Could Boito have done it again? Verdi wrote to Faccio:

> The worst of it is that Boito's regret that he is not able to set it to music himself leads naturally to the supposition that he cannot hope to see it set by me in the way he would like. I admit this completely, and for this reason I turn to you, the oldest and closest of Boito's friends, to ask that when he returns to Milan you tell him – not in writing, but personally – that I give him back his manuscript intact, without a shade of resentment, without rancour of any kind. More, as that manuscript is my property, I offer it to him as a gift if he wishes to set it to music.

A fine letter but it showed that Verdi was very deeply hurt, and Boito was stunned. He did the right thing immediately. He wrote that he had been misunderstood and misquoted. His great desire had been 'to hear, set to music by you, a libretto which I wrote only for the joy of seeing you take up your pen again *on my account*, for the glory of being your working companion. ... You alone can set *Othello* to music; all the dramatic creations you have given us proclaim this truth.' Boito confessed that after working eight years on his *Nerone* he felt 'slowly asphyxiated by an ideal too exalted for my powers. ... I shall finish *Nerone*, or I shall not finish it, but it is certain that I shall never abandon it for another work ...' And then he ends with an impassioned appeal;

For charity's sake, don't abandon *Otello*, don't abandon it! It is pre-destined for you. Create it. You had begun work on it and I was all en-couraged, hoping to see it finished at some not too distant date. You are sounder than I, stronger than I. Your life is tranquil and serene. Take up your pen and write to me soon: Dear Boito, do me the favour of altering these verses etc. I will change them at once, with joy, and I shall know how to work for you, I who do not know how to work for myself, for you live in the true and real world of art, and I in the world of hallucinations.

Boito was appealing to Verdi's emotions but also to the old man's critical intellect when he had brought up the painful subject of the unfinished *Nerone*. But Verdi, always distrustful, was not yet quite convinced. 'All this cast a chill over *Otello*,' he wrote back to Boito. In his despair, and in a moment of genuine inspiration, Boito wrote 'a sort of evil *Credo*, in broken metre, unsymmetrical', and sent it to Verdi:

Please put this fragment together with the other pages of *Otello*. I did it for my own comfort and personal satisfaction, because I felt the need of doing it. You can interpret this need as you like – as puerility, sentimentality, or superstition – it doesn't matter. All I ask is that you do not reply, even to say 'Thank you'. That page is not worth it. If you do, I shall become dis-quieted all over again.

That did it. Verdi at once realised the great beauty of Boito's *Credo* (one of the glories of *Otello*, both for its words and music). He replied:

Since you don't wish it, I won't say 'Thank you'. But I will say 'Bravo!' Most beautiful, this *Credo*: most powerful and wholly Shakespearian. ... If you come to Sant' Agata, as you have given me reason to hope you will, we shall be able to talk about it again, and by then with the necessary calm. So abandon all your disquietude. With kind regards from Peppina, I am always,

Yours affectionately,
G. Verdi

All was well at last, and there was no more misunderstanding. But work on *Otello* proceeded slowly. In Montecatini Verdi consulted Dr Fedeli, a good physician and a wise man. Verdi was worried about his heart since his father had died of heart trouble. Dr Fedeli told him his heart was fine and advised him 'to avoid excessive effort and fatigue' and to write whenever he was in the mood. Verdi's spirits were raised and he went back with Giuseppina. Ever since, the biographers have disagreed about exactly when *Otello* was written. Most probably, much of it was done by October 1885, when Boito came to Sant' Agata and Verdi played for him parts of the first three acts on the piano in his study. In May 1886 Verdi conceived the wonderful entrance of Otello in the first act, with the stunning 'Esultate!' that has been the perdition of many tenors.

Verdi was now completely absorbed by his work. In July Clarina Maffei died in Milan. Verdi went there but arrived too late; she did not even recognize him. Verdi was saddened; she had been his closest woman friend all these years. On 1 November Verdi wrote to Boito: 'It is finished. . . . Here's health to us . . . (and also to Him . . .) Goodbye . . . G. Verdi.' On 18 December he sent the last pages from Genoa to Ricordi. Verdi was sorry to see his beloved child depart. To Boito he wrote: 'Poor Otello! . . . He won't come back here any more!!!' Boito replied: 'The Moor will come back no more to knock on the door of

Verdi's note to Boito on the completion of *Otello*.

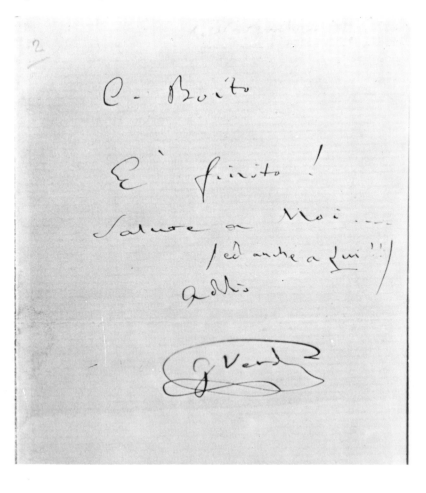

the Palazzo Doria, but you will come to meet the Moor at La Scala. *Otello* exists. The great dream has become reality.'

Verdi's contract with La Scala stipulated that he had the right to withdraw his opera even after the dress rehearsal. This time he wanted to be absolutely sure that everything was done his way. No outsiders were permitted to attend rehearsals, and as the day of the premiere approached there was an enormous amount of speculation. Tension grew. It was rumoured that Verdi, dissatisfied with the way Francesco Tamagno, who was singing Otello, killed himself with his sword in the last act, had taken the sword and performed the scene himself, rolling down the steps of the bed. Not bad for a man of seventy-four. Victor Maurel, more arrogant than ever, was Iago, and went so far as to write a book about the experience a year later. Some people in Milan talked about Tamagno and Maurel as the 'creators' of *Otello* in the way that some today speak of Bernstein's or Karajan's, rather than Verdi's *Falstaff*.

Franco Faccio conducted the world premiere on 5 February 1887. It was by all accounts the musical sensation of the decade. Everybody was happy that Italian opera was not yet dead, and that Verdi had written his best and final work. The ovations started in the first act, after the fire chorus and Iago's drinking song. When Verdi took a curtain-call at the end of the act, 'an immense shout makes the theatre rock. … Verdi bends his head slightly and smiles, the frantic enthusiasm of the huge gathering bringing tears to his eyes.' This was written by an eyewitness, Gino Monaldi, not always the most reliable commentator but absolutely right in this case. Several weeks later, when the nineteen-year-old Arturo Toscanini (who had played second cello in the orchestra) went home to Parma in the middle of the night, he was still so excited that he woke up his mother, saying, 'Get down on your knees, Mamma, and say *Viva Verdi!*' Which poor Signora Toscanini duly did.

Many years later Toscanini told another anecdote about *Otello*. Verdi had marked in his last two scores a dynamic range from *ppppp* to *fff*. He knew that no one could execute even a triple piano, with voice or instrument, but that was how he felt about it. When young Toscanini saw a phrase in his cello part marked *pppp*, he tried to play it that way. Verdi stopped the rehearsal and told Faccio to repeat the phrase: he could not hear the cello. Faccio asked Toscanini to play it louder because 'Verdi must hear the notes'. Years afterwards, Toscanini, then himself conducting at La Scala, told the story to Verdi. The old Maestro sighed: 'True, but who can hear the difference in an opera house?' Verdi had learnt to be realistic and resigned himself to making essential compromises. Twenty years later Toscanini, the perfectionist, no longer made them.

Verdi was depressed after the exhilaration of the first night of *Otello*. After the cheering and the bows at La Scala his party went back to the hotel. Only members of the small inner circle came up to his suite: Peppina, of course, Teresa Stolz, Boito, Ricordi, Faccio and Tamagno.

Verdi was melancholy. He said he felt as though he had fired 'his last cartridge'. They tried to talk him out of it but the wise old man shook his head sadly: 'Oh, glory, glory. I so loved my solitude in the company of Otello and Desdemona! Now the crowd, always greedy for something new, has taken them away from me.' And then he said something that raised their spirits and moved Boito to tears, 'My friends, if I were thirty years younger I should like to begin a new opera tomorrow, provided that Boito wrote the libretto.' Verdi and Boito had become deeply attached to each other. It was almost a father-and-son relationship, quite different from the one Verdi had had with Muzio. Verdi often said that Boito's share in *Otello* was equal to his.

Boito had achieved almost the impossible: without violating the genius and spirit of Shakespeare, he had condensed five acts of poetic language into a much shorter work, with time for the arias and lyrical passages. He had created unity of place by omitting Shakespeare's first act in Venice and concentrating the action in Cyprus. He condensed the time-scheme, and gently shaped the characters for the composer's needs, without basically changing them. Ever since people have argued which is the greater work, Shakespeare's drama or Boito's and Verdi's opera.

Verdi's music is miraculous and words have never explained it. *Otello* has the 'endless melody' that Wagner had talked so much about. It is the greatest Italian tragic opera. Like *Tristan*, its German counterpart, it is a great love-story, with the orchestra providing dramatic continuity and psychological insight. Verdi had translated Shakespeare into music. 'One seems to hear the overtones of Shakespeare,' the British actor Anthony Asquith said. One hears them in the chromatics of Iago's drinking song, in Desdemona's pure love, in Otello's wild outbursts of jealousy. All human emotions, both good and bad, are distilled into music by a man of seventy.

Boito would never forget the first night of *Otello*, for a very private reason. That night he and Eleonora Duse fell deeply in love. They had met briefly three years earlier and Boito had ever since admired the great actress. She was twenty-seven; he was forty-four. Both later knew that they had been under the spell of *Otello*. The emotional range and the agonies of their deeply romantic, intensely sexual relationship became known only after their letters were published in the 1950s. The great passion lasted only two years. Duse referred to the first, the year after *Otello*, as 'the year of the dream'.

OPPOSITE Verdi's villa at Sant' Agata and his bedroom.

14
FALSTAFF: TUTTO E FINITO

Falstaff, Verdi's last work, is a greater miracle than even *Otello*. Not because it was written by a man ten years older, close on eighty. Italians, blessed with creative longevity, have performed miracles before. Monteverdi wrote *Poppea* when he was seventy-five, Michelangelo and Titian lived to eighty-nine and ninety-nine respectively and never stopped working. And outside Italy, Haydn wrote his last two string quartets when he was eighty, and he had developed this fine, subtle form of music almost single-handed from its beginning to its zenith. Yet age and genius are not correlated, for Mozart wrote his great, mature, comic masterpiece, *Le Nozze di Figaro*, when he was thirty.

The first of the many wonders of Verdi's final gift to us is that he began writing it at all. For more than two years after *Otello* he wrote no music. He had glory, money, and the relative pleasures of old age – why should he once more seek the loneliness of his study, the tortures of creation? He and Peppina had established an agreeable routine. They would go to Montecatini and listen to the doctors though they knew the doctors could not really help them, except to alleviate the aches and pains of old age. In Sant' Agata Verdi liked to walk through his fields, talking to his men. In the afternoon Maria Carrara-Verdi would come with her family. And once in a while he would go to Milan. There intimate friends would visit him and Peppina: Teresa Stolz, plumper, less attractive, and now completely accepted by Peppina; Giulio Ricordi; and Boito. Sometimes Carlo Gatti went up. Umberto Giordano, the composer of *Andrea Chénier*, might drop by. He lived in the house, having married the daughter of the hotel proprietor. There would be the latest La Scala gossip, which Verdi enjoyed.

Yet he did give up the easy life of the wealthy retired man once more to involve himself in the doubts, the sleepless nights, the solitude, the hopes and fears of the creative artist. Because Verdi had fallen in

OPPOSITE Victor Maurel as the first Falstaff.

love with Falstaff – Shakespeare's, but especially Boito's – whom he and Boito among themselves called *'Pancione'*, 'Big Belly'. Did he identify himself with Falstaff? In appearance, the two were quite different. Verdi was frail and slim and not exactly a noisy, drinking man. But emotionally and spiritually Verdi was fond of the wise and witty clown who can laugh about himself, and who knows that 'the whole world is a joke', and not always a good one, either. Exactly what Eleonora Duse had meant when she wrote to Boito, 'How sad is your comedy!'

After *Otello* there was never any tension between Verdi and Boito. Their friendship was complete and serene. Again, as in the case of *Otello*, Verdi might not have done *Falstaff* without the tender persistence of Giuseppina, the shrewd prodding of Giulio Ricordi, and above all without Boito, who knew that there was still a great comic masterpiece contained in Verdi's genius. Boito understood, as only a poet can, that now was the time to do *Falstaff*, when Verdi had the distilled wisdom which comes after a long life of sorrows and joys. There had been some talk of a comic opera, perhaps based on *Don Quixote*, but Verdi had ignored all such suggestions. He spent his time supervising the small hospital in Villanova d'Arda, near Sant' Agata.

Then, on one of his trips to Milan, Verdi and Boito discussed the idea of *Falstaff*; the exact day is unknown. In July 1889, when he and Giuseppina were once again in Montecatini, he received Boito's outline libretto. Verdi was delighted with it:

Excellent! Excellent! Before reading your sketch I wanted to re-read the *Merry Wives*, the two parts of *Henry IV* and *Henry V*, and I can only repeat: Excellent. One could not do better than you have done. ... We now have very different matters to discuss so that this *Falstaff*, or *Merry Wives*, which two days ago was in the world of dreams, now takes shape and becomes reality! When? How? ... Who knows? I'll write to you tomorrow or the next day. ... Greetings from Peppina. Farewell.

Affectionately,
G. Verdi

Then came some sombre second thoughts, and the next day, on 7 July, he wrote to Boito:

I said yesterday that I would write to you today. ... As long as one wanders in the realm of ideas, every prospect pleases, but when one comes down to earth, to practical matters, doubts and discouragements arise. ... In outlining *Falstaff* did you never think of the enormous number of my years?
I know you will reply exaggerating the state of my health, which is good, excellent, robust. ... But suppose I couldn't stand the strain? And failed to

finish it? You would then have uselessly wasted your time and trouble! For all the gold in the world I would not wish that. The idea is all the more insupportable to me if you, in writing *Falstaff*, had ... to distract your attention from *Nerone*, or delay its production.

How are we to overcome these obstacles? Have you a sound argument to oppose mine? I hope so but I don't believe it. Still, let's think it over ... and if you can find one [argument] for me, and I some way of throwing off ten years or so, then ... what joy, to be able to say to the public: *Here we go again!!*

Boito understood that Verdi was already won over but being honest towards himself and towards Boito, he just needed an alibi. He replied that old age was no excuse: 'All your arguments – age, strength, hard work for you, hard work for me, etc, etc – are not valid and are not obstacles to a new work.' He thought that 'writing a comic opera I don't believe will tire you.... I shall say that notwithstanding *Falstaff* I shall be able to finish my own work [*Nerone*] within the term promised. I am sure of it.'

That was really all Verdi needed. He answered by return:

Amen! So be it! We'll write this *Falstaff* then. We won't think for the moment of obstacles, of age, of illness. I wish though to keep it the most profound secret, a word I underline three times to tell you that no one must know anything about it! But wait! ... Peppina knew it, I believe, before we did. Be sure, however. She will keep the secret: when women have the talent for secrets, they have it in greater measure than men.

And now a last word. A very prosaic word, yet, especially for me, necessary. But no, no.... Today *Falstaff* is too much in my mind and I could not talk to you of anything else....

The 'very prosaic word' was written on the following day, 11 July:

I continue yesterday's letter. When you have finished your work you will cede the rights to me for the sum of ... (to be fixed later). And if ever, through age or disability, or for any other reason, I cannot finish the music, you will recover your *Falstaff*. I myself offer it to you, to remember me by, and you will make whatever use of it you think fit....

Verdi was right about Peppina. She kept the secret. Even Giulio Ricordi did not know about *Falstaff*. Boito outlined the new project with a true poet's sensitivity:

I should like, as one sprinkles sugar on a tart, to sprinkle the whole comedy with that gay love [of Nannetta and Fenton].... During the first few days I was in despair. To sketch the characters, to weave the plot, to extract all the juice from that enormous Shakespearian orange without letting the useless pips slip into the little glass, to write with colour and clarity and brevity, to delineate the musical plane of the scene, so that there results an organic unity that is a piece of music and yet is not, to make the joyous comedy live from beginning to end, to make it live with a natural and communicative gaiety, is difficult, difficult, difficult. And yet it must seem simple, simple, simple.

This is one of the finest definitions ever written of the work of a librettist-poet; aspiring members of the difficult craft should learn it by heart. On 1 August Boito wrote that he was ready and asked Verdi to return the original sketch, since 're-reading it and thinking it over I shall work more easily'. On 18 August Verdi wrote: 'You are working, I hope? The strangest thing of all is that I am working too! I am amusing myself by writing fugues! Yes, sir, a fugue ... and a comic fugue which would not be out of place in *Falstaff*!'

There was no libretto yet but Verdi had already conceived the wonderful fugue, 'Tutto nel mondo è burla' ('The whole world is a joke'), which concludes *Falstaff*. On 17 March 1890 Verdi wrote, 'The first act is finished, without any alteration at all to the poetry – just as you gave it to me. ...' An incredible statement when one remembers the trouble Verdi had given his earlier librettists, and Boito too when they collaborated on *Otello*. Verdi asked for no major changes in Boito's text. Except that after completing the score he was a little bothered by the way Boito had placed the accents on some English words – 'Falstaff,' 'Norfolk,' 'Windsor' – and asked the poet to make some slight changes in the verse. Verdi was a perfectionist about *Falstaff*, knowing well that he was working on a perfect libretto. An English writer, Francis Toye, admits, 'I would venture to assert that on the whole Boito's *Falstaff* is a better comedy than *The Merry Wives of Windsor*; the action is less diffuse; the intrigue more tidy and concentrated.' With an uncanny sense of drama, Boito omitted some things, reduced the number of characters, and invented other things, such as the comedy between Falstaff and Ford, and the charming love-story of Nannetta and Fenton – for which the eighty-year-old Verdi created the most tender love music ever written. Boito did wonders too with the development of the characters. Boito's Falstaff is hardly the buffoon from *The Merry Wives* but rather the wiser Falstaff from *Henry IV*, more philosopher than clown.

Verdi worked slowly on *Falstaff* but enjoyed the work enormously. He rarely worked for long periods, never more than two hours a day, because the doctors had told him not to overdo it; he wanted to preserve his strength as long as possible (twenty years earlier, he had composed the beautiful score of *Aïda* in four months!). Listening to the glorious fusion of words and music in *Falstaff* one would not know that much private unhappiness occurred in the two years during which Verdi worked on it. Franco Faccio was suffering from

Verdi and Boito at Sant'Agata.

paralysis and became insane. The doctors could do nothing for him and it seemed the end would never come. Boito suffered with his friend. 'There is no hope of saving him, he would be better off dead,' he told Verdi; 'Let us hope that the end comes quickly.' It did not; Faccio's agony lasted until late in July. Boito, in despair, had escaped into work; he sent Verdi a new text for the fugue. Verdi wrote: 'That poor Faccio! It's not a year since he came here [Sant' Agata] and, walking late one day in the garden, I spoke to him in frank, sincere, and perhaps also rather harsh words, for which I now reproach myself. . . .'

In November 1889 La Scala revived *Oberto*, Verdi's first opera, exactly fifty years after the premiere. Verdi always disliked honours and anniversaries, and he did not attend the performance. At Sant'

231

Agata he received messages from the King, the Prime Minister, from the famous and the unknown who admired him as the greatest living Italian. The following year Verdi was grieved by the death of Emanuele Muzio, who had been so close to him. Muzio's last years in Paris were unhappy. He had married a much younger woman in America, and they had had a child who died. Muzio's wife had left him, and he lost his position when the Théâtre-Italien in Paris was closed. He supported himself by giving lessons until his death, in a Paris hospital; there was no one with him on his last days. In his will Muzio said, 'It is my absolute wish that all Verdi's letters be burnt, because I don't want them to become objects of gift or commerce, to be traded for profit. ...' The letters were burnt. Muzio's wish was respected but it has created a gap in the Verdi documents. Now the last friend from the old days was gone. Only Giuseppina was still with Verdi. She had heard the first performance of *Oberto*, fifty years before, and as he worked on *Falstaff* he must have prayed that it would be granted to both of them to attend the first performance of his last work.

There were days when Verdi was 'unable to warm up the engine', as he said to Boito; and days 'when Big Belly doesn't move, but sleeps and is in a bad humour, while at other times he shouts, runs, jumps. ... If he continues I'll have to put on a straitjacket,' as he wrote to Ricordi. The score of the first act was sent to Ricordi in August 1892 and the third act in September; it is not known exactly when the whole work was finished. (Even after the Scala premiere, Verdi made two important revisions in one copy of the score, now the only one in existence, after he had ordered the earlier ones destroyed.) No one has been able to explain why Verdi composed the first part of the second act after nearly everything else was completed.

Late in 1892 Verdi invited some of the singers to come to Genoa and began coaching them in their roles. His contract again gave him the right to withdraw the opera even after the dress rehearsal, if he was not completely satisfied. He had total and absolute control over every detail of the production. He no longer had problems with managers, stage designers, chorus masters, conductors, arrogant prima donnas and vain tenors. La Scala was his house, and La Scala did more for him than for any other composer, before or since.

Rehearsals of *Falstaff* started on 3 January 1893, when the Milan climate is damp and raw, and lasted almost five weeks, until the opening night on 9 February. Verdi was at the theatre every day, sometimes for seven or eight hours. If there was a special rehearsal after dinner, he would go back again. He was happy, almost exhilarated. He enjoyed life and his work; his appetite was good. A true Parmigiano, he had always liked good food, and occasionally fooled around in the kitchen in Sant' Agata, upsetting the servants by making

OPPOSITE Three of the first cast of Falstaff: top to bottom, Virginia Guerrini (Meg), Adelina Stehle (Nannetta), Giuseppina Pasqua (Mistress Quickly).

LEFT Verdi watches Falstaff through a peephole in the stage manager's office.

233

Verdi with friends at Montecatini, a spa to which he went for relaxation. Teresa Stolz sits at his right.

his special risotto for himself. He liked his wine and a good cigar. In Milan he found time to receive friends and admirers, and even journalists, whom he had never liked. They wrote long articles about the incredible octogenarian, about his meals, his habits, his sense of humour. Some medical authorities were quoted as calling Verdi a 'phenomenon'. In truth he was not so much a biological phenomenon as a spiritual and emotional one.

Verdi was happy because he had reached his personal fulfilment, as artist and man. He knew in his heart that he had created a masterpiece; he was more certain than ever before. He indicated it only to Boito, who was not at all surprised, and to Giuseppina, who was so pleased with her Verdi that she even forgot her arthritis for a few hours. Verdi had visualised the production of *Falstaff* long before the

Scala premiere. Ideally he would have liked to stage the opera at his home in Sant' Agata, with a relatively small orchestra of virtuosi, in an intimate setting, surrounded by the landscape he loved; but, as a realist, he knew this was impossible.

He let it be known, through Ricordi, that permission to produce *Falstaff* would be withdrawn unless it was done exactly the way he wanted. He told his friends that he would rather destroy the score than permit its maltreatment in the opera houses of the world, and he said he was not prepared to be upset by bad productions as he had been so often in the past. He knew that only his physical presence could prevent this, and he was there all the time. For the first and last time in his life he permitted what he called 'personal exhibition', but some people who knew him might have seen a sly twinkle in the old Maestro's eyes as he answered silly questions and listened to empty speeches honouring him. He was delighted to hear that visitors from all over the world had come to attend the first three performances, at which he would be present.

The premiere, on 9 February 1893, was the musical event of the 1890s, just as *Otello* had been for the 1880s. Edoardo Mascheroni conducted. He was Verdi's choice, after the death of Franco Faccio, an early, pre-Toscanini perfectionist. The performance was not perfect however. The orchestra did not play brilliantly throughout, the double-bass section had difficulties in the final act, and some critics thought that the large stage of La Scala was simply too large for the witty, intimate comedy, which did not surprise Verdi. Some people who had been at the *Otello* premiere felt that there was not quite the same passionate enthusiasm; but a comedy arouses less emotion.

Yet the success was enormous, no one doubted that Verdi had created a very great masterpiece and there was no more comparison with Wagner. Later, some authorities were to see some relationship between *Meistersinger* and *Falstaff*, but there is none. Falstaff is closer to the surprisingly humorous, exhilarating moments in Beethoven's late quartets than to Wagner. *Falstaff* is incomparable, though it has something of the celestial airiness of Mozart's *Figaro*. The success of the premiere was best summed up by Boito, in a letter to his friend Camille Bellaigne, the French critic, who had not been present: 'what you cannot imagine is the immense intellectual pleasure that this Latin lyric comedy produces on the stage. . . . Come, come dear friend, to hear this masterpiece; come to spend two hours in the gardens of the *Decameron*. . . .'

And when it was all over and he had taken the last curtain-call and appeared on the balcony of his hotel, what was Verdi thinking? Would there be another opera? Could there be? Boito had translated *Antony and Cleopatra* for Eleonora Duse and spoken of it with Verdi, and there was talk, once more, about *King Lear*; but Giuseppina did not want Boito to discuss any new plans. She said, 'Verdi is tired'. Verdi himself, shrewd and pious in his own way, knew that the gods had given him much; they must not be challenged. When some months later Emma Zilli, one of the 'merry wives' in *Falstaff*, wrote to send her Christmas greetings, he replied:

Do you remember the third performance of *Falstaff*? I took leave of you all, and you were all somewhat moved, especially you and Giuseppina Pasqua. ... Imagine what that farewell was for me. It meant, 'We shall never meet again as artists ...'. My memories always go back to that third night, which meant, *Tutto è finito*.

It was all over. Twenty-five years later Toscanini found a note in Verdi's hand in his *Falstaff* score which begins:

> Tutto è finito!
> Va, va, vecchio John ...
> Cammina per la tua via,
> Fin che tu puoi ...

> All is ended!
> Go, go, old John ...
> Be off on your way,
> As far as you can ...

Verdi had written at the top, 'The last Notes of Falstaff'.

Falstaff will never have the popularity of *Aïda*, *Rigoletto*, *La Traviata*. It is musical caviar, a 'Latin lyric comedy' with an 'immense intellectual joy', as Boito had said. It is Italian rather than English, but it has an almost universal meaning and even its gayest moments always contain the tears that characterise immortal comedy. It is sheer poetry magically turned into music, but it demands much from the listener. To appreciate the finesse and subtlety of *Falstaff* takes concentration and patience. It is a very fast-moving opera. Musical gems suddenly appear, and are as suddenly gone, a few moments later. Falstaff's 'Quand' ero Paggio', perhaps the finest, and certainly the best-known passage of the opera – not even a number, or aria – lasts less than a minute. There are no popular arias that people can hum, such as 'La donna è mobile'. But there is the magnificent monologue on 'Honour', with the wonderful woodwind passages and trills, which has been called by many the counterpart of Iago's *Credo* in *Otello*, and in fact is even finer, even more subtle. There is the magnificent 'Va, va, vecchio John', which is Falstaff's and Verdi's personal farewell. There is the laughter of the merry wives, unlike anything ever written for the voice. And there is passion, too, in Ford's

'Jealousy' monologue. But all this beauty comes and goes, and is brought out only in the transparent texture if the performers are capable of making it transparent. As Boito said, long before the opera existed: 'difficult, difficult, difficult,' to make it 'simple, simple, simple'.

The cunning old Maestro, who never ceased to watch the box-office takings, soon knew that this masterpiece, unanimously praised by all the critics, would never make as much money as some of the earlier operas which the critics had called 'vulgar'. It must have been an amusing thought for the old man.

A signed photograph of Verdi
in old age.

15
APOTHEOSIS

There was one more thing to be done. Verdi, a poor boy who had become a rich man, had a strong sense of his social responsibilities, rare in Italy where inherited privileges are unchallenged because the country has never had a social or political revolution. Earlier Verdi had set up scholarships for students in Busseto. He built three new dairy farms which would employ some two hundred people and might prevent, as Verdi hoped, 'emigration from my village'. This was at the time when poor Italians despaired about their homeland and went to America as steerage passengers. Verdi, who could get furious about an impresario or a publisher who in his opinion was trying to cheat him, reduced the rents on his farms when times were bad. He started a new system of irrigation and reclaimed swamps along the Po river. He agreed with Garibaldi, who had said that the gap between the very poor and the very rich was a serious threat to the recently unified country.

Today Italian Communists who love Verdi claim that it can be proved that Verdi was an 'early Communist'. He took a lasting interest in the small hospital he had built near Sant' Agata. Peppina had bought furniture and linen, and everything else that was needed. Two months after the opening Verdi wrote to the hospital's director:

I think it right to warn you that I have had bad reports from the hospital. ... I hope they are not true. They are saying 1. that the food is poor, 2. the wine even more so, though the cellar is well stocked, 3. that the milk is not fresh milk, 4. that the oil is of the commonest kind . . . and so on.

I hope that none of this is true, and that you will be so kind as to reassure me at once with a few words.

One day in 1900, the biographer Eugenio Checchi reports, Verdi, then eighty-seven, was asked by a friend which of his works he liked best. Verdi did not name any of his thirty-two operas, or the *Requiem* or any of the other works he had composed. Instead he said: 'Of all my works the one that is dearest to me is the Home I built in Milan for old artists who were not favoured by fortune and not endowed with the virtue of thrift. Poor, dear companions of my life! Believe me, friend, this Home is really my most beautiful opera.' This was the man who would not permit his servants to leave Sant' Agata and could be a tyrant at home. Verdi was complex.

He was referring to the Casa di Riposa per Musicisti ('House of Rest for Musicians') where men and women, hundreds of them, have spent the last years of their lives in peace and without having to worry about money. They were, in accordance with Verdi's instructions, 'Italian citizens who have reached the age of sixty-five, have practised the art of music professionally, and find themselves in a state of poverty.'

The project dated from 1889 when Verdi had bought a piece of land on the Piazza Michelangelo Buonarroti, where he planned to build a hospital and convalescent home. He consulted Camillo Boito, an architect and Arrigo's brother, but he told no one that he had bought the land. As soon as Arrigo Boito and he had finished *Falstaff*, he talked again to Camillo Boito and to Emilio Seletti, his lawyer. Instead of a hospital Verdi would now build an old people's home. He was

The Casa di Riposa per Musicisti, built and endowed by Verdi for the care of impoverished elderly musicians.

always quite thorough about business affairs. He knew the Home had to have a sound financial basis.

In 1895 Camillo Boito showed him the first plans. Verdi immediately put 150,000 gold lire into a special account in the Banco Popolare. The house was finished in 1899 but Verdi died before it was officially opened, on 10 October 1902. By that time he and Giuseppina were buried in the crypt of the 'Casa Verdi', as the Milanese called it. There has never been an empty room at the Casa Verdi since it was opened. Verdi had the idea that the pensioners would want to share double rooms so they would not be lonely, but it turned out that nearly all preferred to live alone. The building originally had two storeys; a third was added in 1937. A hundred rooms, occupied by sixty men and forty women, the precise ratio that Verdi had stipulated. He had also set up the order of preference according to which people were to be admitted: composers first, then singers, conductors, chorus masters, orchestral players and so on. There has always been a long waiting list. In his will Verdi had left certain royalties to the Home for perpetuity. At first this income was sufficient, but later war, inflation and devaluation began raising havoc with the Home's finances and now the copyrights on Verdi's last works, *Otello* and *Falstaff*, have expired. However, many private benefactors have come to the Home's assistance; one of the most generous was Arturo Toscanini.

Today the Home is being supported by the city and the state. One of the Casa Verdi's house rules is that the male pensioners must wear 'Verdi hats', the wide-brimmed black felt hats with crushed crowns which Verdi is wearing in many of his photographs. He had adopted the style from the peasants in his native Parma.

Wagner built himself a shrine in Bayreuth, mostly with other people's money, to glorify and perpetuate his memory. Verdi used his money and part of his life-savings to help his 'poor, dear companions'.

Even after *Falstaff* Verdi remained astonishingly active. In the autumn of 1894 Giulio Ricordi went to Paris to help Verdi with the first French production of *Otello*. On 29 September he wrote to Giacomo Puccini;

Verdi, who in a few days will have completed eighty-one years, is rejuvenated. ... Yesterday he was 'crazy' enough to arrange, preside at, and conduct the following rehearsals: twelve o'clock the chorus, from one to two the orchestra, from two to half past two dance rehearsal, from half past two to half past five the soloists at the piano, third and fourth acts!! I cry, Hosanna!!

By the way, Tuesday, 9 October, Verdi has his eighty-first birthday. If you want to telegraph to him here a word of congratulation, I am sure it will please him very much. Although very busy, he has already mentioned you twice, asking what you are doing. ...

Ricordi wanted to get Verdi and Puccini together; he knew the 'emperor' of the House of Ricordi might help the 'crown prince'. The next year, 1895, Verdi and Giuseppina went again to Montecatini. Ricordi suggested that Puccini, then thirty-seven, pay Verdi a visit: 'I am certain that it would give him the greatest pleasure.' But none of Puccini's biographers mentions a personal meeting between the men. Puccini had a signed photograph of Verdi, which is however no proof that they met. Puccini, like many other younger musicians in Italy, was too awed by Verdi to try to meet him. But Puccini was always aware of Verdi. When Ricordi received the score of *La Bohème*, he found 'all kinds of possible and impossible indications. It is a forest of p-pp-pppp, of f-ff-fff-ffff, of slowing-up and of going ahead so that the conductors will lose their heads.' Puccini replied: 'As for the pp's and ff's of the score, I have overdone them, because, as Verdi says, when one wants *piano* one puts ppp.' In Puccini's score of the fourth act of *La Bohème*, the B minor chord indicating the moment of Mimi's death is marked *ppppppp*, seven times *piano*, which is even more than Verdi used.

One January morning in 1897 Giuseppina found Verdi in his bed in their large apartment in Genoa. He was unable to move or to speak. Giuseppina called Maria Carrara, who was staying with them. Should they get a doctor? The publicity might be terrible. While they were arguing, Verdi gave a sign that he wanted to write. They gave him paper and pencil, and he wrote 'caffè'. They brought him a cup of strong coffee and he felt better. A few days later he seemed to have recovered completely. Only Boito, Ricordi, and Mascheroni, who was conducting in Genoa, were told about the 'attack'. In Montecatini, in July, it was noticed that Verdi walked briskly and held himself straight, but Giuseppina walked with difficulty, supporting herself on his arm. Verdi seemed in good form. A woman wrote to him that she had loved *Aïda* and asked for some 'explanations' and he asked her to leave him alone. He complained he was stared at 'like a beast', and he could not stand autograph-hunters.

They returned to Sant' Agata. Giuseppina had bronchitis and stayed in bed. She got up after a few weeks and said she felt better, but she had no appetite and Verdi was worried about her. In November she was worse and the doctor said it was pneumonia. She wrote her last letter on 1 November, to her her sister Barberina:

Today is All Saints Day, but every day to me seems a day of mourning! You, at least, take every care of yourself, so that you can enjoy a few days of sunshine, and excuse me if weakness obliges me to write infrequently. Give my regards to Maria. To you, from the depths of my heart a kiss and an embrace from your affectionate sister.

Peppina Verdi

Giuseppina died, at four in the afternoon, on 14 November 1897. She was eighty-two. Verdi was said to be 'silent, erect, unable to speak'. In her will Giuseppina asked for a simple funeral: 'I came poor into this world, and I want to leave it the same way.' (To Teresa Stolz she left a watch covered with brilliants and some other jewelry.) 'And now: Farewell, my Verdi. . . . As we were united in life, may God lead our spirits together again in Heaven!'

A simple service was held in the cathedral of Busseto. Many local people attended. Among the older ones some may have remembered how the Bussetani had moved demonstratively away from Giuseppina Strepponi when she had come there to pray, forty-seven years ago, because she had not been married to Verdi. The proud woman had never forgiven them. Now she took leave of Busseto for ever. Teresa Stolz, Ricordi, and a few other intimates accompanied the coffin to the cemetery in Milan for burial.

In his infrequent later letters Verdi does not mention Giuseppina, but she was never far from his thoughts. Once he writes, 'Great grief asks for silence, isolation, I would even say, the torture of reflection.' Then he writes to Boito, 'I am feeling the burden of age. Life is departing.' And to Mascheroni, 'I am not sick, but I am too old! . . . It is very hard.'

Verdi's last compositions were his *Pezzi Sacri* ('Sacred Pieces'). Back in 1888 he had written the *Laudi alla Vergine Maria*, for four women's voices, after a text from his beloved Dante's *Paradiso*, and the following year the *Ave Maria*, for four unaccompanied voices. In 1895 and the following year he wrote his *Te Deum*, and in 1896–7 the *Stabat Mater*, for chorus and orchestra. There has been much speculation whether Giuseppina's influence had made him write his religious pieces. Boito, who knew Verdi so well, did not think so. Years later, he wrote to his friend Bellaigue:

This is the day that he loved best of all the days of the year. Christmas Eve recalled to him the holy marvels of childhood. . . . He lost his belief early, like all of us, but he retained, more than the rest of us perhaps, a regret for it all his life.

He gave the example of Christian faith by the moving beauty of his religious works . . . by the ordering of his funeral, found in his will: one priest, one candle, one cross. He knew that faith is the sustenance of the heart. . . . In the ideal, moral and social sense he was a great Christian, but one must be very careful not to present him as a Catholic in the political and strictly theological sense of the word: nothing could be further from the truth.

Boito asked Verdi for permission have the *Sacred Pieces* performed by the Société des Concerts, at the Paris Opéra, at Easter 1898, and Verdi agreed. He wanted to go but the doctors were against it. The

Sacred Pieces are beautiful music but less dramatic than the *Requiem*. A performance at La Scala in 1899 was not sold out. Verdi had no illusions. His eyes were bad, he was having trouble with his hearing, but his mind was clear. 'When the public does not run to a new production, it is already unsuccessful,' he told Boito; 'No indulgence or pity. Better to have them whistle!'

Verdi spent much time in Milan, where he felt less lonely than in Sant' Agata. Boito, Ricordi, Stolz saw him almost every day. At eighty-five, he seemed in fine shape. He loved to play a Beethoven sonata on the piano. Sometimes he played a composition for four hands with a visitor. 'Verdi is marvellously well,' Boito told Bellaigue; 'He plays the piano, he sings, eats as he pleases, walks, and argues. I shall see him this evening.'

Verdi and Boito had come a long way. Verdi's first letter to Boito, addressed 'Dear Sig. Boito', written on 15 August 1880, was signed 'Yours Sincerely, G. Verdi', and included a postscript: 'Allow me most sincerely to congratulate you on the success of *Mefistofele* in London.' His last letter to Boito, dated 20 October 1900, says:

Dear Boito,

I shall be brief because writing makes me tired. And let it be said once and for all, whenever you please and your engagements permit you to come to Sant' Agata, it will always be a joy to me and to us all. . . . I am not really ill but my legs barely support me, and my strength diminishes from day to day. The doctor comes twice daily for the massage but I feel no improvement. . . . With a warm handshake, I am,

Yours affectionately,
G. Verdi

Verdi was eighty-seven, feeling lonely and often depressed, asking himself why he was still around. In December he went to the Grand Hotel in Milan and spent Christmas there with Maria Carrara and his friends. At La Scala's museum in Milan is kept the writing-desk that had been in the hotel rooms where Verdi spent his last days. His pencils are still on top of the desk, a paperweight and a knife with the inscription 'Souvenir de la Tour Eiffel', unused envelopes and postcards, a French-Italian dictionary, a small Italian railway timetable, and a set of patience cards – a lonely old man's pastime. Each little thing appears to have its place in the ensemble; the pencils were carefully sharpened, the unused envelopes were neatly stacked.

On the morning of 21 January 1901 Verdi had a stroke. He remained motionless and unconscious, except for brief moments, during the next six days. A great drama, almost reminiscent of a Verdi opera, was staged around him. The hotel ordered black drapes. A priest was called and administered extreme unction. The Milan city council had straw mats placed in the street beneath his bedroom to

OPPOSITE Verdi's desk at the Grand Hotel in Milan, now kept in the La Scala museum.

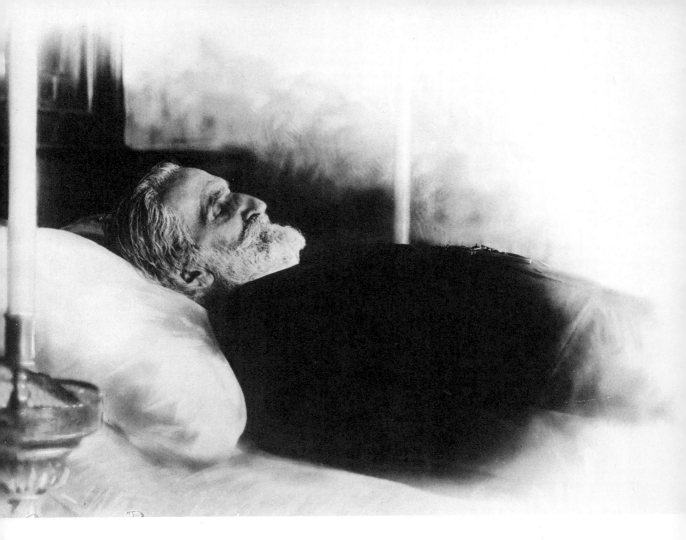

The death of Verdi.

dull the sound of the horses' hooves and the carriage wheels. Close friends stayed in the drawing-room near the bedroom. They watched him anxiously and talked to the doctors in whispers. Then word was sent to acquaintances waiting in the corridor, and they gave the news to people in the lobby and in the street.

Verdi did not hear the people. His heart was still beating but he was already elsewhere. No one understood this better than Boito, who wrote to his friend Bellaigue, much later:

He died magnificently, like a fighter, formidable and mute. The silence of death had fallen on him a week before he died. . . . His resistance was heroic. The breathing of this great chest sustained him for four days and three nights. On the fourth night the sound of his breathing still filled the room but the fatigue . . . Poor Maestro, how brave and handsome he was, up to the las moment. . . .

My dear friend, never have I experienced such a feeling of hatred for

246

death, of contempt for that mysterious, blind, stupid, triumphant and craven power. . . .

Now all is over. He sleeps like a King of Spain in his Escorial. Under a bronze slab that completely covers him . . .

The sound of breathing stopped at three in the morning, on 27 January 1901. Verdi was dead.

Carlo Gatti attended Verdi's funeral. The last time I saw the old biographer, who knew so much about Verdi, he talked about that day:

It was in the Milan city cemetery. Verdi had left instructions that there must be neither music nor singing. He wanted it all very simple. . . . The day was dark and damp and foggy. Half the people of Milan were there. No one was permitted to approach the grave, and we all stood at a distance, silently crying. Verdi had decreed there must be no music but he couldn't

The graves in the Milan city cemetery where the bodies of Verdi and Giuseppina were first laid, before their removal to the crypt of the Casa di Riposa.

247

The funeral procession passes
through Milan.

decree there should be no weeping. Then, suddenly, there rose from among
the crowd a chorale – soft at first, then louder and louder as it swept through
the throng. It was the 'Va, pensiero', from *Nabucco* that had made Verdi a
national symbol, almost sixty years ago.

Gatti cleared his throat.

Well, we had to obey his last will. But a month later, on 28 February 1901,
the coffin was taken out of its modest grave and buried in the crypt of the
Casa Verdi, and the second funeral was an impressive demonstration of
Italy's devotion to its dead Master. Toscanini conducted nine hundred
voices in the 'Va, pensiero', while the bodies of Verdi and Giuseppina were
carried from the cemetery to the Casa. The people of Italy had done as Verdi
wished, but now they did what they felt they had to do.

ACKNOWLEDGMENTS

I remain particularly grateful to the late Carlo Gatti whose *Verdi*, two volumes (Alpes, Milan, 1931) remains *the* standard biography. It was Gatti who encouraged me to do a book on Verdi as we rode from Gatti's home in Milan to Villa Verdi in Sant'Agata. Gatti predicted that each generation would take 'a new and fresh look' at the genius of Verdi. He was right; I wrote this book, twenty years later, when I feel I understand Verdi better than twenty or fifty years ago. Thus the bibliography on Verdi is growing and the conscientious biographer's thanks are due to many of his predecessors. Particularly to Gaetano Cesari and Alessandro Luzio who published *I Copialettere di Giuseppe Verdi* (Milan, 1913), Verdi's copybooks of his and Giuseppina Strepponi's letters; to Frank Walker (*The Man Verdi*, Knopf, New York, 1962) whose invaluable, scholarly research debunked many Verdi myths and legends; to George Martin (*Verdi, His Music, Life and Times*, Dodd, Mead & Company, New York, 1963); and to *The New Yorker* for permission to use some material from *The Black Felt Hat*, my report on Carlo Gatti and Sant'Agata.

There are other Verdi books, such as Ferruccio Bonavia, *Verdi* (Dobson, London, 1947); Luigi Agostino Garibaldi, *Giuseppe Verdi nelle lettere di Emanuele Muzio ad Antonio Barezzi* (Fratelli Treves, Milan, 1931); Massimo Mila, *Giuseppe Verdi* (Laterza, Bari, 1958); Francis Toye, *Giuseppe Verdi, His Life and Works* (Knopf, New York, 1946); and Franz Werfel and Paul Stefan edited *Verdi, The Man in His Letters* (Fischer, New York, 1942). It has been said that the best books about Verdi have been written by non-Italians who are more detached about the great composer than his compatriots. Verdi remains an elusive subject. Owing to his passion for privacy some aspects of his life may never become known, and important letters – written by or to him, or about him – are still hidden in various places. His life was often as dramatic as the libretti of some of his operas; there is no need to invent things about him or 're-create' his thoughts and speeches. I have stuck to the facts and nothing but the facts. Whenever possible I went back to the original sources. One must mention the archives of La Scala's Museum in Milan, of Villa Verdi in Sant'Agata, and the publications of the Institute of Verdi Studies in Parma. And there is always Verdi's wonderful music, never 'autobiographical' in the narrow sense of the word, but always helping us to understand the man and the composer.

Photographs and illustrations were supplied or are reproduced by kind permission of the following: Aldo Garzanti Editore (from *Verdi nelle immagini* by Carlo Gatti): 24, 63, 103, 111, 124, 141, 241; Biblioteca del Risorgimento Italio, Rome: 106; Biblioteca Nazionale Braidense, Milan:

INDEX